Dear Reader,

Defining literary movements is not the easiest task. I have yet to read a satisfactory definition of "Beat Generation," for example, even after spending my whole adult life studying it. Some are better than others and I have attempted my own, but it is imperfect and many would disagree with it. Who should be included? Who should be excluded? When did it begin and end? Has it ever really ended? These are questions impossible to definitively answer.

And what of the San Francisco Renaissance? It overlapped with the Beat movement of course, confusing matters, but did the writers later labelled "Beat" start it with the 6 Gallery reading or did they merely enter an existing literary scene? If the latter is true, then to what extent did they reshape it? It is hard to dispute the importance of Allen Ginsberg's time in San Francisco both for the poet and the poetry scene there, but beyond that there are many questions and uncertainties.

This issue of *Beatdom*, which is released to coincide with the 70th anniversary of the 6 Gallery reading, will not definitively answer any of the above but in its various essays it will discuss important questions and shine a light into overlooked corners. As always, in choosing the various contributions for this issue, I opted for a wide range of material that have different focuses and styles and which sometimes disagree with one another. I have also pushed for the inclusion of writers we have not featured so heavily in previous issues of the journal.

In this issue of *Beatdom*, Thomas Antonic and Ryan Mathews look at female poets who were in San Francisco arguably doing the things for which the male Beat writers later became famous. Yorio Hirano concludes his two-part philosophical discussion of Robert Duncan's poetry and I more broadly examine the pre-6 Gallery poetry scene, looking at Duncan and Rexroth and others who laid the groundwork for the San Francisco Renaissance. Leon Horton looks at Rexroth and Ferlinghetti's jazz-and-poetry nights at The Cellar and James K. Hanna explores the clash of personalities (or perhaps egos) that took place when Kerouac entered Rexroth's world. We have essays on the woman Kerouac wrote about as "The Good Blonde" and the links between Trappist monk Thomas Merton and the bohemian poets of the Bay, as well pieces focused on Ginsberg's "Howl," on Michael McClure, and on the influence of Asian religions and philosophies.

In editing this issue, I have tried to avoid extensive repetition but this is of course unavoidable in certain cases, and so there will be multiple references to the 6 Gallery reading, The Cellar readings, *The Dharma Bums*, Kenneth Rexroth's Friday-night salons, and so on. What is repeated here is typically of such significance that repetition was necessary but still I hope each essay brings something new in terms of opinion and focus.

We also have a review of a new book from Gregory Stephenson. This book is not explicitly about the San Francisco Renaissance but it is a study of *The Dharma Bums*, which was possibly the first book to mention that movement. You will also find several poems throughout this issue of the journal, all of which relate to the poets of San Francisco.

As always, our aim is to educate, enlighten, but above all to provoke discussion. I hope we have succeeded.

David S. Wills
Editor

P.S. In addition to our old website, www.beatdom.com, we have recently begun using Substack. This began as a means of operating a mailing list, which otherwise proved prohibitively expensive. However, as I have explored the platform, it has become clear to me that it is a superior way of reaching a wide audience and sharing long-form essays. It is easier to maintain than the old website and allows for informing *Beatdom*'s subscribers about important updates related to the journal. If you are interested in signing up, you can do so—for free—at www.beatdom.substack.com. We will probably post one or two lengthy, investigative essays per month over the coming years, the sort of content that falls outside the scope of these themed issues of the journal and is too short to publish as a book. Our old website will remain online but may function more as an archive of old material.

BEATDOM
FOUNDED 2007

EDITOR - DAVID S. WILLS
COVER DESIGN - WAYLON BACON

PUBLISHED BY BEATDOM BOOKS
WWW.BEATDOM.COM

TABLE OF CONTENTS

ESSAYS

Blowing Beats in the Basement: Rexroth, Ferlinghetti, and the Poetry Readings in the Cellar
    by Leon Horton..1

The 6 Gallery Reading and the San Francisco Renaissance
    by David S. Wills..23

"Before That Whole Beat Thing Happened": ruth weiss' First Years in San Francisco
    by Thomas Antonic...45

Madeline Gleason: The Romantic Rhyming Radical
    by Ryan Mathews..63

Rexroth and Kerouac: An Antidote of Sorts
    by James K. Hanna...75

The Monk in the "Beat-Fold"
    by John Marshell..81

In Search of the Good Blonde
    by Brett Sigurdson...97

The San Francisco Renaissance and Far Eastern Religions
    by Peter Oehler...115

Beginner's Mind: A Re-reading of Allen Ginsberg's Revolutionary "Howl"
    by Jonah Raskin...129

A.D. Winans on the Counterculture
   by A.D. Winans..145
Festivals of Poetry, 1947-1952
   by Tom Cantrell..153
"It's Not My Scene": The Evolving Poets and Poetics of
   the Berkeley and San Francisco Renaissances and the
   Beat Generation
   by Ryan Mathews..155
Duncan Among The "Stars": An Essay on Robert Duncan's
   Poetics of "Open Form" (Part II)
   by Yorio Hirano..189

MEMOIRS
The Beat Poet Spills It Out
   by Henri Bensussen...141
Ghost Mantras: Michael McClure Remembered
   by D.S. Black..229

POETRY
Poem for ruth weiss
   by A.D. Winans..96
Remembering Bob Kaufman
   by A.D. Winans..128
Lifting the Light from the Jade Green Waves Below
   by Paul W. Jacobs (Jake)..150
Poems for Jack Micheline
   by A.D. Winans..184

REVIEWS
To Find Dawn's Moon
   by David S. Wills..187

David S. Wills is the editor of *Beatdom* and the author of books on William S. Burroughs, Allen Ginsberg, Haruki Murakami, and Hunter S. Thompson. His latest book is the first comprehensive study of the 6 Gallery reading.

Leon Horton is a UK-based countercultural writer, interviewer, and editor. He is the editor of the acclaimed essay/memoir collection, *Gregory Corso: Ten Times a Poet*, and interviewer of author Victor Bockris for *The Burroughs-Warhol Connection*. A regular contributor to *Beatdom* and *Rock and the Beat Generation*, his essays, features, and interviews have also been published by *International Times*, *Beat Scene*, *Erotic Review*, and *Literary Heist*.

Thomas Antonic, PhD, Beat scholar, filmmaker, poet, musician, currently working on a criticial hybrid edition of ruth weiss' complete works and her biography. His publications include *Amongst Nazis: William S. Burroughs in Vienna 1936/37* and *ruth weiss: Beat Poetry, Jazz, Art* (co-edited with Estíbaliz Encarnación Pinedo). *The Three Wives of Queer William S. Burroughs* will be published by Beatdom Books in 2026.

Ryan Mathews—a native of Northern California, currently in exile in Detroit—is a published poet, essayist, and nonfiction bestselling author as well as an artist, philosopher, and futurist. His essays on obscure Beat figures have appeared in previous issues of *Beatdom* and *Beat Scene*.

James K. Hanna is a Pittsburgh-based writer. His essays on Jack Kerouac have appeared in *New Oxford Review*, on *Dappled Things*, and on his Substack: "The Obscure, Forgotten, and Undiscovered."

John Marshell is an independent researcher and writer with current interests focused on Thomas Merton and Asian religions. He has recently completed a Masters in Comparative Religion from Western Michigan University.

Brett Sigurdson is a faculty member of the Liberal Arts Department at Alexandria College in Minnesota. His published work includes contributions to *Rethinking Kerouac: Afterlives, Continuities, Reappraisals* and *The Cambridge Companion to Jack Kerouac*. He is currently revising his dissertation on Jack Kerouac for publication as a monograph.

Peter Oehler, born in 1962, lives in Frankfurt/Main. Educated as an engineer in electrical engineering, he is a freelance lecturer at a technical university and author with focus on Greece, refugees, Beat Generation, and reviews.

Jonah Raskin is the author of *American Scream: Allen Ginsberg's "Howl" and the Birth of the Beat Generation*. The chief book reviewer for *Beat & Rock & Roll*, he is a professor emeritus at Sonoma State University. He is the author of books about Jack London and Abbie Hoffman, and a poet who performs his work in San Francisco where he lives.

A.D. Winans is a native San Francisco poet and writer whose work has been translated into 14 languages. Awards include a PEN National Josephine Miles Award for excellence in literature and a PEN Oakland Lifetime Achievement award. His work has appeared in hundreds of literary magazines and anthologies including *City Lights Journal*, *Beat Scene*, *Beatitude*, and *Beatdom*. He edited *Second Coming Magazine* and Press for 17 years. He was friends with Lawrence Ferlinghetti, Gregory Corso, Jack Micheline, Bob Kaufman, Harold Norse, David Meltzer, and ruth weiss.

Tom Cantrell is the author of a biography of TV producer Roy Huggins, *The Mysteries of Roy Huggins and the Deportation of Harry Carlisle*. He contributes articles to *Paperback Parade* magazine on authors of interest to collectors of vintage paperbacks.

D.S. Black is an archives whisperer by day, a somnobiographer of night. He was born in Toronto, raised there and in Manitoba. Now lives in Berkeley, California.

Henri Bensussen has published poems in *Blue Mesa Review*, *Common Ground Review*, *Sinister Wisdom*, *Into the Teeth of the Wind*, among others; essays & fiction in Lisa Locascio, ed., *Golden State 2017: Best New Fiction and Nonfiction from California*, *Rooted 2: the Best New Arboreal Nonfiction 2023*, etc. *Earning Colors*, a chapbook of poems, was published by Finishing Line Press in 2014.

Paul W. Jacob (Jake) is a poet/writer and professor of Spiritual Literature and Sacred Wisdom. He has had several books of creative nonfiction and poetry published by presses in the United States and Canada. Jake and his wife, Jess, are the co-founders of Feed The Way, a charitable organization whose mission is to provide meals, daily necessities, human companionship, and spiritual care for our homeless brothers and sisters out on the streets.

Yorio Hirano is professor emeritus at Sugiyama Jogakuen University. He has published numerous works on Charles Olson, Robert Duncan, and Ezra Pound. His most recent publications include "Charles Olson's epic and Edward Dorn's mock-epic: from *The Maximums Poems* to *Gunslinger Book I-IIII*" in 2023 and his Japanese translation of Olson's magnum opus, *The Maximus Poems*, in 2012.

Matz McLaughlin is a writer, junior associate professor at Tokyo University of Science (TUS), translator, and scholar of the Beat Generation and modernist writers. He is currently conducting doctoral research on the vanished Beat poet Lew Welch at Université Libre de Bruxelles (ULB).

BLOWING BEATS IN THE BASEMENT:

REXROTH, FERLINGHETTI, AND *POETRY READINGS IN THE CELLAR*

BY LEON HORTON
ARTWORK BY MARK ILOTT

They are queuing down the sidewalk outside The Cellar, North Beach, in February 1957; some five hundred more than the one-fifty or so crammed inside. Down the stairs, the smoke-filled jazz club is heaving, standing room only, knee deep at the bar. On the tiny stage the Cellar Jazz Quintet are hunched up close, waiting, tuning, vamping 'til ready. The lights dim to a spot. The crowd falls silent. A solitary trumpet note, mournful and sustained, heralds a moustached, slightly patrician poet clutching a sheaf of papers. He stares imperiously across the room at expectant faces veiled in coils of smoke that kiss the rarefied air and starts to recite: "They are murdering all the young men. / For half a century now, every day, / They have hunted them down and killed them." The poet is Kenneth Rexroth. The poem: "Thou Shalt Not Kill":

> They are killing them now.
> At this minute, all over the world,
> They are killing the young men.
> They know ten thousand ways to kill them,
> Every year they invent new ones.[i]

Poet Robert Duncan called it "excited and straight out."[ii] Charles Olson called it "gruesome."[iii] William Carlos Williams called for it to be posted on college campuses across the country.[iv] Quite why Rexroth chose this antiwar poem to perform and record to jazz accompaniment across six nights at The Cellar jazz club remains unclear. "Thou Shalt Not Kill (A Memorial for Dylan Thomas)" to give it its full title, written "at white heat"[v] according to Henry Miller, is a blistering jeremiad, a savage indictment of the horrors of the 20th century, a cry of rage against the dying of the light. Lawrence Ferlinghetti, Rexroth's fellow performer at The Cellar, called it a "much fiercer castigation of American consumer society than 'Howl'"[vi] and with lines like "Three generations of infants / Stuffed down the maw of Moloch" it can be regarded as a forbearer to Allen Ginsberg's more famous poem.[1]

Perhaps its anti-establishment theme was the reason Rexroth chose it. Perhaps, having witnessed the success of "Howl," he sought to appeal to a hipster audience, for as critic and jazz enthusiast Ralph J. Gleason observed in the liner notes for the subsequent LP *Poetry Readings in The Cellar* (Fantasy Records, 1958), "During each of the half dozen evenings devoted to the jazz and poetry experiments the club was packed. San Franciscans of every strata of society came to hear what was obviously a new and intriguing artistic excursion."[vii] And as Barry Silesky noted in *Ferlinghetti: The Artist in His Time*, "Only about a hundred could fit into the room, but on the very first night, some five hundred more lined up outside to get in and a fire marshal had to be called to clear the hallway. It seemed to everyone an idea whose time had come, and the idea spread quickly."[viii]

What is jazz poetry? Rexroth both posed and gave his answer to that question in his essay "Jazz Poetry," published in March 1958 in *The Nation*. "It is the reciting of suitable poetry with the music of a jazz band, usually small and comparatively quiet. Most emphatically, it is not recitation with 'background' music."[ix] More formally, jazz poetry has been defined as "poetry that demonstrates jazz-like rhythm or the feel of improvisation."[x] By that definition, "Thou Shalt Not Kill" bears little resemblance to jazz poetry, since, as Sascha Feinstein observed in *Jazz Poetry: From the 1920s to the Present*, 'It does not include direct references to jazz or experimental techniques in rhythm, meter, or form that

---

1   For a detailed account of the similarities between these two poems, see David S. Wills' essay "Thou Shalt Not Howl": https://beatdom.substack.com/p/thou-shalt-not-howl

might call attention to the music's influence." That said, Feinstein conceded the piece succeeded "because of its length, which enabled the players to interact more organically with the reader. More important, the use of repetition as a frame… allowed the musicians to anticipate the rhythm of the poem…"[xi]

Rexroth was no stranger to jazz poetry, or "poetry-and-jazz" as he preferred to call it—to its experimental nature, its possibilities and limitations. He had performed to jazz accompaniment in Chicago alongside Langston Hughes (an early exponent of jazz poetry who led the way with the Harlem Renaissance in the 1920s) and with Maxwell Bondenheim in Greenwich Village. He had written extensively about jazz and championed the likes of Charles Mingus, one of the greatest jazz composers of them all. "The combination of poetry and jazz with the poet reciting, gives the poet a new kind of audience," he wrote in "Jazz Poetry." "Not necessarily a bigger one, but a more normal one—ordinary people out for the evening, looking for civilized entertainment."[xii] Rexroth, not for the first time, had seen which way the wind was blowing. And for a brief moment in the late 1950s, it blew across the bay into San Francisco.

> They are stoning Stephen,
> They are casting him forth from every city in the world.
> Under the Welcome sign,
> Under the Rotary emblem,
> On the highway in the suburbs,
> His body lies under the hurling stones.

The poem references persecuted saints, Stephen, Sebastian, and Lawrence (with perhaps just a nod to D.H. Lawrence), but Rexroth chose another Lawrence as his running man for those six nights. "Rexroth picked me out of nowhere," Ferlinghetti recalled in *The Paris Review Interviews: Beat Writers at Work*. "I was completely unknown except for a little self-published book of poetry here at City Lights called *Pictures of the Gone World*. In 1958 [sic], just when *Coney Island of the Mind* was coming out, he asked me to perform with him at the Cellar Jazz Club here in North Beach."[xiii] In an interview with Jerome Rothenberg and David Antin, conducted in 1958 but not published until 2003, Rexroth explained his reasons for choosing Ferlinghetti: "Larry came to it late and didn't really know much about jazz to start with. But he's a good foil for me. We work well together."[xiv] Ferlinghetti, in awe of Rexroth, was happy to play second fiddle: "Rexroth was the great master, and I was just a kid."[xv]

"If you think that will open your eyes,"[xvi] says Adam to Eve in the hand-drawn poster advertising the night, "you should dig those Wednesday night Poetry and Jazz Sessions at the Cellar." "Rexroth and Ferlinghetti and the Cellar Jazz Quintet, too!" chimes the serpent coiled around the Tree of Knowledge. "I read you, man, loud and clear," says Eve, about to bite down on a red apple. Rexroth and Ferlinghetti were reading if not singing from the same song sheet when it came to their feelings about modern poetry. "It is very important to get poetry out of the hands of the professors and out of the hands of the squares," Rexroth told Ralph J. Gleason. "If we can get poetry out into the life of the country it can be creative. Homer, or the guy who recited Beowulf, was show business. We simply want to make poetry a part of show business."[xvii] Ferlinghetti agreed: "The jazz comes in as part of the attempt to get the audience back."[xviii] "The real problem in putting jazz and poetry together," Rexroth informed Gleason,

> is in finding people who are flexible enough. You have to find people who can play different kinds of jazz and you can't have a jazz bigot... lots of musicians are anti-verbal, you know. The group at The Cellar is young and flexible and they stay put. This is a tremendous advantage. Where bands understand poetry and poets understand jazz, it will catch on.[xix]

The Cellar, a former Chinese restaurant, was turned into a jazz club by musicians Wil Carlson, Jack Minger, and Sonny Nelson in 1956. It quickly became a fixture on the North Beach scene. "At the Cellar, you walk down a flight of old wooden stairs, through an art gallery and into the subterranean improvised, timbered, rectangular room," ran a report by Allen Brown in the *San Francisco Chronicle*, June 15, 1958, "where the reading of poetry to modern jazz was born in San Francisco. Four men—two of them bearded, one mustached—are playing instruments."[xx] The musicians, the Cellar Jazz Quintet, were comprised of band leader Bruce Lippincott (tenor sax), Dickie Mills (trumpet), Bill Weisjahns (piano), Bob Lewis and/or Jerry Goode (bass), and club co-owner Sonny Nelson, billed as Sonny Wayne (drums). "Those days in 'North Beach' San Francisco were never boring!" Nelson wrote in a missive (collected in the Sonny Nelson Papers at the San Francisco History Center). "And the days and nights at the 'Jazz Cellar' unforgettable."[xxi]

One night in 1956, a young waitress got up on the stage and started to recite her poetry as the band played. Her name (she always insisted on using lower case) was ruth weiss. Dubbed "The Goddess of the Beat Generation" by *Chronicle* columnist Herb Caen, weiss had been reciting poetry to jazz since 1949. Her performance went down a storm with the audience and soon the management were advertising Wednesdays as "Poetry and Jazz Night." "She was a big part of it, believe me," Sonny Nelson informed Preston Whaley Jr. in *Blows Like a Horn: Beat Writing, Jazz, Style, and Markets in the Transformation of U.S. Culture*. "We had huge crowds. Locals came to hear the sessions and soon so did celebrities such as Lenny Bruce, Dizzy Gillespie, widely read local critic Ralph Gleason, Charles Mingus, and William Carlos Williams."[xxii] "Once a week, on Wednesday, I did poetry and jazz," weiss told Nancy M. Grace in *Breaking the Rule of Cool:*:

> I did this for months, and then I started inviting other poets. I did this for about two years or so.... Well, it was only after that that some of the other well-known poets, whose names I'm not going to mention because everyone knows them, ended up doing the same thing. Only they were smart. They recorded them and got records out of it. So nobody knows that I did this, innovate jazz and poetry in San Francisco in 1956 at The Cellar.[xxiii]

One of the records weiss was referring to was, of course, Fantasy Records' *Poetry Readings in The Cellar*. Founded by brothers Max and Sol Weiss (no relation) in 1949, Fantasy Records was something of an oddity among independent jazz labels: they made money. With Dave Brubeck—then an unknown pianist—as one of their talents, they made a lot of money. "We weren't die-hard jazz fans, never were, still aren't," Max Weiss told Ted Gioia in *West Coast Jazz: Modern Jazz in California 1945-1960*. "Anything that sold, we would sell."[xxiv] The brothers were quick to spot the potential of the "poetry-to-jazz" that Rexroth and Ferlinghetti were laying down at The Cellar and a deal was struck to record and press an LP on Fantasy's signature red vinyl. Each poet occupied a single side. Side A was given to "Thou Shalt Not Kill."

> You,
> The hyena with polished face and bow tie,
> In the office of a billion dollar
> Corporation devoted to service;
> The vulture dripping with carrion,
> Carefully and carelessly robed in imported tweeds,
> Lecturing on the Age of Abundance;

It isn't difficult to imagine, with the accusatory, repeated use of the word "you" in part I of the poem, that the audience might have felt it was to them he was pointing the finger, but Rexroth was venting spleen at the invisible "behemoths" of corporate America—the hyenas and the vultures and the jackals, the rich and the all-powerful stoking bonfires of destruction as they watched it rain down on the poor from their glass towers.

> The jackal in double-breasted gabardine,
> Barking by remote control,
> In the United Nations;
> The vampire bat seated at the couch head,
> Notebook in hand, toying with his decerebrator;
> The autonomous, ambulatory cancer,
> The Superego in a thousand uniforms;
> You, the finger man of behemoth,
> The murderer of the young men.

On *Poetry Readings in The Cellar*, it is difficult to ascertain the atmosphere in the club the night the recording was made, all but impossible to gauge the audience reaction. They simply aren't present. There are no whoops of encouragement; none of Kerouac's "Go, Go, Go!" that greeted "Howl" on its first performance. Rexroth's paced delivery is raw, nearly hysterical at times, as befits the words, and his habit of extending vowel sounds and pausing when the end of a line coincides with the end of a sentence produces a suitably oratorical tone. The musicians syncopate well with the material, counterpointing in the spaces in and around Rexroth's performance, but without the atmosphere—the audience—it might just as well have been recorded in a studio.

According to Feinstein, "Rexroth feared, and rightfully so, that his performance would be cast off as being careless, undignified and trite."[xxv] To counteract this, he insisted on very precise, careful composition, far removed from what we think of as improvisation.

"We have found that the effects we want are obtained by making sure that each musician knows exactly what the poet is doing—what he means, and what technical effects he employs," Rexroth wrote of his working methods in "Jazz and Poetry" for *Esquire*. "Each musician has a sheet with the text in front of him, which he uses as a cue sheet and for all sorts of marginal musical notation. Then comes plenty of careful rehearsal, each one taped and played back and carefully analyzed... the constant effort is to increase spontaneity, not to limit it. We find, like all artists, that you have to work hard to obtain freedom of expression."[xxvi]

In Part II of "Thou Shalt Not Kill," Rexroth asks what happened to all the poets who died young or in obscurity:

> What happened to Robinson,
> Who used to stagger down Eighth Street,
> Dizzy with solitary gin?
> Where is Masters, who crouched in
> His law office for ruinous decades?
> Where is Leonard who thought he was
> A locomotive? And Lindsay,
> Wise as a dove, innocent
> As a serpent, where is he?
>   Timor mortis conturbat me.

Each of the six stanzas in Part II ends with the same refrain, *Timor mortis conturbat me*: "the fear of death disturbs me." Taken from a phrase more commonly found in medieval Scottish and English poetry, "Sinning daily, and not repenting, the fear of death disturbs me" is a Catholic prayer for the souls in purgatory and Rexroth makes full use of the religious rhetoric. He sounds like a soon-to-be-defrocked priest in the pulpit, wondering aloud if his own future lies along a similar path as Edna Millay ("who took / Her last straight whiskey"), Lola Ridge ("alone in an / Icy furnished room"), and Max Bodenheim ("butchered in stinking squalor"). The artist's destiny in an uncaring world illustrates Rexroth's feelings about his own future. *Timor mortis conturbat me*.

> How many stopped writing at thirty?
> How many went to work for Time?
> How many died of prefrontal
> Lobotomies in the Communist Party?
> How many are lost in the back wards

> Of provincial madhouses?
> How many on the advice of
> Their psychoanalysts, decided
> A business career was best after all?
> How many are hopeless alcoholics?

In Part III, Rexroth fires off a litany of dead poets and long-forgotten artists, each name thrown into the "maw of Moloch" with a cymbal crash from Sonny Nelson: "René Crevel! / Jaques Riguard! / Antonin Artaud!" Rexroth piles the bodies high. "Essenin! / Robert Desno! / Saint Pol Roux!"

"You don't always get what you want, of course, but we're learning," Rexroth told Rothenberg and Antin. "What I try with my own stuff is to work the poem to a slow climax through a series of quiet painful dissonances."[xxvii] For some, "painful" was an apt description of Rexroth's voice. It has often been criticized for its whining, jarring quality—hardly conducive to a jazz poetry recital. For poet David Meltzer, who would also perform to jazz at The Cellar, it was "unintentionally comic" and had "a droning patrician W.C. Fields bluster and mashed potato hauteur."[xxviii] For Steven Watson in *The Birth of the Beat Generation,* it sounded "like a B gangster pitcher."[xxix] That said, Rexroth's voice on *Poetry Readings in The Cellar* retains a powerful intensity and, as William Everson noted, "He delivers his pronouncements with such verve, even aplomb, that you sat there wondering, utterly charmed but rather bedazzled by the pyrotechnics."[xxx]

In Part IV, Rexroth names the guilty—the engineers of this post-war industrial nightmare:

> You killed him,
> Oppenheimer the Million-Killer,
> You killed him,
> Einstein the Gray Eminence.
> You killed him,
> Havanahavana, with your Nobel Prize.

And driving forward, grinding against the inhumanity that values greed over life, he proffers his own violent offensive:

> I want to pour gasoline down your chimneys.
> I want to blow up your galleries.
> I want to burn down your editorial offices.

> I want to slit the bellies of your frigid women.
> I want to sink your sailboats and launches.

The poem comes to a climax, Rexroth competing with the band, louder and louder, as he reduces the horror-makers of the modern world to their favourite Ivy League clothing:

> And all the birds of the deep sea rise up
> Over the luxury liners and scream,
> "You killed him! You killed him.
> In your God damned Brooks Brothers suit.
> You son of a bitch."

Robert Duncan, in the audience that night, was amused by the last line of the poem as he was wearing a Brooks Brothers suit.[xxxi] Painter John Allen Ryan had also been in the audience, as he told Allen Ginsberg:

> Last night Rexroth and Ferlinghetti had a whing-ding at the Cellar, backed by Bruce Lippincott and the Cellar Quartet [sic]. Rexwrath came on like Elvis Presslay, doing the rhumba, and the flashbulbs blinded everybody and the police came and made half of the people go away because of the fire regulations and only one exit, so they did a second performance later and Hub Crehan tried to have a fight with me over some chick named Kitty and Rex was very angry with him and Betty Keck who is the waitress there now sat and drank free beer because there were so many people that she couldn't get through to serve them.[xxxii]

The night was heady. The audience was drunk. "Thou Shalt Not Kill" hit the sweet spot. And it had only just begun.

The poet stares across the sea of heads as his friend and mentor leaves the stage. A camera flashes blind. The applause turns into small talk, laughter, and the clink of glasses. The band plays under. A shaft of house light cuts through the fog of smoke and time. Familiar faces lean forward. There is Michael McClure and Lenore

Kandel. There is Shig Murao,[2] Now it is his turn. Now it is his time. Lawrence Ferlinghetti pushes his way to the stage, takes his place at the music stand, and gives a nod to the band.

> I am leading a quiet life
> in Mike's Place every day
> watching the champs
> of the Dante Billiard Parlor
> and the French pinball addicts.
> I am leading a quiet life
> on lower East Broadway.
> I am an American.
> I was an American boy.[xxxiii]

Side B of *Poetry Readings in The Cellar* belongs to Ferlinghetti. Three poems, all taken from his soon-to-be-published collection, *A Coney Island of the Mind,* make the final cut: "Autobiography," "The Statue of St. Francis," and "Junkman's Obbligato." In "Autobiography," Ferlinghetti, in direct contrast to Rexroth's bombast, is showcasing a reflective, lyrical form, conversational in both tone and tempo. The poem explores themes of loss, disillusionment, and the search for identity in the aftermath of World War II, but unlike "Thou Shalt Not Kill," Ferlinghetti doesn't rail against the evils of society so much as subvert them through the lens of satirical humour and a resigned voice:

> I got caught stealing pencils
> From the Five and Ten Cent Store
> The same month I made Eagle Scout.
> I chopped trees for the CCC
> And sat on them.
> I landed in Normandy
> in a rowboat that turned over.
> I have seen the educated armies
> on the beach at Dover.

He is drawing on his formative years, his own experiences in a bombed-out Europe, and the poem resonates with and amplifies

---

2   McClure, Kandel, and Murao were photographed together at the event by Gerhard Gsheidle. The photograph can be seen in Lawrence Ferlinghetti and Nancy J. Peters, *Literary San Francisco: A pictorial history from its beginnings to the present day.*

the fragmented feelings of a generation still grappling with guilt and remorse in the atomic age. Hiroshima and Nagasaki are never far away.

"'Autobiography' is perhaps the first poem in the English language to be written specifically to be read with a jazz accompaniment,"[xxxiv] Gleason wrote in the liner notes—a bold claim, half of which is true. "It really developed right along with The Cellar sessions," Ferlinghetti affirmed. "When you do it this way, the poetry reads better as a result. Once it goes through the test, this oral test, then it makes it that way, you don't have to worry about it on the page."[xxxv] In a short preface to the "Oral Messages" section in *A Coney Island of the Mind*, where both "Autobiography" and "Junkman's Obbligato" are to be found, Ferlinghetti wrote: "These seven poems were conceived specifically for jazz accompaniment and as such should be considered as spontaneously spoken 'oral messages' rather than as poems written for the printed page. As a result of continued experimental reading with jazz, they are still in a state of change."[xxxvi]

This "state of change" indicates Ferlinghetti's openness to improvisation. Unlike the carefully rehearsed, notated, buttoned-down performance of Rexroth, Ferlinghetti is much looser in the collar, something appreciated by the musicians. "If we listen to each other, we can get a kind of question and answer thing going underneath, all without any key," band leader and tenor sax player Bruce Lippincott told Gleason. "It comes down to a different approach to jazz, in a way. The idea of responding, not in a preordained way, but in a question and answer, sort of relative pitch way, a very direct way."[xxxvii]

This "question and answer," as Lippincott saw it, is a fugue-like technique, where a melody or phrase is introduced by one part (the poet), picked up by others (the band), and developed by interweaving the parts. After Ferlinghetti recites "I have heard a hundred housebroken Ezra Pounds. / They should all be freed. / It is long since I was a herdsman," Dickie Mills and Sonny Nelson answer with a vaudevillian trumpet and snare drum, engaging with and complementing Ferlinghetti's delivery. It is most successful, according to Gleason, when "Ferlinghetti reads a passage and then pauses while the band improvises four bars of jazz on the chords of 'I Got Rhythm.'"[xxxviii]

Writing a "San Francisco Letter" for the second issue of *Evergreen Review* in 1957, Rexroth described his comrade-at-arms as "a lazy-looking, good natured man with the canny cocky eye of an old-time vaudeville tenor," adding, "There is a lot more real bite to Ferlinghetti and a deeper humour." Rexroth was unequivocal in his praise for Ferlinghetti's poetry: "so easy and relaxed, is constructed of most complex rhythms, all organized to produce just the right tone."[xxxix] Like Rexroth, Ferlinghetti utilizes anaphora (the repetition of a word or phrase at the beginning of successive clauses) to great effect. Swapping Rexroth's "You" and "They" for the more personal, first person "I" (an all-seeing "I"), Ferlinghetti gives the musicians a point to which they can easily return, and builds rhythm into the poem. For the audience, it affords a sense of intimacy.

> I have wandered in various nightwoods.
> I have leaned in drunken doorways.
> I have written wild stories
> without punctuation.
> I am the man.
> I was there.
> I suffered
> somewhat.

Ferlinghetti's language—simple, lyrical, colloquial—is the American idiom of the streets, and found, according to Gleason, "considerable acceptance from the jazz musicians themselves."[xl] Ferlinghetti attributed this to "the way I was writing poetry all along, by using the common speech and having no allusions in there that the average under-read citizen wouldn't be able to understand."[xli] In "Note on Poetry in San Francisco," written about the same time, Ferlinghetti saw a rejection of classical form in favour of the colloquial as his modus operandi: "For it amounts to getting the poet out of the inner esthetic sanctum where he has too long been contemplating his complicated navel. It amounts to getting poetry back into the street where it once was, out of the classroom, out of the speech department, and—in fact—off the printed page."[xlii]

Where Rexroth named other writers in his litany of the forgotten dead, Ferlinghetti brings them back to life in paraphrased lines such as "I looked homeward / and saw no angel" (Thomas Wolfe), "I have wandered lonely / as a crowd" (William Wordsworth), and "I too have ridden boxcars boxcars boxcars" (Allen Ginsberg). "You can have all kinds of allusions," he told Gleason, "to 'Waiting for Godot,' Joyce or Hamlet or anything else as long as it has a public surface, too, which doesn't depend on this."[xliii]

Ferlinghetti's light vocal touch and easy cadence on *Poetry Readings in The Cellar* counterpoints Rexroth's venomous screech, but it still invited some criticism. On September 16, 1957, James Laughlin of New Directions (who were looking to publish *A Coney Island of the Mind*) wrote to Ferlinghetti and mentioned he'd heard the Fantasy recording, praising it on one hand as "powerful stuff" but adding that he didn't care for the "monotony of the verbal tone." "Both you and Kenneth seemed to have your voice at the same pitch all the way through. Good old Dylan, as I recall, used to put a lot of variation into his readings, almost as if he were an actor acting the lines, and I think that helped to put it across... I think some variation in pitch and force would help."[xliv]

"This is, er, 'The Statue of St. Francis.' It really happened," Ferlinghetti informs the audience on *Poetry Readings* before slipping smoothly into Poem #6 from the main body of *A Coney Island of the Mind*. The musicians improvise around the words, seemingly without predetermined chord patterns or rhythms. "We set up as the first rule—listen to each other," Lippincott revealed. "And second—respond with our instruments as emotionally as possible to the *words* of the poem and also the prearranged form."[xlv]

>   They were putting up the statue
>   of Saint Francis
>   in front of the church
>   of Saint Francis
>   in the city of San Francisco
>   in a little side street
>   just off the Avenue
>   where no birds sang
>   and the sun was coming up on time
>   in its usual fashion
>   and just beginning to shine
>   on the statue of Saint Francis
>   where no birds sang[xlvi]

The prearranged form—the layout of "The Statue of Saint Francis" as seen on the page—is revealing. It is not indented to the left margin as with "Autobiography" and "Junkman's Obbligato," not specifically written as an "oral message" meant for jazz, but splashed across the page in left and right lines. As Barry Silesky observed in *Ferlinghetti: The Artist in His Time*, "Ferlinghetti wanted to use the page as a canvas. Rather than being restricted to the left margin, these poems were designed to use the whole page... Poetry happens not only in the language, but between the lines, in the white space."[xlvii] This was in tune with the idea of improvisation and "between the lines, in the white space" was a place the musicians could hang their playing, as Lippincott explained:

> ...for this many lines we will have the drums swelling and rolling and the bass will enter at the bottom and bowed. Prearranged that way—letting the instruments know when they are to enter and what they are to do. Then you begin to see music differently. It becomes more visual and broader. You give it a new dimension with a much stronger visual element, rather than just an auditory one. Any really aware musician is attracted by this.[xlviii]

With "Junkman's Obbligato" (a poem that owes much to T.S. Eliot and "The Love Song of J. Alfred Prufrock") Ferlinghetti is straight out of the traps: "Let's go / Come on / Let's go." Dickie Mills' trumpet establishes the rhythm, while Ferlinghetti, at a slow tempo, slurs the words like a drunken street philosopher calling out in vain at passers-by.

> Let us arise and go now
> to where dogs do it
> Over the hill
> where they keep the earthquakes
> behind the city dumps
> lost among gasmains and garbage.[xlix]

The influence of Eliot and the opening lines of Prufrock ("Let us go then, you and I / When the evening is spread out against the sky"[l]) is palpable. "I actually had to put T.S. Eliot books out of the house because my poetry was so influenced," Ferlinghetti later admitted in *Interview Magazine*. "Everything I wrote sounded like Eliot."[li] The world of "Junkman's Obbligato" is Eliot for a post-war generation—a city wasteland of "automobile graveyards," "garbage fires," and "broken bibles," of "Sleep in phone booths / Puke in pawnshops / wailing for a winter overcoat." It is poetry for the Beat Generation.

> Let's go
> smelling of sterno
> where the benches are filled
> with discarded Bowling Green statues
> in the interior dark night
> of the flowery bowery
> our eyes watery
> with the contemplation
> of empty bottles of muscatel.

Nelson's drums enter at the start of the second stanza, producing a marching sound that threatens to overpower Ferlinghetti's rising inflections. Ferlinghetti, in the guise of The Junkman—the buyer and seller of human detritus—implores the world about him to see itself. He is Diogenes, living in a garbage can, shouting at the American dream:

> Let us arise and go now
> under the city
> where ashcans roll
> and reappear in putrid clothes
> as the uncrowned underground kings
> of subway men's rooms.
> Let us feed the pigeons
> at the City Hall
> urging them to do their duty
> in the Major's Office.

The Junkman is a character fit for jazz. The Junkman is a metaphor for life, with just a sniff of heroin perhaps, and while he is guilty of romanticizing poverty, Ferlinghetti imbues the character with a genuine sadness as he sees better worlds in the flames of oil drum fires. The Junkman dreams of escaping the screaming urban urgency of the city.

> Goodbye I'm walking out on the whole scene.
> Close down the joint.
> The system is all loused up.
> Rome was never like this.
> I'm tired of waiting for Godot.

The Junkman, his delivery sobering, plays to the brooding instruments that cloud the atmosphere and complement his ominous tone. His words are loaded with warnings ("Another flood is coming / though not the kind you think") and consumer references ("let us not wait for the cadillacs"), metaphors for the ultimate capitalist con, boulders for burdens. He is Sisyphus, "a social climber / climbing downward / And the descent is difficult."

"Junkman's Obbligato" is perhaps the most successful of the four poems featured on *Poetry Readings in The Cellar*, thanks to the way Lippincott and the band work with it and to Ferlinghetti's rendering of a character immediately recognizable to both poetry and jazz milieus. The Junkman has seen down the alleyways and backstreets of life. He buys and sells what others discard. He has known "whores third hand" and seen "under Brooklyn's Bridge / blown statues in baggy pants." The world fascinates and repulses him.

The Junkman imagines a pastoral paradise far away from the city—a place he calls "Manisfree," the Arcadia of Greek legend. "Let us arise and go now / to the Isle of Manisfree / and live the true blue simple life". The longing in his voice is carried by a faint trumpet softly fading with the last words of the poem. He is Theocritus, the poet, dreaming:

> of wisdom and wonderment
> where all things grow
> straight up
> aslant and singing
> in the yellow sun
> poppies out of cowpods
> thinking angels out of turds.
> I must arise and go now
> to the Isle of Manisfree
> way up behind the broken words
> and woods of Arcady.

"Broken words" or no, Ferlinghetti made a suitable mark on the jazz poetry scene with "Autobiography" and "Junkman's Obbligato," which in turn would play their part in making *A Coney Island of the Mind* such a success. He would have hated the classification, but both those poems, and many others in the collection, are prime cuts of Beat.

After the act come "the facts," and sometimes it is better to experience than explain. "The audience every night thinks it is wonderful," Rexroth wrote in the *Evergreen Review*. He continued:

> Musically, we are still working on it. The problem is that jazz is not really improvised cold, but begins with at least the chord patterns of tunes known to the whole band. Each jazz number has a specific shape based on the 33-34-36 bar popular tune. Our problem is to keep it free and flexible and continuously developing and not allow the form to conflict with the form of poetry... We have felt that this was best worked towards by using head arrangements at first and keeping the whole thing fluid and spontaneous until we had a better insight into the specific problems. Understand – this is spoken poetry, not sung. Anyway – so far it has been a great show, received with wild enthusiasm. Last week we really got it. Every number had fluidity, invention, drive, and form, and furthermore, it swung. And if it don't swing, it ain't it. I hope some record company takes us up soon. It should make not just a very popular twelve-inch disc, but it might well start a craze.[lii]

Poetry Readings in The Cellar is an important if flawed recording, but it provides only a whisper of what the Wednesday "Poetry and Jazz" nights at The Cellar were truly like. At just over 42 minutes, the LP leads us to speculate as to what other poetry Rexroth and Ferlinghetti performed over the six nights. Since they were all "conceived specifically for jazz," we can assume Ferlinghetti recited the poems from the "oral messages" section of *A Coney Island of the Mind*, namely: "I Am Waiting," "Dog," "Christ Climbed Down," "The Long Street," and "Meet Miss Subways." But was that all? And what other choices did Rexroth make?

It is known that Rexroth liked to perform works by other writers at this time. In "The Sounds of the Fury" published in the *Prairie Schooner* in 1959, Harry Roskolenko recalled that he "left many of his work sheets behind in my apartment," mentioning "aside notes to the musicians"[liii] on Carl Sandburg's "Mag" and translations of Pablo Neruda. Furthermore, a photograph taken at The Cellar by *LIFE Magazine's* Nat Farbman clearly shows

17

Rexroth reading from the anthology *New Directions 15*, which includes his own translations of several French poets, with two poems—"Epitaph" and "Last Poem"—by the surrealist poet Robert Desnos. Since Desnos (who died in a Nazi concentration camp) is one of the poets mentioned in the litany of the dead in "Thou Shalt Not Kill" it seems only logical that Rexroth would tie these in.

On the opening night, sound artist and humourist Henry Jacobs made a recording that, unlike the Fantasy record, captures the essence of the evening: the audience, clinking glasses, small talk, and the ring of the till. This remarkable recording, which puts the listener in the room, was released as a bonus CD with Jacobs' 2010 album *Around The World With Henry Jacobs*. We can now say with certainty that on the opening night Rexroth performed "For a Masseuse and Prostitute" and "Between Myself and Death" (from *The Signature of All Things*, 1950); "Quietly," "The Old Song and Dance," and "She is Away" (from *In Defence of the Earth*, 1956); along with "A Singing Voice" and "A Dialogue of Watching." For his part, Ferlinghetti recited "Sometime during Eternity" (poem #5 in *A Coney Island of the Mind*, 1958) and "Just as I used to Say" and "The World is a Beautiful Place" (poems #2 and #25 from *Pictures of the Gone World*, 1955).

It is difficult to assess the overall success of jazz poetry at The Cellar, but the idea travelled well enough. Lawrence Lipton in *The Holy Barbarians* saw what Rexroth and Ferlinghetti were doing as "a restoration of poetry to its ancient, traditional role as a socially functional art allied with music in a single, reintegrated art form." Lipton would soon follow their example with his own jazz poetry nights in Venice West. With much the same result.

> We turned to jazz music because jazz is the musical language of America in our time. Modern poetry was born at the same time as modern jazz was born and both have had a similar history. Both have had the same friends and the same enemies. Both aimed at freeing their art from the straitjacket of the printing press: in the case of poetry, from the printed page, in the case of jazz, from the printed score. They belong together.[liv]

In *West Coast Jazz: Modern Jazz in California 1945-1960*, Ted Gioia offered a gushing summation of the jazz poetry experiment, albeit as a postscript note: "Beatniks met jazz musicians on a square and even basis at this Green Street club. It even became a setting in the novel *Desolation Angels* by the quintessential beat writer Jack Kerouac—who once got thrown out of the Cellar. The attempt by poets Kenneth Rexroth and Lawrence Ferlinghetti to mix their poetry recitations with live jazz music, from February 1957, was a seminal event in San Francisco's cultural history."[lv]

Not everyone who saw Rexroth and Ferlinghetti perform, or who listened to *Poetry Readings in The Cellar* a year later, was impressed by the results. Barry Silesky in *Ferlinghetti: The Artist in His Time* felt inclined to blame the band. "The music at The Cellar was loose, improvisational, 'semi-spontaneous,' but the musicians were generally more interested in their own self expression than in creating an ensemble that supported or harmonized with the poetry. Neither Ferlinghetti nor Rexroth had any musical training, and most aficionados felt the performances weren't particularly successful, despite their popularity at the time."[lvi] ruth weiss, who had started it all, took a swing: "Ferlinghetti and Rexroth were poets who read over jazz, but jazz was a part of me; I swung."[lvii] David Meltzer in *Reading Jazz* was equally unreserved in his opinion: "[they] seemed separate from the music, the jazz only background to the poem, not interactive with it"[lviii] and amplified his feelings in his 2001 essay "Poetry & Jazz":

> The Beats were over-the-hill guys; they didn't, like, swing. Rexroth, Ferlinghetti, and Kenneth Patchen read alerting and often alarming words while the musicians played in the background. Listen to the "live" Fantasy recordings of Rexroth and Ferlinghetti. Both are formidable poets, public charmers and disarmers, but neither seemed connected to the jazz comped behind their words. The words came first, music second. As a greenhorn poet, my jazz poets were singers. Whatever poetry was, it wasn't jazz.[lix]

Kenneth Rexroth and Lawrence Ferlinghetti shared a core belief about poetry: they wanted to pry it from the deaf ears of the academies and the silence of the printed word and "sing it" in the streets. Jazz poetry was merely part of that desire, not the whole of it. In a 2000 interview for *Elsewhere*, Ferlinghetti reflected on the experiment: "There were a few tracks where we really hit it, but generally it was a disaster, murder on the poetry. Musicians were like, 'Man, go ahead and read your poems, but we got to blow.' So the poet ends up trying to be heard above the din, like he's hawking fish on the street corner."[lx] It was left to Kenneth Rexroth, who, despite his initially barbed comments about those who took up the mantle, was moved to write on the liner notes for his 1960 Fantasy Records LP *Poetry and Jazz at the Blackhawk*: "Now the fad has died away and the permanent, solid achievements remain. The form is not going to revolutionize either jazz or poetry, but it is going to stay with us, and both jazz and poetry are going to have one new way of expressing themselves, and so are going to be just a little richer. This is as it should be, because jazz poetry is fun to listen to, and it is even greater fun to do."[lxi]

In the final analysis, those six nights of poetry-and-jazz and the resultant LP *Poetry Readings in The Cellar* are perhaps best judged not by their quality or success in terms of synthesis, but by what this hybrid "experiment" kick-started. Many more jazz poetry nights sprang up across the country; many more albums were released. In the coming years Kenneth Patchen, David Meltzer, Allen Ginsberg, and the king of them all, Jack Kerouac, would perform their poetry to jazz music. They were by no means the first, Rexroth and Ferlinghetti, but thanks to those smoke-kissed nights down in the basement with the Cellar Jazz Quintet in the spring of 1957, neither would they be the last.

ENDNOTES

i   Kenneth Rexroth, "Thou Shalt Not Kill", *Poetry Foundation*, archived from the original. Accessed 4 May 2025. http://www.poetryfoundation.org/archive/poem.html?id=171537.
ii   Robert Duncan, *An Open Map: The Correspondence of Robert Duncan and Charles Olson* (Albuquerque: University of New Mexico Press, 2017), p.63
iii   Charles Olson, *An Open Map*, p.73.
iv   Linda Hamalian, *A Life of Kenneth Rexroth* (New York: W. W. Norton & Company, 1991), p. 231.
v   Henry Miller, *Time of the Assassins: A Study of Rimbaud* (New York: New Directions, 1962), p. viii.
vi   Lawrence Ferlinghetti in (ed.) George Plimpton, *Beat Writers at Work* (New York: Random House, 1999), p. 345.
vii   Ralph J. Gleason, liner notes, *Poetry Readings in "The Cellar"* (Fantasy Records, 1958), Fantasy 7002.

viii   Barry Silesky, *Ferlinghetti: The Artist in His Time* (New York: Warner Books, 1990), p. 89.
ix   Rexroth, "Jazz Poetry," *The Nation*, March 1958.
x   Barry Wallenstein, "JazzPoetry/Jazz-Poetry/'JazzPoetry' ???," *African American Review*, vol. 17, no. 4, 1993, pp. 665-671. Accessed 8 July 2025. *JSTOR*, https://doi.org/10.2307/3041904.
xi   Sascha Feinstein, *Jazz Poetry: From the 1920s to the Present* (Westport, CT: Praeger Publishers, 1997), p. 69.
xii   Rexroth, "Jazz Poetry," *The Nation*.
xiii   Ferlinghetti, *Beat Writers at Work*, p. 344.
xiv   Rexroth, interview with Jerome Rothenberg and David Antin, 1958. Accessed 6 June 2025. www.jacket2.org/commentrary/jerome-rothenberg-david-antin-first-interview-kenneth-rexroth-1958-redux.
xv   Silesky, *Ferlinghetti: The Artist in His Time*, p. 47.
xvi   Original Poster for The Cellar, Sonny Nelson Papers (SFH 78), San Francisco History Center, San Francisco Public Library.
xvii   Gleason, liner notes.
xviii   Ibid.
xix   Ibid.
xx   Allen Brown, "The Beatniks," *San Francisco Chronicle*, June 15, 1958, reprinted in (eds.) William Hogan and William German, *The San Francisco Chronicle Reader* (New York: McGraw Hill Book Company, 1962), p. 40.
xxi   Sonny Nelson missive, Sonny Nelson Papers (SFH 78), San Francisco History Center.
xxii   Preston Whalley Jr, *Blows Like a Horn: Beat Writing, Jazz, Style, and Markets in the Transformation of U.S. Culture* (Cambridge, Massachusetts: Harvard University Press, 2004), p. 66.
xxiii   ruth weiss in (eds.) Nancy M. Grace and Ronna C. Johnson, *Breaking the Rule of Cool: Interviewing and Reading Women Beat Writers* (Mississippi: The University Press of Mississippi, 2004), p. 71.
xxiv   Ted Gioia, *West Coast Jazz: Modern Jazz in California 1945-1960* (Berkeley and Los Angeles: University of California Press, 1992), p. 64.
xxv   Feinstein, *Jazz Poetry: From the 1920s to the Present*, p.68.
xxvi   Rexroth, "Jazz and Poetry," *Esquire*, May 1958.
xxvii   Rexroth, interview with Rothenberg and Antin, 1958.
xxviii   David Meltzer, *San Francisco Beat*, p. 229.
xxix   Steven Watson, *The Birth of the Beat Generation: Visionaries, Rebels, and Hipsters, 1944-1960* (New York: Pantheon Books, 1995), p. 199.
xxx   Hamalian, "Everson on Rexroth: An Interview," *Literary Review*, vol. 26, no. 3, 1988, p. 424.
xxxi   Hamalian, *A Life of Kenneth Rexroth*, p. 407.
xxxii   John Allen Ryan, letter to Allen Ginsberg, Allen Ginsberg Archive, S1b5f15.
xxxiii   Ferlinghetti, "Autobiography," *A Coney Island of the Mind* (New York: New Directions, 1958), p. 60.
xxxiv   Gleason, liner notes.
xxxv   Ibid.
xxxvi   Ferlinghetti, Preface to "Oral Messages," *A Coney Island of the Mind*, p. 48.

xxxvii Gleason, liner notes.
xxxviii Ibid.
xxxix Rexroth, "San Francisco Letter," *Evergreen Review*, vol. 1, no. 2, 1957, p.12.
xl Gleason, liner notes.
xli Ibid.
xlii Ferlinghetti, "Note on Poetry in San Francisco" reprinted in (ed.) Ann Charters, *Beat Down to Your Soul* (New York: Penguin Books, 2001), p. 168.
xliii Gleason, liner notes.
xliv James Laughlin, letter to Lawrence Ferlinghetti, September 16, 1957, reprinted in Neeli Cherkovski, *Ferlinghetti A Life: Expanded Edition* (Boston, Massachusetts: Black Sparrow Press, 2022), p. 82.
xlv Gleason, liner notes.
xlvi Ferlinghetti, "The Statue of St Francis" (Poem #6), *A Coney Island of the Mind*, p. 17.
xlvii Silesky, *Ferlinghetti: The Artist in His Time*, p. 55.
xlviii Gleason, liner notes.
xlix Ferlinghetti, "Junkman's Obbligato," *A Coney Island of the Mind*, p 54.
l T. S. Eliot, "The Love Song of J. Alfred Prufrock," *Selected Poems* (London: Faber and Faber, 1961), p. 11.
li Christopher Bollen, "Lawrence Ferlinghetti," *Interview Magazine*, December 1, 2012. Retrieved June 7, 2025. www.interviewmagazine.com/culture/Lawrence-ferlinghetti
lii Rexroth, "San Francisco Letter," *Evergreen Review*, pp. 13-14.
liii Harry Roskolenko, "The Sounds of the Fury," *Prairie Schooner*, vol. 33, no. 2, 1959, p. 150.
liv Lawrence Lipton, *The Holy Barbarians* (New York: Mansfield Publishing, 2009), p. 222.
lv Gioia, *West Coast Jazz*, p. 372.
lvi Silesky, *Ferlinghetti: The Artist in His Time*, p. 90.
lvii weiss, quoted in Art Peterson, "The Cellar," *The Semaphore*, no. 194, 2011. Accessed through https://www.foundsf.org/index.php?title=The_Cellar&oldid=27257
lviii Meltzer, *Reading Jazz* (San Francisco: Mercury house, 1993), p. 178.
lix Meltzer, "Poetry & Jazz" reprinted in (ed.) Charters, *Beat Down to Your Soul*, p. 398.
lx Graham Reid, "Lawrence Ferlinghetti Interviewed (2000): The angry old man," *Elsewhere*, July 7, 2010. Retrieved June 3, 2025. www.elsewhere.co.nz/writingelsewhere/469/lawrenceferlinghetti-interviewed-2000-the-angry-old-man/
lxi Rexroth, liner notes, *Poetry and Jazz at the Blackhawk* (Fantasy Records, 1960). Fantasy 7008.

THE 6 GALLERY READING AND THE SAN FRANCISCO RENAISSANCE

BY DAVID S. WILLS

Most of what has been written about the 6 Gallery reading in the past is questionable at best and in my latest book, *A Remarkable Collection of Angels*, I have offered for the first time a comprehensive study of that landmark event, setting it in its proper historical context, dispelling many myths, and establishing a number of key facts. The following essay is not an excerpt from that book but it draws upon the same research and pushes in a slightly different direction. It asks whether the San Francisco Renaissance was really born that night and, if so, what changed in the city's literary scene.

Although the 6 Gallery reading is an event surrounded by an incredible amount of myth and uncertainty, there is little disagreement that it was an important moment in the history of the Beat Generation. We can debate the extent to which is really pushed Lawrence Ferlinghetti into publishing Allen Ginsberg's poem, "Howl," and argue over the degree of impact it had on the reputations of the five young poets who took to the stage that night, but it is hard to deny that it marked a turning point. Prior to that evening, the writers we now consider as making up the Beat Generation had little in the way of literary reputations, with just a handful of readings and publications between them. A few months later they were all locally famous and two years on they were nationally known. It is hard to deny that the 6 Gallery reading more than any other single event seems responsible for their sudden success. It also marked a drastic and consequential expansion of a socio-literary group. In the words of Bill Morgan, "That night the Beat Generation was made whole. This extended family would grow over the next few years to accommodate a few other names, but the group's original nucleus of Kerouac, Ginsberg, and Burroughs was forever united with the San Francisco poets by this reading."[i] Indeed, Gary Snyder said that the 6 Gallery reading "was the beginning of the Beat Generation."[ii]

Few would agree with Snyder's claim but there is far more acceptance of something that Jack Kerouac wrote in his 1958 novel, *The Dharma Bums*. In chapter two, he said that the 6 Gallery reading was "the birth of the San Francisco Poetry Renaissance,"[iii] and this statement is widely accepted. However, over the years there have been various problems noted with this idea, and these include the fact that San Francisco had a poetry scene prior to the 6 Gallery reading and the use of the word "renaissance."[1]

Although the name and concept of the "San Francisco Renaissance" has been widely accepted, there has been some criticism. Ann Charters, in an early biography of Jack Kerouac, called it "a later journalist's term," which is true in that later journalists (as well as academics) used it to neatly categorise a group of writers and to label a sort of cultural atmosphere that

---

1   There is also the problem of categorising a movement that emerged unplanned, had no officially elected leader, and which overlapped with several other such movements. Some believe the San Francisco Renaissance essentially morphed into a nationwide movement and thus the name is misleading. That highlights the problem of separating it from the Beat and beatnik phenomena but it is not really within the scope of this essay to discuss such matters.

arose in a certain place at a certain time. Robert Duncan, who arguably was part of the movement (if we could call it that), complained that "[t]he term [...] shows that someone didn't know what a renaissance was at all. What did it mean? That we revived the Yukon poets or something?"[iv]

I would respectfully disagree with both critiques. In terms of Charters' criticism, she is suggesting that a single journalist at a later date named the group, but in fact the term was used by participants in the movement during the movement and it was also very widely discussed in the local media at that time. Thus, it was not exactly "a later journalist's term." Additionally, Ginsberg referred to it as a "renaissance" as early as March 1956. He seems to have been quoting or at least paraphrasing Kenneth Rexroth, who then used the full term "San Francisco Renaissance" in his introductory letter to the second issue of *Evergreen Review*, which was dedicated to the "San Francisco Scene" in 1957. In the summer of 1957, the San Francisco media began using the term and by the end of that year both Ginsberg and Kerouac were using it in their correspondence.[2]

As for Duncan's complaint, it actually seems to show that *he* did not understand the word "renaissance." He seems to believe it means a revival of something previously lost. This is of course what people mean when talking about *the Renaissance* that took place in Europe beginning in the 14th century, but any dictionary will tell you that *a renaissance* (as a common noun, not a proper one) means something a little different. Coming from the U.K., I tend to look to the Cambridge Dictionary, which says a renaissance is "a new growth of activity or interest in something, especially art, literature, or music," but even the American Merriam-Webster Dictionary says that it is "a movement or period of vigorous artistic and intellectual activity." Both would affirm that "San Francisco Renaissance" seems to be an apt description. In fact, Duncan himself used the term "Berkeley Renaissance" to refer to an earlier poetic movement of which he was a part, so it is unclear why he felt the term was apt for one but not the other.

Charters also noted that "[p]oetry had no need to be reborn in San Francisco since it had always been alive there,"[v] which is

---

2   I will note here that various participants seemed to favour the term "revolution" rather than "renaissance." Ginsberg used this in a 1957 article, and Ferlinghetti and Whalen both referred to the movement that way. However, all three (as well as others who used this word) seemed to refer to a larger cultural movement, perhaps somewhere between what we know today as the San Francisco Renaissance and the Beat Generation.

absolutely true but Kerouac was not saying it had been "*re*born." He merely noted that a new movement had been created in the city in October 1955. Still, this is a point that others have made and it is what this essay will mostly discuss. Although Kerouac did not explicitly state that the city gained its *first* poetic scene that night, one might come to that conclusion after reading a number of Beat histories. There are various enthusiastic quotes from the participants of the 6 Gallery reading that suggest they breezed into the city and started a movement in a sort of cultural wasteland, but this was far from true. San Francisco and the wider Bay Area had a literary scene before they appeared and it is worth asking whether the 6 Gallery reading began the San Francisco Renaissance or it was merely an important event in a renaissance that had already started, much as it was not the founding of the Beat Generation but certainly a key moment in its history.

THE SAN FRANCISCO POETRY SCENE PRE-6 GALLERY READING

Due to the later importance of the Beat poets, especially Allen Ginsberg and Gary Snyder, there is a tendency to look back on the 6 Gallery reading as the birth of *something*. After all, those two poets had met only one month earlier and Kerouac had met Snyder and Whalen just a few weeks before. The reading was also the debut of the era's most important poem and Beat mythology would have you believe that it was not going to be published until Ginsberg read it for an approving audience.[3] Books about the Beat writers, or about American literature more generally, often give the impression that the Beats arrived in San Francisco and created a poetry scene from nothing, and sometimes even those same writers seem to have suggested this. Snyder, for example, remarked that "[p]oetry suddenly seemed useful in 1955 San Francisco. From that day to this, there has never been a week without a reading in the Bay area."[vi] The use of "suddenly" of course suggests that poetry had not been of much value and his claim about readings implies that the 6 Gallery was the first such event.

---

3   It is debatable and hard to say definitively whether or not "Howl" would have been published but certainly Ginsberg and Ferlinghetti had reached an agreement long before the 6 Gallery reading. It is likely that the success of this event made Ferlinghetti more enthusiastic about it, though. Ginsberg also had at least one other publisher keen to put out an edition of his poem.

If one reads selectively, one can find similar claims among the poets who had lived in the city before the Beat writers. Ferlinghetti, for example, who had arrived in 1951, said that he came to a "provincial" city. Rexroth, who had sort of washed up in San Francisco by accident several decades earlier complained that not only did the city lack a literary scene but he struggled even to buy recently published books there.[vii] Major publishing houses apparently thought so little of the Bay Area that they wouldn't ship their books to local booksellers. Yet one could look to the same writers and find proof of the opposite. Indeed, in the same sentence as he called San Francisco "provincial," Ferlinghetti said it had "a wide open, non-academic poetry scene."[viii] Rexroth worked hard to help forge a literary scene and once he had done—with himself at the centre, of course—he raved about it to friends in other parts of the country. Ginsberg acknowledged when he arrived in the middle of 1954 that it had an incredible arts scene with "wild surrealist movies, art shows, jazz bands, hipsters, parties, cellar lounges filled with hi fidelity Bach etc."[ix] He went on to say, "All in all a very active cultured city the rival of NY for general relaxation and progressive artlife."

Perhaps this should not be surprising, for San Francisco had long since attracted writers. Jack London, Ambrose Bierce, Bret Harte, Mark Twain, George Sterling, and Gertrude Stein had all lived in or visited the city, staying at or visiting the famed Montgomery ("Monkey") Block, a magnet for literary types in the late 19th and early 20th centuries. But that was long before Ginsberg arrived and even if that one iconic building had possessed a certain allure for writers, evidently allowing for some kind of literary atmosphere, there was not much of a scene and little evidence of any wild poetry readings. The city was not known for publishing houses or magazines in the way it would be in the mid-20th century. When we look back at Ginsberg's initial impression of the city, we see that he was impressed by its cultural output, but notably he made no reference to literature. He only commented on music, film, and art. Even a year later, after much effort seeking out a literary scene, he complained that the city had no good writers.

There was, however, something of a literary scene and Ginsberg knew this; he just wasn't all that impressed by it. It seems to have started in the mid-forties, during or slightly after World War II. This was not exactly a San Francisco literary movement but rather one spanning the whole Bay Area and it was certainly more limited in scope than what we generally think of as the San Francisco Renaissance, comprising just a small number of writers scattered across the region and doing very little in terms of reading and publishing their work. In fact, although some of these people lived in San Francisco, it might be better to use the term Robert Duncan and others used at the time: the Berkeley Renaissance. This was used as "a joke [...] but it was not entirely a joke,"[x] according to Jack Spicer's biographers. The group was made up of Duncan and Spicer, as well as Robin Blaser, but there were other poets active at that time, and although there was no coherent movement, they did socialise and collaborate to a small degree. There were writers in Berkeley, Oakland, Sausalito, and San Francisco, as well as others slightly further afield, including Henry Miller, who famously resided at Big Sur, a few hours down the coast.

In 1944, Bern Porter and George Leite began *Circle* magazine from daliel's bookshop in Berkeley. There were nine issues between 1944 and 1946 and then a tenth in 1948. The list of contents shows many of the poets who made up the loose literary scene of the mid-forties and some that would later be associated with or even central to the San Francisco Renaissance: Miller, Rexroth, Duncan, Porter, William Everson, Philip Lamantia, Kenneth Patchen, Thomas Parkinson, Douglas MacAgy, W. Edwin Ver Becke, Weldon Kees, Rosalie Moore, Gil Orlovitz, Harold Norse, and more.

In April 1947, Madeline Gleason organised a two-night Festival of Poetry at the Labaudt Gallery in San Francisco. This event featured many of the aforementioned poets and also James Broughton, another relatively prominent local writer (albeit far better known as a filmmaker) who was friends with Duncan and Gleason. It was such a success that the event became an annual festival held until 1952.[4] Duncan reflected on this many years later, calling it "the first such Readings presented in the contemporary world."[xi] He was referring to "modern poetry," but it not entirely clear from his description what exactly he meant by that term. A quick search of the archives of several local newspapers shows that poetry readings were not uncommon in the first half of the twentieth century, and in the 1920s, various such announcements spoke of "modern" and "contemporary" poetry being read.

Still, there was not much of a scene and the small number of poets that lived in the Bay Area had few outlets for their work aside from ten issues of *Circle* and five annual poetry festivals. Mostly, they met at Kenneth Rexroth's house, with his living room the venue for twice-monthly literary salons throughout the forties and

---

4   There is more about this event on pages 151-152. There is more on Madeline Gleason's role in Ryan Mathews' essay on pages 64-74.

fifties. The self-professed "cultural minister of San Francisco,"[xii] and possibly the whole West Coast, Rexroth had a modest national reputation by the post-war period and he possessed many contacts among the country's best-known poets and publishers, chief among them being James Laughlin, the founder of New Directions. By the mid-forties, his Friday-night soirées were arguably at the heart of San Francisco's poetry scene, and Duncan said that by the time Ginsberg arrived in the city, "Kenneth Rexroth was its Prophet."[xiii] According to his biographer,

> Rexroth was "at home" Friday evenings. Usually an invitation was required, but it was easy to obtain by telephoning in advance. Started as a literary soirée of sorts, this occasion turned into regular gatherings for philosophical discussion, storytelling, as well as gossip and social banter. Overall they provided what Berkeley poet, professor, and scholar Thomas Parkinson describes as "genuinely intellectual discussions," as well as a sense of community for San Francisco's poets and philosophical anarchists.[xiv]

Indeed, whilst these gatherings perhaps became more focused on writing at time went by, they began as more political in nature. I have mentioned that when Rexroth arrived in the city, he was disappointed by the lack of forums for writers, and certainly his early efforts joining or creating communities tended to be more political (he was an anarcho-pacifist) than literary. In the mid-forties, he was hosting these Friday-night salons and over the coming decade they grew to be utterly central to the city's poetry scene.[5]

In Berkeley, the miniature scene seems to have lasted until around 1951 at the latest and in San Francisco there really was little more than Rexroth's salon and Gleason's annual Festival of Poetry. In the early fifties, the Berkeley poets moved across the

---

5   Rexroth's salon is a fascinating area of discussion that probably warrants a whole essay or even a short book. I recommend, for starters at least, that people read Linda Hamalian's accounts in her excellent biography of him. It discusses the origins to some degree and provides important details, such as the periods when he stopped hosting and when he began charging an entry fee. There is more in an essay that appeared in *Beatdom #24* as well.

water and so the San Francisco poetry scene—such as it was—expanded a little, but still "scene" seems rather a grand term for the scattering of writers inhabiting the city at the time. In fact, the cultural world of San Francisco then was very much dominated by the visual arts. From 1945 to 1950, Douglas MacAgy's tenure as director of the California School of Fine Arts had injected into the city a spirit of creativity and it became a hotbed of artistic activity. It developed several distinct painting movements and attracted painters and sculptors from around the world. It drew the likes of Mark Rothko, Salvador Dali, and Man Ray, each of whom taught classes at the Calfornia School of Fine Arts (C.S.F.A.) at MacAgy's invitation, as well as Marcel Duchamp, who participated in a public round-table discussion again at MacAgy's invitation. MacAgy did not believe in a division between the arts and neither did many of the students at his school. It was common for artists to dabble in multiple disciplines and so cross-pollination became common. Painters wrote poetry and poets painted pictures. Playwrights and filmmakers and photographers and dancers infused the scene with the respective innovations in their fields. Artists mingled and co-habited. Innovations in one discipline influenced another. These people drank together, smoked pot together, listened to jazz and talked politics and screwed each other. That is to say that whilst there was no major writing scene, the writers were part of a wider arts movement.

Many of those we think of now as writers or publishers were at the time at least partially visual artists or concerned with visual arts. When Lawrence Ferlinghetti arrived in the city, he thought of himself primarily as a painter and quickly became a critic for an arts magazine. Michael McClure moved to the Bay Area with the intention of studying under the various famous painters at C.S.F.A. and Rexroth was as much a painter as a poet. Bern Porter, an important local publisher, who would produce books by many of the best West Coast writers, owned an art gallery in Sausalito, as did W. Edwin Ver Becke, another *Circle* contributor and performer at the Festival of Poetry.

Ver Becke's name is not well known now but he was part of the literary and artistic scenes of the Bay Area in the forties and early fifties. In 1952, he opened an art gallery and theatre at 3119 Fillmore Street, an address familiar to those who know about the Beat Generation, for it was where Ginsberg first read "Howl" at the 6 Gallery. But this was several years earlier and the building had no history of art or poetry. It had been home to many businesses, including restaurants and wine merchants and laundries and—

most recently—a pest-control business. Ver Becke saw its potential as a home of the arts and launched an organisation called the San Francisco Community Theater, whose performances of popular Broadway plays earned such terrible reviews that they only lasted a few months before disbanding. Ver Becke handed the keys to Robert Duncan, his husband Jess, and their friend Harry Jacobus, then fled the city to become a drama teacher further down the coast.

Duncan, Jess, and Jacobus opened a gallery called King Ubu in December 1952. They ran it for exactly one year and during that time they seem to have used it to build upon an idea Duncan had come up with shortly before they founded the gallery, which was to fuse a multitude of art forms in a single print publication called "The Artist's View." Whilst the gallery of course featured paintings, sculptures, and other forms of visual art, it was also a venue for poets and playwrights. Deborah Remington, an artist who exhibited her work there and then co-founded the 6 Gallery, remembers it being primarily a place for poetry, where art was merely used to decorate the walls.[xv] This seems rather an overstatement and certainly there is a long catalogue of exhibitions of visual art that can be found in various places, including newspaper archives; however, it does seem to have been true that many poetry readings took place there. They even had a small, moveable platform that could be rolled into the middle of the gallery for poets to stand on and read.

King Ubu opened in December 1952 and closed in December 1953. Ten months later, the 6 Gallery took over, founded by five C.S.F.A. students and their teacher, Jack Spicer. The King Ubu gallery had had a strong focus on poetry because of Robert Duncan and it was mostly due to the influence of his friend Jack Spicer that the 6 Gallery had a similar attitude. Spicer taught a range of classes at C.S.F.A., where the five artists (Remington, Wally Hedrick, John Allen Ryan, Hayward King, and David Simpson) were studying as of 1954. In June of that year, they all decided to start an art gallery and from the very beginning Spicer pushed for it to include poetry. This would include live readings, recordings, and written poetry affixed to the walls. I wondered if perhaps the five painters simply took from C.S.F.A. or King Ubu the idea of fusing the arts and that is why poetry featured so prominently in their early efforts to promote the gallery, or perhaps it was partly due to Ryan, who was as much a poet as a painter, but David Simpson—the last-surviving member of that group—told me that it was Spicer's doing. He "came in as a poet," Simpson said, "as a full-fledged member, and was influential in expanding away from just painting and sculpture [and it was under] his influence that we accepted readily that poetry readings would be a good idea."[xvi]

Due to poor record-keeping and the use of limited postcard advertising, there is not much evidence to confirm what poets read at the 6 Gallery and when they performed. We know from a newspaper report that Spicer read his work aloud early on, which is hardly surprising, and it does seem to have been well-received, but only the exhibitions, which usually lasted for a month and were each begun with a big drunken party, were announced in the local media. Everything else comes from people's memories. These memories speak of a gallery where all arts—and sometimes even strange behaviours and concepts that might later be termed "happenings"—were considered valid and welcome. There were nude dancers, experimental films, and men talking with birds on a stage. There were no doubt several forays into theatre, given that they had a stage and professional theatre lighting, but again little evidence exists. All we have are references in interviews conducted many years later.

There is, however, one play that took place there rather infamously. It was not a fully staged show but instead a reading of a script. On January 20, 1955, Duncan and his King Ubu friends returned to put on a performance of *Faust Foutu*,[6] and this reading featured a number of artists and poets who would later become quite famous. It became locally renowned because, at the very end of it, Duncan took off his clothes in what was widely seen as a brave poetic act. However, even that is probably only remembered today because of one audience member: Allen Ginsberg.

THE SAN FRANCISCO POETRY SCENE POST-6 GALLERY READING

In January 1955, Ginsberg was a relative newcomer to San Francisco, having arrived in the middle of the previous year. He had initially stayed with Neal and Carolyn Cassady in San Jose, journeying into San Francisco on Mondays, but soon he found himself living in North Beach, where he lived for roughly a year. Ginsberg was always quick to find the local literary scene and this time was no different. He soon attended Rexroth's salon and a class taught by

---

6   This was not, as most sources claim, the debut of this particular play. Duncan had performed it at least twice before, including at King Ubu.

Duncan, although he was quite dismissive of both men at first. He became a regular at The Place, a bar that was popular among writers and artists, including Spicer and the 6 Gallery founders, and spent much time at City Lights, which had opened a year before he arrived in the city. It stayed open until midnight and allowed people to sit and read without the pressure to buy anything.

Ginsberg's social circle expanded quite rapidly in San Francisco and it encompassed the expected mixture of hipsters, criminals, and writers, along with a number of visual artists, such as Robert LaVigne, through whom he met his long-term partner, Peter Orlovsky. He struggled to meet writers that he respected, though. He quickly introduced himself to Rexroth and Duncan, both of whom he flattered to their faces but bitched about behind their backs. He admired Duncan's poetic gesture of stripping off on stage but they had very different views on poetry. Ginsberg met Michael McClure and got along well but was not particularly impressed with his poetry, and he reconnected with Philip Lamantia, whom he had known in New York, but again he was largely unimpressed by his writing, calling it "bullshit" because the poet was "hung up on being a cabalistic type mystic."[xvii] (This was a complaint also made by Rexroth, one of Lamantia's biggest supporters. He blamed Lamantia's "mystic temperament"[xviii] for a lack of consistency and the weakness of his mid-fifties poems.)

It was only after he wrote the start of "Howl" in August 1955 that Ginsberg began to feel more positively about the San Francisco poetry scene, and that's because he began looking for places to read his work, and this led him to organise the 6 Gallery reading, which is where he finally found like-minded poets whose work and personalities he truly admired. He made a poetic breakthrough in early June, pushed forward throughout July, and then in August wrote a first draft of Part I of "Howl," then quickly began redrafting and expanding the poem. His letters from this period show great enthusiasm after a period of depression and self-doubt, and this excitement pushed him to look for places to read his work.

At some point earlier that summer Ginsberg had been asked to arrange a poetry reading by Wally Hedrick, who was then the director of the gallery, but he initially refused. However, with "Howl" taking shape he "changed [his] fucking mind" and set about organising an event that would prove suitable for such a revolutionary work. He could not of course read it at a small, stuffy event alongside conventional rhyming poets for an audience of shirt-and-tie professors. No, he needed a bohemian audience and fellow poets with challenging, innovative works. For all he felt McClure's poetry was lacking and Lamantia could be inconsistent and poor, he invited them for at least they would produce original and challenging poetry. (They were both better connected in the arts scene than Ginsberg, too, which was likely another reason.) Ginsberg then turned to Rexroth, who almost certainly knew more poets than anyone else in the city, and Rexroth pointed Ginsberg in the direction of his present protégé, a young man named Gary Snyder. Incredibly, the two young poets had not yet met, and by a lucky coincidence they had each moved to Berkeley quite recently, so Ginsberg took his address and paid him a visit.

The reason Ginsberg and Snyder had not met was probably because Snyder spent so much time in the mountains or at school in Berkeley, whereas Ginsberg had been more of a North Beach hipster during his time in San Francisco. Snyder was back from a stint in the mountains and preparing for another semester studying Asian languages. Like Ginsberg, he viewed the Bay Area as lacking any sort of coherent, popular poetry movement marked by regular events beyond the dozen or so people that would meet at Rexroth's house twice a month. He liked that there was a Buddhist organisation in town that had a journal in which poetry was published, but still it was too "square" for him. Snyder was at this point in his life eager to move to Japan to study Zen but he had been blacklisted by the F.B.I. and was awaiting permission to go abroad.

Ginsberg met Snyder at the latter's tiny house in Berkeley on September 8. They shared their work and immediately became close friends, with Ginsberg almost overwhelmed by Snyder's force of personality and his esoteric interests. (His good looks probably didn't hurt, either.) Snyder was likely the first poet in San Francisco that Ginsberg really admired, on both a poetic and personal level. This is evident from his letters, but perhaps McClure summed it up best when he said, years later, that "Allen had respect for Gary in a way that he didn't for some other people. He wanted to learn from Gary."[xix] His poetry was already quite mature and he oozed a self-confidence that Ginsberg envied. Snyder took to Ginsberg and immediately agreed to be part of the reading.

The final poet added to the bill was Philip Whalen, who was not asked so much as told he would participate. Snyder had already shared some of Whalen's work with the local poetry community by sending it to Rexroth and reading it at one of his Friday-night salons, and it seems that it was reasonably well received. Although Snyder was much younger than his friend, he often acted as a big-

Collage by David S. Wills

brother figure and pushed him to do things that he felt would be beneficial for the otherwise shy and bookish man. "This town and these new people will do Philip much good,"[xx] Snyder wrote in his journal.

Whalen arrived in the city on September 21 and it was around this time that Jack Kerouac—having travelled up from a stint in Mexico City, where he had written *Mexico City Blues*—got into town. Ginsberg had hoped his old friend would read with him on stage but Kerouac was cripplingly shy and refused. Though confident in his work, he struggled to read it in public unless very drunk. He was keen to attend, though, and he happily accompanied Ginsberg on a trip into San Francisco on September 23. They met Snyder and Whalen and then attended Rexroth's salon. Aside from Snyder and Ginsberg, who as we've seen met two weeks earlier, this was the first meeting of these men and they immediately formed an intense group friendship. They helped each other with their poetry and exchanged ideas about many subjects, with Snyder acting as "the old man"[xxi] in spite of being the youngest. The others were keen to learn about Asian culture, Native American lore, the American wilderness, and more. Their bond was so intense and their friendship so filled with revelry that unfortunately these four writers—normally so quick to record the minutiae of their lives—did very little in the way of journalling and letter-writing over this crucial period, making it quite hard to establish exact dates and details.

On October 7, six poets stood on a tiny stage at the back of the 6 Gallery. Rexroth was the "introducer" and the other five read. Lamantia went first, reading some poems by John Hoffman, a friend who had died several years earlier. Lamantia had recently been stung by a scorpion and converted to Catholicism, coming to view his body of work as blasphemous, and it was only at the prompting of Rexroth and Ginsberg he participated at all. McClure read next. He was the only one of the poets for whom this was truly the first reading, as the others had a small amount of experience already. Philip Whalen followed with a number of short, strange poems that some found difficult to understand, before Ginsberg stole the show. He almost certainly read a few other poems prior to "Howl" and it seems likely he read an early version of "Part II," though all this must be inferred from a few scattered contemporary documents as no one recorded the reading. Snyder followed up with an excellent reading of "A Berry Feast" and the first part of *Myths & Texts*.

Many books suggest that the poets woke up the next

morning famous and that the San Francisco Renaissance had been established. There is some truth in this but it is at the same time a bit of an exaggeration. The 6 Gallery reading had been packed to capacity, and that meant probably somewhere in the region of 150 people had crammed into the building.[7] There were painters and poets and professors and all sorts of bohemian intellectuals present, some of whom were quite influential, such as Ruth Witt-Diamant. They were all very impressed by what they saw and heard and they began to spread word of a big change. Poetry had suddenly leapt off the page and now it was in oral form. It had felt like a jazz concert rather than the sort of stuffy, pretentious, sedate readings they were used to.

Although the poets did not become instant celebrities, the reading undoubtedly did impact their lives and propel them in the direction of literary success. Most famously, Ferlinghetti claimed to have gone home and sent a telegram to Ginsberg offering to publish "Howl." This may or may not have happened. Certainly, they already had an agreement and there was no good reason for him to spend so much money, but it is possible he did so out of sheer enthusiasm and perhaps a fear that another offer might come after the successful debut of "Howl." In addition to the prospect of publication for "Howl," there were reading opportunities for all the poets except Lamantia, who had decided he wanted no part of the ensuing poetic scene. The others were asked to perform individually at the San Francisco Poetry Center, and these readings were well attended and prominently advertised in major media outlets. I should note, though, that Snyder had been asked *before* the reading, seemingly due to a request from Rexroth. The others, however, were invited on the basis of their performances that night.

For these young poets, who were all relative newcomers to the city, the following weeks and months were filled with poetry readings and collaboration. They quickly became known throughout San Francisco and Berkeley, and whilst it is an exaggeration to say that this all happened overnight, it certainly happened quite quickly. By March of the following year, which is to say just five months later,

---

[7] It is hard to know for sure how many people were present. Estimate range from 100 to 250. The gallery could definitely hold 150 people but 250 seems rather a stretch, even though the theatre group that previously occupied 3119 Fillmore did claim this as the capacity. Having considered many factors and asked various people about occupancy, it is my belief that roughly 150 people were in attendance on October 7.

the 6 Gallery poets were minor local celebrities. People travelled from across the country and even from Canada to hear them read and to record their work. Ginsberg was even invited to lead a poetry workshop.

But it wasn't only these poets. Poetry readings all of a sudden began occurring around town and before long poets tended to be accompanied by jazz musicians. They were boozy, raucous events that happened late at night. Disaffected youths stood on small stages and read passionate screeds filled with four-letter words. Jack Goodwin, a composer who attended many of these readings, including the 6 Gallery one, recalled some years later:

> During the following year, this Dionysian, public, confessional, Howl-type reading caught on like the Plague. It blew so loud that the public actually discovered poetry. The show moved out of the small conference room into the gymnasium. People brought gallons of wine and responded, cruised and fought.[xxii]

It didn't take long before the poetic developments of San Francisco began to catch the attention of the wider public. As early as April 1956, just six months after the 6 Gallery reading, the *San Francisco Examiner* was reporting on the exciting literary scene. It featured exuberant quotes from visiting poet Richard Eberhart, who said that it was now at the forefront of American poetry:

> It's the nearest thing to a group movement I've seen. I've met more poets here than anywhere else on my present trip. Back East they are more individualistic; they don't go around in packs. Here you get two or three hundred together to hear a reading. It's very vigorous, and most promising.[xxiii]

Eberhart would go on to report positively on the "movement" (it was not yet being called a "renaissance") for the *New York Times* and Michael Grieg would similarly report for *Mademoiselle*, but what was most frustrating for the local poets was that all these accounts were fixated on the small group of outsiders who had breezed into the city and captured everyone's attention.

We have seen already that there was a small, scattered poetry scene in the city before the 6 Gallery reading and indeed it had certainly grown a lot between Rexroth's arrival and October 1955. But of the prominent poets at that time (including Rexroth, Duncan, Spicer, Blaser, Broughton, Gleason, and Parkinson), only Rexroth was on stage that night, and he was in the capacity of elder statesman. He was, in fact, old enough to be the father of any of the other five poets. Unfortunately for the local poets, on the night of the city's greatest poetic event, Duncan was in Europe whilst Spicer and Blaser were on the East Coast. After years of forging a scene, they just happened to be absent the night it all changed.

When Duncan and Jess returned from Spain in the middle of 1956, after just a year away from San Francisco, they found themselves "in Ginsbergenlandt."[xxiv] He said later it had been "like an invasion."[xxv] This was a phrase used by other people on the scene and it reflects the sudden role Ginsberg had taken. Those who wrote about San Francisco in late 1955 and early 1956 describe a poetry world that revolved around "Ginsberg and his chorus of howling boys,"[xxvi] stomping around town and reciting their most provocative work from the pulpit at The Place. Although Ginsberg never thought of himself as a leader, he did view himself as an organiser and it was clear others saw him in much the same way. Like Rexroth, he pushed to create a culture open to poetry and he was savvy enough to build on the momentum generated by his initial success.

The old guard were unimpressed. Duncan didn't care for their style and attitude towards poetry. Spicer hated Ginsberg and everything the Beats represented, and he would go around screaming "FUCK GINSBERG!"[xxvii] at the top of his lungs. Kenneth Patchen, another major local poet, also disliked the Beats and the feeling was mutual. Even Rexroth, who had been the M.C. at the 6 Gallery reading, and who had initially been delighted to see a poetic scene form, soon felt his eminence challenged by these young upstarts. He was growing old and facing numerous personal problems, and the young poets drew all the attention. One of them even started screwing his wife, which seems to have temporarily pushed him over the edge into a dangerously unstable mental state.

For his part, Ginsberg had not attempted in any way to supplant the major San Francisco poets. He had merely arrived and then brought together all the hip young writers in the area as a means of furthering the cause of poetry (whilst conveniently finding himself an audience). He wanted that movement to include many of the poets who resented or hated him, but their jealousy only grew as Ginsberg built upon his successes and became the leading poet, drawing bigger audiences, and then, in late 1956, releasing the poetry book of the era, one that would become nationally infamous the following year after the government waged a doomed war against it. Rivalries developed. Bitterness was felt. Animosity grew among those who felt they deserved the limelight. Some felt that Ferlinghetti's legal defence of Ginsberg was proof of a sort of hostile takeover of the scene, with the most business-savvy of the poets working together for their own success at the expense of others. Before long, gawking tourists were flooding the city in the hopes of snapping photos of real-life beatniks and the police were rounding up and often beating those who looked bohemian.

By the time things really got ugly, though, Ginsberg had already left the city. He had arrived in the middle of 1954 and then left towards the end of 1956, with the 6 Gallery reading more or less marking the halfway point in his stay there. It was not only Ginsberg who left, though. Snyder left in early May 1956 and spent the next decade in Japan. Whalen stuck around until 1957. Kerouac only really spent brief periods there, coming and going like a drunken dervish.

It is difficult to say exactly when that term "San Francisco Renaissance" was first used, but it was in general use by the middle of 1957. Ginsberg had initially noted there being a "a semimajor renaissance"[xxviii] of poetry in late March 1956 but he attributed it to Rexroth. It's not entirely clear if the exact wording was Rexroth's or the concept but by 1957 Rexroth was using the term "San Francisco Renaissance" in his introductory letter for the second issue of *Evergreen Review*, which was devoted to the "San Francisco Scene" (which was, all things considered, probably a better name).

When that issue of *Evergreen Review* was published, it included a balance of older San Francisco poets (Duncan, Everson, Broughton, Rexroth) and also the 6 Gallery poets except for Lamantia. Even so, when the scene was discussed in the wider media, it was the newcomers who got the attention and it was their style of poetry that came to be associated with the city. No wonder there was a degree of hostility among the local poets. They had fostered a small but growing poetry scene over a period of many years and then a group of outsiders held one reading that changed everything and quickly fled the city. The San Francisco Renaissance would forever be associated with "Howl"-inspired poems and live readings that sought to recapture the atmosphere of the 6 Gallery reading. People would hear the name and think first of Allen Ginsberg, a man who only inhabited the city for two years but arguably had a greater impact than poets who spent decades there.

There are various explanations put forth for the change that took place, with perhaps the most convincing being the development of (or return to) poetry in oral form. Ferlinghetti believed that was the difference. "The printing press has made poetry so silent that we've forgotten the power of the oral message,"[xxix] he said. "Up to the Beat poets, or up to the poets of the late 1950s, poetry was a great big mumble. Poets were contemplating their navels or talking to themselves in a low mumble and no one was listening because they weren't saying anything relevant to the average person in the streets. Allen Ginsberg comes along with 'Howl' and he's saying something very important to everybody." Although the 6 Gallery poets wrote their poems down, it was their live performance that excited people and over the next few years San Francisco would become famous for such events. The 6 Gallery reading was a red-wine-fuelled event where people socialised and cheered on the readers. It was wild and fun. Looking at descriptions of later readings, one gets the feeling that this all grew out of the 6 Gallery reading and that is a claim many have made, but is it entirely true?

I do not want to downplay the importance of the 6 Gallery reading, for it was undeniably influential and certainly had a major role in inspiring similar events in the coming months and years, but we should briefly return to January 1955, when Ginsberg sat in the audience as Robert Duncan stripped at the end of his highly experimental play, *Faust Foutu*. A daring artistic work had been performed in front of an audience at the very same venue where Ginsberg first read "Howl." It was performed by an array of talented and experimental artists, who entertained an audience filled with bohemian intellectuals eager for something challenging and new. It was not poetry, exactly, but it was poetic.

Two days later, on January 22, Weldon Kees and Michael Grieg (whose article on the Beats would help them go mainstream in 1957) inaugurated a series of events called Poets' Follies. It was established partly in opposition to the recently created Poetry Center, whose sponsorship of poets like Auden did not impress Kees. As with Ginsberg and his 6 Gallery reading, Kees and Grieg wanted to defy the establishment. In the words of Kees' biographer, it would be "a stage show that was part poetry, part theater, minstrel show, and chautauqua."[xxx] It would be fun and wild and different, a thumb in the eye of academic pretensions. Poets would read as dancers interpreted their work and there was a jazz band playing. One of the poets that night was Lawrence Ferling (who had recently changed from Ferling to Ferlinghetti and was now going back to his earlier name). There was a computerised "brain" that took classic poems and cut them up into new ones, perhaps beating Burroughs and Gysin to the punch. There was a stripper (who kept her clothes on but bared her soul) and the first acting performance from Phyllis Diller. Whereas Rexroth M.C.'d the 6 Gallery reading, this was introduced by R.H. Hagan, a prominent columnist.

It was every bit as groundbreaking as the 6 Gallery reading, even if it lacked a single work with the force of "Howl." Kees killed himself a few months later but the Follies continued in early 1956, showing a film he had made featuring the bridge from which he had leaped to his death. There was even a "serious counterpart"[xxxi] to the Follies that began in the summer of 1955, just before Kees' suicide. Clearly, there was something happening in the city. Crowds were drawn to experimental, challenging art. The city had seen whole new painting movements emerge and was leading the way in collage. There were innovative sculptors and even artists like Jay DeFeo whose work blurred the line between painting and sculpture. Bern Porter had been publishing avant-garde poetry and Lawrence Ferlinghetti was about to dive into that, too, with City Lights' Pocket Poets series, the first of which was published in the middle of 1955. In other words, the literary scene in the city was already developing. It might have taken Ginsberg and his friends to give it that crucial shove, but there was already enough momentum that it is not implausible that it would have happened, perhaps on a smaller scale, with their efforts.

CONCLUSION

Jack Kerouac famously wrote that the San Francisco Renaissance was born on the night of the 6 Gallery reading and for seven decades that has largely been seen as the truth, but of course it was not born in a vacuum. We typically do not look at the Beat Generation as being created on any one particular night but instead recognise a great many significant moments in its creation and development, with certain of them being of particular importance, and perhaps that is how we ought to view the 6 Gallery reading and the San Francisco Renaissance, too.

There had been some form of Bay Area poetry movement brewing for a full decade, pushed on by great creative leaps in all the other art forms, and perhaps with the infusion of new blood from other parts of the country in the form of Ginsberg, Kerouac, Snyder, Whalen, and McClure, the San Francisco scene had its pivotal moment, becoming a revolution or renaissance. Undoubtedly Ginsberg had a talent for self-promotion and for networking, and this catapulted him to the forefront in a way few other writers could have imagined. He parlayed his success into a group achievement and so, even after he fled the city before the scene imploded under the weight of public scrutiny and the dreaded beatnik phenomenon, he would be forever tied to its creation.

Some continuity existed in the form of Rexroth and Ferlinghetti, who partially endorsed the newcomers and performed alongside them, but they were keen to distance themselves. Then again, when it comes to literary movements, it does not always help to distance yourself. The media, the academy, and society at large will pretty much categorise as they please. Both men were lumped in, as were numerous other poets who did not wish to be aligned with Ginsberg and his friends. They all benefited to some degree, though. The success of the 6 Gallery reading allowed for many more public readings. It helped local publishers and little magazines. The forging of a scene brought unwanted attention but it also allowed poets to reach bigger audiences. Some of them took advantage of this; others did the opposite. Ferlinghetti became nationally renowned and Spicer spent the rest of his lift cursing the Beats. Others were resentful at first and appreciative later.

Considering all of this, it seems that one could make a pretty strong argument for a number of contradictory positions regarding the role of the 6 Gallery reading in the history of the San Francisco Renaissance, but there is no doubting that it was should be viewed as a landmark in literary history. Whether it birthed or merely changed a poetry scene, it was a night of astounding cultural importance.

ENDNOTES

i   Morgan, Bill, *The Typewriter is Holy: The Complete, Uncensored History of the Beat Generation* (Free Press: New York, 2010), p.104

ii   Qtd in Weidman, Rich, *The Beat Generation FAQ: All That's Left to Know About the Angelheaded Hipsters* (Backbeat Books: Montclair, 2015), p.90

iii   Kerouac, Jack, *The Dharma Bums* (Penguin: New York, 2006), p.9

iv   Ellingham, Lewis, and Killian, Kevin, *Poet Be Like God: Jack Spicer and the San Francisco Renaissance* (University Press of New England: Hanover, 1998), p.78

v   Charters, Ann, *Kerouac: A Biography* (Straight Arrow Books: San Francisco, 1973), p.249

vi   Qtd in Schumacher, Michael, *Dharma Lion: A Biography of Allen Ginsberg* (University of Minnesota Press: Minneapolis, 2016), p.216
vii   Hamalian, Linda, *A Life of Kenneth Rexroth* (W.W. Norton & Company: New York, 1991), p.54
viii   Morgan, Bill, and Peters, Nancy J., *Howl on Trial: The Battle for Free Expression* (City Lights Books: San Francisco, 2006), unpaginated
ix   Ginsberg, Allen, and Ginsberg, Louis, *Family Business: Selected Letters Between a Father and Son* (Bloomsbury: New York, 2002), p.29
x   *Poet Be Like God*, p.xi
xi   Bertholf, Robert J., *Robert Duncan: A Descriptive Bibliography* (Black Sparrow Press: Santa Rosa, 1986), p.A46
xii   Bartlett, Lee, *Kenneth Rexroth and James Laughlin: Selected Letters* (W.W. Norton: New York, 1991), p.241
xiii   *Robert Duncan: A Descriptive Bibliography* , p.A46
xiv   *A Life of Kenneth Rexroth*, p.147
xv   Johnson, Ronna C., and Theado, Matt, *Journal of Beat Studies #11* (Pace University Press: New York, 2023), p.62
xvi   Interview with author
xvii   Gifford, Barry (ed.), *As Ever: The Collected Correspondence of Allen Ginsberg & Neal Cassady* (Creative Arts Book Company: Berkeley, 1977), p.123
xviii   Suiter, John, *Poets on the Peaks: Gary Snyder, Philip Whalen & Jack Kerouac in the North Cascades* (Counterpoint: Washington D.C., 2002), p.304
xix   "Interview with Michael McClure," by John Suiter, December 9, 2000
xx   Journal entry, October 2, 1955
xxi   Journal entry, November 3, 1955
xxii   Manuscript version of "Dress Rehearsal: Or, Life Among the Founding Fathers," by Jack Goodwin
xxiii   *The San Francisco Examiner*, April 9, 1956
xxiv   Bertholf, Robert J. and Smith, Dale M. *Open Map: The Correspondence of Robert Duncan and Charles Olson* (University of New Mexico Press: Albuquerque, 2017), p.101
xxv   Gifford, Barry, and Lee, Lawrence, *Jack's Book: Jack Kerouac in the Lives and Words of his Friends* (Hamish Hamilton: London, 1979), p.200
xxvi   Jack Goodwin to John Allen Ryan, December 3, 1955
xxvii   John Allen Ryan to Allen Ginsberg, February 14, 1957
xxviii *Family Business*, p.37
xxix   Silesky, Barry, *Ferlinghetti: The Artist in his Time* (Warner Books: New York, 1990), p.88–89
xxx   Reidel, James, *Vanished Act: The Life and Art of Weldon Kees* (University of Nebraska Press: Lincoln, 2003), p.327
xxxi   *The San Francisco Examiner*, May 31, 1955

"BEFORE THAT WHOLE BEAT THING HAPPENED"
RUTH WEISS' FIRST YEARS IN SAN FRANCISCO

BY THOMAS ANTONIC

The following is an excerpt from an in-progress biography. Biographical details are based on over forty hours of unpublished interviews that I conducted with ruth weiss between 2012 and 2018, which I do not refer to as sources within the text. Additional sources, i.e. interviews conducted by others or weiss' autobiographical writings, are of course given. weiss' memories in old age were not always accurate. Sometimes she provided two quite different versions of an event. In such situations, I had no choice but to choose the more plausible version (and possibly mention the second version in a footnote). It was hardly possible to interview other contemporary witnesses in order to make any corrections, as most of the protagonists are no longer alive. One exception was Mel Weitsman (1929–2021), with whom I was able to have a long conversation in Berkeley in 2017. However, whenever possible, I also tried to cross-check weiss' statements through publications (such as biographies, interviews and autobiographical testimonies), unpublished letters and journals, etc.

INTRO: FAST FORWARD FROM CHICAGO VIA NEW ORLEANS TO SAN FRANCISCO

From 1948 to 1949, the 20-year-old ruth weiss (1928–2020; name always lowercase) lived at the Art Circle, a rooming house exclusively for artists, in a Victorian building on Chicago's Near North Side. She had left home at eighteen, at first taking a dorm room for a bit more than a year while nominally attending Wright Junior College (now Wilbur Wright College)—an alibi of sorts—

though even then she already knew she wanted to devote herself entirely to poetry. The Art Circle offered about twenty-five rooms at seven dollars a week and a large common room with a stage, where residents and visitors met daily to trade ideas across disciplines: musicians tried out new compositions or jammed, visual artists showed recent work, and poets read their latest pieces.

It was against this backdrop that ruth weiss stepped onstage one day to recite her poetry while a jazz combo from the south of Chicago was waiting behind her for their turn. Whether from boredom or a sudden spark, the saxophonist eventually lifted his horn and sounded a note. The drummer followed with brushes and within moments the whole band was improvising behind weiss as she performed. From that moment, Jazz & Poetry was born—a form that, a few years later, became a hallmark of the Beat Generation and drew worldwide attention.[1]

From then on, weiss shared the stage with jazz musicians whenever she could—first in Chicago, then in New Orleans' French Quarter, where she lived in 1950–51, and finally in San Francisco. She reached the city in August 1952 after hitchhiking across the United States with her typewriter and 60 dollars. Her last ride, a hunter who drove her from Fresno to San Francisco and to whom she'd said she was a poet, dropped her at Broadway and Columbus in North Beach and said, "This is where you belong."

In the first interview I conducted with her, weiss said: "Actually I came to San Francisco before that whole Beat thing happened, or what they call it. It was in full bloom I would say about 1955, but I was already in San Francisco in '52, living in North Beach. I was already living there when the other Beats arrived."[i]

1010 MONTGOMERY, THE BLACK CAT, AND ENCOUNTERS WITH PHILIP WHALEN

On arriving, she headed straight to the Black Cat, a bar she already knew by reputation from Chicago and New Orleans. Open since 1906 at 710 Montgomery in the "Canessa Building" (two blocks from where the Transamerica Pyramid now stands), it was a gathering place for artists, intellectuals, sailors, and sex workers.

---

1   ruth weiss' innovation of Jazz & Poetry happened, of course, independently from Langston Hughes who did something similar in New York at the same time but didn't release any recordings of his poetry with musical accompaniment prior to 1958, and independently from similar endeavors, for example Pierre Reverdy's recording of his poem "Fonds Secrets" in Paris, 1937, of which hardly anyone in the US was aware.

Above all, it was renowned for its openness toward homosexuals, one of the very few places that encouraged people to acknowledge their orientation in the 1950s, when persecution was common and police raids were frequent. Regulars included John Steinbeck, Jack London, Truman Capote, and William Saroyan; in 1930, Diego Rivera and Frida Kahlo kept a studio next door. In 1945 the Austrian émigré and Holocaust survivor Sol Stoumen took over the bar. The walls were painted black and hung with portraits, some of whose subjects weiss recognized among the patrons, and the floor was strewn with sawdust.[2]

At the bar, weiss fell into conversation with a man and mentioned she'd just arrived and needed a room for more than a few days because at that point she already sensed she wanted to stay in the city. He offered to drive her around to look for a place. She agreed and after a beer they set off. Barely two blocks later she spotted a "Room for rent" sign at 1010 Montgomery. She jumped out of the car and rang the bell. The landlord showed her a spacious first-floor room with a fireplace for twenty-five dollars a month. She had exactly twenty-five dollars left, and—frugal from the road—she seized the chance. Someone at the Black Cat had also told her she could donate blood once a month in San Francisco for twenty-five dollars; she did so the very next day, which covered meals and beer for a few weeks. Everything else could wait; before job-hunting, she needed a roof over her head.

However, on her third morning, after a late night at the Black Cat, the roar of a garbage truck jolted her awake at four a.m., and she realized it clattered by twice a week right beneath her big window. That same day she asked the landlord for something quieter. He showed her a tiny attic room, just large enough for a mattress on the floor and a box from Chinatown to set her typewriter on, with a small window opening onto an atrium. The place had three clear advantages: it cost only ten dollars, it was quiet, and just outside she could step onto the roof overlooking the Bay Bridge, where what looked like a phone booth turned out to be a shower, quickly her favorite feature. "Because," she said, "I would come home absolutely smashed at two in the morning with the fog coming in and I'd take a shower with the steam and the fog. It was wonderful. It sobered me up enough so that I didn't have to stumble over everything. That was so beautiful."

---

2 For more information on the Black Cat see Christopher Agee's *The Streets of San Francisco*, p.84-87; and Bill Morgan's *The Beat Generation in San Francisco: A Literary Tour*, p.34.

According to weiss, a few days later she heard typing somewhere in the building. She knocked to introduce herself, and a man with wavy dark hair and horn-rimmed glasses opened the door, introducing himself as Philip Whalen. Whalen had graduated with Gary Snyder from Reed College in Portland, Oregon, in 1951 (Lew Welch had also been a classmate) and had recently moved there after spending a few months in Los Angeles. Memory may be hazy, however, because it is known that Whalen lived together with Gary Snyder in an apartment one block farther north, at 1207 Montgomery.[ii] Maybe she heard Whalen's typewriter out of the open window of his apartment at 1207 and decided to knock or maybe Whalen visited a friend or acquaintance at 1010 and happened to open the door when weiss knocked. Whatever the case may be, whenever weiss and Whalen met, either at 1010 or in the immediate vicinity, they would exchange a few friendly words. However, this acquaintance could not be described as a close friendship. Whalen did not introduce her to the art scene nor to his friends like Gary Snyder, nor was he able to help her getting published. weiss did not consider her own poems to be ready for print at the time, and Whalen did not aspire to a career as a poet either and had to wait another seven years for his first volume of poetry, which was published by Auerhahn Press in 1959.

At that time, weiss was not so keen to gain a foothold as a young poet in San Francisco. She was much more interested in living the bohemian life to the full. She became a regular at the Black Cat and soon became part of the inner circle there. Sol Stoumen often invited her and some of his other favorite guests to spend a few days at his weekend house in Mill Valley on the other side of the Golden Gate to recover from the rigors of nightlife in the city. He simply handed them the key and sent them on their way. When she wasn't at the Black Cat or in Mill Valley, weiss roamed the city at night on long walks. She found many other bars where she felt comfortable and met new acquaintances. One such bar was Jimbo's Bop City in the Fillmore District, where jazz was played every night from two to six in the morning. In between visits to bars, she would go out alone or in the company of friends and strangers, drink beer in parks, or smoke a joint on Telegraph Hill. An excerpt from her autobiographical long poem "I Always Thought You Black" (in the volume *Can't Stop the Beat*, 2011) illustrates what a typical night might have looked like for ruth weiss in 1952:

THE BLACK CAT. a bar that is legend. marbles of memory pinged me there. mention san francisco and someone would say THE BLACK CAT. in chicago. in new orleans. even in new york. [...]

it's 2 a.m. you don't have to go home but you can't stay here the bartender shouts over the last drink.

i'm in the street. with the crowd. someone sez let's go to THE GOURMET.

i'm sitting on someone's lap in a cab. we pour out of the cab. – 8 or 9 of us – a MARX BROTHERS movie. we're at THE GOURMET. a gay after-hours in the fillmore. a dance-palace.

i never stop dancing. the bottle passes under the table to fill our soda set-ups.[iii]

By donating blood regularly, weiss had 15 dollars a month left over after deducting her rent, so she could just about make ends meet. She didn't need more than 50 cents a day for food. She was often bought alcoholic drinks in the bars, and as a slow drinker three pints were often enough to last her a whole night. From Chicago, she still had a card from the Waitress Union, which enabled her to find odd jobs all over the country to earn a little extra money. Sometimes she also found jobs by visiting bars that happened to be looking for a waitress or bartender, such as the House of Blue Lights on a block between Kearny and Montgomery Streets on Pacific Avenue, which was known as the International Settlement. She often took the ferry from San Francisco to Oakland and back just to have a beer on the boat and indulge her thoughts. To explore the city, she would take a random bus, ride to the end of the line, take a long walk, and then ride back to North Beach. She took plenty of time to get to know Chinatown, where she bought rare types of paper in all kinds of colors for very little money. It was a new world for her—one she had never experienced in Chicago. She worked on poems in her room during the day, and when she wasn't waiting tables or having fun with people, she would sit in the corner of a bar in the evening and write into the night over several beers.

Virtually none of this early poetry found its way into her later books. Over a hundred unpublished poems from her early years in San Francisco are preserved in the ruth weiss Papers. One example is the following short poem, written one night at the Vesuvio

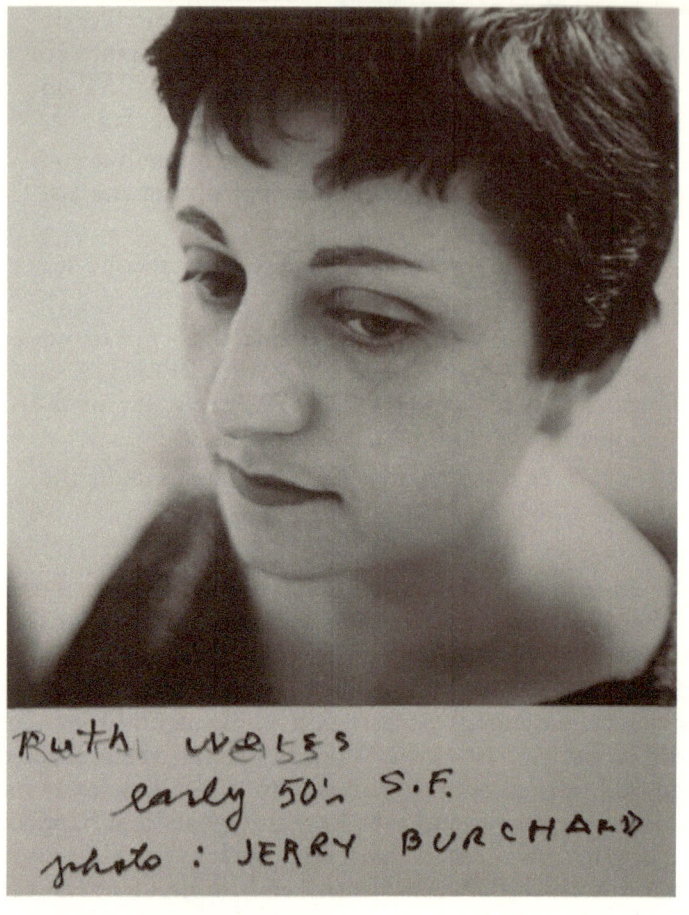

Ruth Weiss
early 50's S.F.
photo: JERRY BURCHARD

Café on the corner of Broadway and Columbus, which was later frequented by Kerouac and other Beats and also happened to be run by an Austrian, Leo Riegler:

>   *tear a sudden*
>   *page*
>   *the ball*
>   *bounces between*
>   *those who talk*
>   *too well ...*
>   *at a moment*
>   *talk*
>   *cannot ---*[iv]

The poem is typical of weiss' style at the time and provides a snapshot of how closely the young poet observed interpersonal interaction.

ON PINE STREET WITH LAURA ULEWICZ

The mood was not always exuberant. ruth weiss was plagued by fears for the future, worried that her financial situation could become even worse than it already was, and that blood donations and odd jobs as a waitress could hardly be a permanent solution. Despite many new acquaintances and her sociability, the newcomer often felt lonely, as can be seen in many of her poetic works from this period.

Even at the age of 85, she recalled this time in the poem "At 85 in 2013", which testifies to how important it was for her to write poetry in which she could find stability:

>   *my feet upon the earth*
>   *those lines pounding in my head*
>   *as i pounded on cement*
>   *along market street in san francisco*
>   *at 25 in '52*
>   *looking only at my feet*
>   *looking for a way to earn my keep*
>   *as door upon door slammed behind me*
>
>   *what am i doing here?*
>
>   [...]
>   *my feet upon the earth*
>   *the poem kept me going*
>   *the poems kept me going*

One of her first acquaintances, which developed into a friendship, was a now-forgotten artist named Marianne Hahn, a Holocaust survivor who had come to San Francisco in the late 1940s. She had a number tattooed on her forearm as an indelible mark of her time in a concentration camp. When weiss met her by chance, Hahn was already over eighty years old and lived in a room in a stately home that she had decorated in a very European style.

She was always elegantly dressed and used to drink sherry with weiss. She painted abstract pictures and portraits and constantly hung new works on her walls. One of her friends was the biologist Rachel Carson, whose book *Silent Spring* was a bestseller in 1962. weiss visited Hahn regularly, at least once a week, and they often talked about ecological problems that depressed Hahn, although as a young woman weiss couldn't understand how someone could survive a concentration camp and then become depressed about such "banalities" as environmental pollution. In any case, this friendship lasted for three years. Hahn died in 1955 at the age of 89.

By the end of the year 1952, weiss' financial situation had improved with a steady job as a waitress at a jazz club called the Tin Angel at the end of Broadway at 981 Embarcadero, which was known as a meeting place for lesbians until it closed in 1962. It achieved a certain degree of fame through live recordings, including those of folk singer Odetta, and was immortalized in Jerry Stoll's book *I Am a Lover* (1961). weiss worked at the Tin Angel for a few months and met Laura Ulewicz, among others, who was to become a close, long-term friend. The Detroit-born poet, daughter of Polish immigrants, was two years younger than weiss and had come to San Francisco in 1950. Ulewicz was acquainted with Kenneth Rexroth and many others, and from the late 1950s was involved for many years with the poet Jack Gilbert, who in turn was a close friend of Allen Ginsberg and Jack Spicer. She was never successful as a poet herself but played a significant role as an intermediary. After her arrival, she worked as a "camera girl in nightclubs and strip joints"[vi] on the Barbary Coast and felt like she was in heaven in North Beach "until the scene was promoted in the media as the 'Beat Generation' and the streets were suddenly full of pushy men eager for free love."[vii] This dark side of the Beat hype finally drove her to Seattle in the early 1960s, from where she followed Jack Gilbert to England a little later. A few years later she returned to San Francisco and in 1965 opened the I/Thou Coffee House in Haight-Ashbury, which had replaced North Beach as the hippest neighborhood at the beginning of the hippie era. She organized poetry readings, art exhibitions, and concerts until 1973, when she retired to Locke, a small community in the Sacramento-San Joaquin Delta.

Ulewicz lived in a spacious apartment on Pine Street on Nob Hill with a large spare room that had a balcony with a garden view, an open fireplace and marble stairs, parquet floors, and large mirrors on the walls, and she asked weiss to move in with her in early 1953. The rent was the same as for her attic room at 1010 Montgomery and weiss accepted the offer. Shortly afterwards she met Sutter Marin, a homosexual artist who lived in the same building on the top floor. They met one day outside the building and got talking, whereupon Sutter invited weiss into his studio. An hour-long conversation ensued, and Sutter was to become her closest friend until his death in 1985 as a result of AIDS.

FRIENDSHIP WITH PHILIP LAMANTIA AND GOGO NESBIT

One evening in Jimbo's Bop City in the spring of 1953, weiss met the photographer and poet Goldian "Gogo" Nesbit and her future husband, Philip Lamantia. He had been involved with the Surrealists in New York in the 1940s and was later counted among the inner circle of the Beat Generation due to his participation in the 6 Gallery reading. Only one year older than weiss, he had already published his first volume of poetry, entitled *Erotic Poems*, with Bern Porter in Berkeley in 1946. Porter was also to publish Nesbit's book *Graffiti* in 1955. Lamantia had just returned to his hometown of San Francisco from a trip of several months through Europe and Morocco, where he had visited his friend Paul Bowles. He moved into a room in the so-called "Ghost House," a Victorian villa at 1350 Franklin Street in the Polk Gulch district, which no longer exists today and was already very run-down at the time. Here the poet Robert Duncan, the artist Jess Collins, the filmmaker Stan Brakhage, and the poet and filmmaker Christopher Maclaine also lived.[viii] Shortly after Lamantia's arrival in San Francisco, he met Nesbit and the two immediately fell in love.

Nesbit and Lamantia also immediately hit it off with weiss. After a long, stimulating conversation and a few drinks, Lamantia invited her to the Ghost House for the next evening. At the Ghost House, the conversation from the previous night continued. Lamantia talked at length about his new poetic concepts, which he had just begun to develop after an out-of-body experience and which he had processed into poems, which he later collected under the name *Tau*. He also enjoyed talking about philosophy and even German literature, such as Heinrich von Kleist. Meanwhile, Nesbit showed many of the photographs she had brought with her, which had a lot in common with the work of Edward Weston, under whom she had learned her craft in Carmel in the 1940s: high-contrast and abstract details of nature, often taken in the Monterey or Point Lobos area. weiss also had some poems with her and recited them. Lamantia liked them very much and compared them to those of his friend John Hoffman, who had recently died under mysterious circumstances in Mexico at the age of just 24.

weiss, Nesbit, and Lamantia often spent evenings like the one just described. "We were all three short, in our twenties, and always wore black,"[ix] weiss recalled with a laugh. This cemented a friendship that lasted for many years and continued after Nesbit and Lamantia separated in 1955. Lamantia also took weiss, twice, to the salon evenings held every Friday at Rexroth's house, but she didn't feel comfortable there. This was where, as Bill Morgan puts it, the "lyrical intelligentsia of the city" met regularly, with Rexroth himself setting the authoritarian tone of the discussions and "talking about every conceivable topic, from anarchy to Zen."[x] In addition to Lamantia, regular guests included poets such as Robert Duncan, Lawrence Ferlinghetti, Michael McClure, and David Meltzer. weiss could not do much with this group of people because this scene, as she recalled, "was far too cerebral. Everything was just forced into categories"—something that she herself radically rejected, both in terms of her poetics and in terms of cultural, ethnic or social attributions and thus definitions.

RELATIONSHIP WITH MEL WEITSMAN

Her encounter with Mel Weitsman the following summer proved pivotal. By chance, weiss ran into Charly Stark, a painter she knew from Chicago who had also moved to San Francisco with his wife Suzie. Stark invited her to a party at the home of his friend George Abend and his wife Kitty, who lived in a small alley just off Broadway and would become longtime friends of weiss. Abend, a student of Clyfford Still, went on to establish himself as a California abstract expressionist and a founding member of the audio visual happening group VORTEX. In the 1960s he taught at the Carnegie Institute of Technology in Pittsburgh, and later spent periods in Guadalajara, Big Sur, and Los Angeles.

When weiss arrived at the party, Weitsman, who lived on the first floor of the same house and, like George Abend, had studied painting with Clyfford Still, was there as well. weiss immediately felt drawn to the shy yet striking young man, though the two spent the evening without speaking, trading only intense looks. The next day there was a knock at her door and Ulewicz said that someone named Mel was there to see her. She answered, "Oh, Mel. Tell him I don't want to see anyone." weiss sensed something was taking shape but preferred to stay on her own. Weitsman persisted and asked to see her, so she relented and went downstairs, where he was waiting outside the house. They greeted one another, and he said firmly, "We're going out tonight." She replied, "Excuse me?" He said, "I know a nice Chinese restaurant that I'd like to show you." A few hours later they were seated at Sam Wo in Chinatown, talking over dinner. When I interviewed him sixty-five years later, Weitsman recalled that they could not stop talking and became very close. Soon after, weiss and Weitsman became a couple.

weiss and Ulewicz remained close friends until Ulewicz's death in 2007, but they soon realized that they couldn't live together in the same apartment, so weiss looked for a new place to stay. She found shelter with Marianne Hahn for a few weeks, but that didn't last long, either. During this time, she saw Weitsman frequently and it wasn't long before he invited her to move in with him, even though he only lived in a small room that was also his studio. There wasn't even a shower in the house and weiss regularly visited a public shower not far from the apartment. Weitsman had little ambition to gain a foothold in the art scene, as he disliked having to sell his artwork, and in fact felt negatively about the whole scene with its competition, hypocrisies, and animosities. He hardly ever exhibited his paintings and instead made ends meet with his G.I. Bill (as he had been in the Marines) and odd jobs, working as a cab driver, in a mattress factory, and as a painter and decorator. weiss had since given up her job at the Tin Angel and worked first at a hot dog stand at Aquatic Park, later as an information clerk for a telephone company, and then as a service lady at a gas station.

She wrote a lot in her free time and had her first reading in San Francisco in 1954 at the Artist's Co-op on Union Street. Already then, she performed with her face painted white, which would become one of her trademarks in the 1960s. However, she had to wait another two years before performing again. That was at the jazz club The Cellar in North Beach, in 1956, where she started a weekly Jazz & Poetry performance series, which Ferlinghetti and Rexroth witnessed and adapted to produce their 1957 record *Poetry Readings at The Cellar* with The Cellar Jazz Quintet. Ralph J. Gleason, in the liner notes on the record cover, calls Rexroth the "prime mover" of the Jazz & Poetry experiment in The Cellar—without giving credit to ruth weiss.[3]

The artist couple weiss and Weitsman inspired each other's work. Weitsman painted pictures to accompany weiss' poems,

---

3   See Leon Horton's essay on pages 1-22 for more on Rexroth and Ferlinghetti's readings.

while weiss was inspired to write poems by Weitsman's paintings. They did a lot together, visiting exhibitions, readings, and concerts, taking trips along the California coast in Weitsman's Ford Model A and going to parties. However, nightlife in bars and jazz clubs was mostly reserved for weiss alone, while Weitsman drove a cab at night.

After two years of cramped conditions, the room they lived in became too small for the couple. In addition, weiss needed a break from the constant hustle and bustle of North Beach, which was draining her energy, so they looked for a new place to stay outside the city. They found a small apartment in San Anselmo near San Rafael, north of San Francisco, where Weitsman found a job painting boats. By this time, however, the relationship between weiss and Weitsman had begun to crack and was no longer as harmonious as it had been in the beginning. weiss was particularly troubled by Weitsman's unfounded jealousy, which had developed over time, and there were frequent conflicts when weiss was out alone and came home from a night of drinking. She also realized after a short time that she didn't like the warmer climate in San Anselmo. In fact, she began to hate the place. She said forty years later in an interview that her time there was the low point of their life together. The fact that after a while she increasingly fled to North Beach and spent many nights there, often in the company of her friends Sutter Marin and Laura Ulewicz, didn't make the relationship situation any better.

One day in 1955, her friend Phyllis Holliday visited the couple in San Anselmo. When weiss returned from shopping and saw Holliday and Weitsman sitting next to each other in the kitchen while peeling shrimp, she knew something was going on between them. "I saw them together. I don't think they had slept together or anything like that. I just saw it coming and called her best friend, who was also a good friend of mine, and said, 'Mats, I think Phyllis has just taken over Mel and I need someone to take me back to the city'." Shortly afterwards, Mats turned up and weiss packed all her things. That same day, she left Weitsman and San Anselmo and moved into a room at the Hotel Wentley. The rapprochement between Weitsman and Holliday was a welcome opportunity for weiss to end the relationship and return to her bohemian life, free of any obligations. Of course, neither of them knew that it would only be a longer interruption to their relationship. In 1957, they got back together and were married from 1958 to 1963.

AT THE WENTLEY HOTEL (FRIENDSHIP WITH JACK KEROUAC, NEAL CASSADY, AND PETER ORLOVSKY; ENMITY BETWEEN WEISS AND ALLEN GINSBERG)

The Wentley Hotel at 1214 Polk Street, with Foster's Cafeteria on the first floor, was a well-known meeting place for bohemians, homosexual men, artists, and prostitutes both female and male. With its cheap one-bedroom apartments, it served as long-term accommodation for this clientele as well as for older, already retired people with low incomes. One of the artists who often frequented the cafeteria and lived nearby on Gough Street was Robert LaVigne. Allen Ginsberg met LaVigne there in late 1954 and, through him, Peter Orlovsky, who was to become Ginsberg's life partner. Orlovsky, like Natalie Jackson, who was in a relationship with Neal Cassady for a time in 1955, was a model for LaVigne. In January 1955, Ginsberg had moved into a room at the Wentley and one month later, he found an apartment at weiss' former 1010 Montgomery address. Orlovsky moved in with him shortly thereafter. In August, Ginsberg began writing Part I of "Howl" there and in early September he moved to a cottage in Berkeley, leaving Peter and his younger brother Julius at the 1010 Montgomery apartment.

At this time weiss was living in a room at the Wentley Hotel for 20 dollars a month. LaVigne was still in the area, and it could be that weiss had met Jack Kerouac one night in the cafeteria through him or another friend, possibly also Lamantia, after the latter had spent some time in Mexico and had arrived in San Francisco just before the 6 Gallery reading in early October. Orlovsky, who continued to be in contact with LaVigne and whom weiss met and befriended at the Wentley (most likely in the cafeteria), may also have introduced her to Kerouac. However, weiss could no longer remember the exact circumstances of their meeting, only that the first encounter had taken place in "a bar" and that it had not been in North Beach, but in the Tenderloin, where the Wentley Hotel was located and where LaVigne as well as Cassady and Jackson lived. The other, long-dead contemporary witnesses can no longer be questioned about this and to this date there have been no documents found in any papers, such as letters or diaries, that could provide any information. Kerouac's journals from this period have been lost. The only source is therefore ruth weiss' fragmentary memory, which can at best be cross-checked with Kerouac biographies and similar documents.

What *is* certain is that she and Kerouac got on well at the time and had a lot in common. For example, they had both been hitchhiking for a while, and English was not the native language for either of them—Kerouac was the son of French-Canadian immigrants and had spoken almost exclusively French until he started school, whereas weiss had come to the United States with her parents in 1938 at the age of ten, fleeing the Nazis from Austria—and, in particular, they shared a fondness for the haiku form.

Every time Kerouac turned up at the Wentley to see friends, he knocked on weiss' bedroom door late at night and they would sit down at the table to chat about everything and anything, including various writing methods, such as the pros and cons of giving words free rein when writing poetry or condensing them in a disciplined manner. Kerouac drank wine, weiss her beer. As the night progressed, they always began to write haikus, not together, as weiss explained, but to each other, as a form of poetic dialogue. The haiku form, with its seventeen syllables and three lines, served more as a guideline and was not strictly adhered to, which, according to weiss and many of her colleagues, would not make much sense in a language that's not Japanese. It could therefore also have been a combination of haiku and waka. The latter, thirty-one-syllable form originated in Japan in the seventh century at the latest as a private exchange between friends and lovers. weiss always emphasized, however, that she never had sexual relations with Kerouac. "I was never one of his ladies, which is why we got on so well. He was great, but he never treated his women well."

At dawn, Cassady often appeared and would end up carrying Kerouac, who had fallen asleep drunk, under his arms and bring him downstairs. The three would sometimes drive up Potrero Hill in one of Cassady's "borrowed" cars, with Cassady at the wheel, weiss in the passenger seat, and Kerouac in the back, to watch the sunrise over Oakland on the far side of San Francisco Bay, and a little later they would roar back down Vermont Street, one of the steep winding roads, which at that time was also two-lane with oncoming traffic, at breathtaking speed. While the friendship with Kerouac was intense, in fact it only lasted a few weeks. After Natalie Jackson committed suicide in November[4] and Cassady returned to his wife Carolyn in San Jose, Kerouac returned to the East Coast in the winter of 1955 and he and weiss never met again.

---

4   For details on this tragedy, see "Beat & Damned: The Death of Natalie Jackson," by David S. Wills. It can be read online: https://beatdom.substack.com/p/beat-and-damned-the-death-of-natalie

The haikus written at the Wentley Hotel are lost. Kerouac is said to have once told her that her haikus were much better than his, to which weiss replied: "Yes, but you are a novelist. I've written a few short stories, but I couldn't write a novel because then I'd be responsible for all those characters." In an interview from 2012, she also said that they ultimately lived in two different worlds. weiss could also do little with the novels that made Kerouac world-famous from 1957 onwards. (On the other hand, she was an avid reader of Burroughs' books.) She felt a connection with Cassady, but a close friendship also failed to materialize here—mainly, as weiss explained, because the "wild man" talked incessantly and never let her get a word in edgewise. "It was different with Jack. He also talked incessantly, but he could also listen and it was possible to have in-depth conversations with him."[5]

In stark contrast to her relationship with Kerouac and Cassady, weiss' relationship with Ginsberg was difficult. However, we can only speculate as to the reasons for this, as weiss couldn't explain his antipathy. She was also unable to remember their first encounters and what exactly had happened between them. According to her own statements, weiss was good friends with Peter Orlovsky. Thus, it might have been a case of jealousy on Ginsberg's part. In any case, he and Kerouac must have talked about weiss because in a letter dated October 10, 1956, Ginsberg wrote to Kerouac: "We've [Orlovsky and Ginsberg] also balled Ruth Weiss together, finally, I screw dog her, and she kneeling blows Peter, then we change around. She shy at first but after awhile we all began goofing happily with our cocks and cunts and everybody woke up pleased."[xi] weiss could not explain this statement because, according to her, there would never have been a way in which she could have ended up in such a situation with Ginsberg and Orlovsky. But why would Ginsberg invent this threesome?

The letter also remains a mystery to Ginsberg biographer Bill Morgan:

> It is quite possible that Allen misremembered ruth and was writing about someone else. Allen, especially in the 1950s, often treated women as if they didn't

---

[5] ruth weiss told the story many times almost in the exact same manner. However, once, in conversation with Jerry Cimino after a 2016 Jazz & Poetry performance at Monroe on Broadway in San Francisco, she said: "We wouldn't talk at all. We'd just start writing haiku and exchanging them." (*ruth weiss at Monroe*. DVD, produced by the Beat Museum, San Francisco.)

exist. He wasn't a misogynist as Burroughs was, but he often ignored or overlooked them. It was only later that he realized that women existed, to put it bluntly. There are countless examples in his photo collection where he identified all the people in a group photograph except the women. Or he will write something like "wife of Michael McClure" without bothering to remember her name. It was more a sign of his times than something evil, I think, but it is also evident in his writings. He just didn't think about women, let alone their feelings. All that to say I don't know why he would make that up. Writing to brag to Jack maybe, but usually he didn't do that either. I'd guess just drug-induced mistaken identity, although he did exaggerate from time to time too. But why did he pick on ruth? We'll never know.[xii]

There's no reply from Kerouac that could help clarify the matter, as the two friends met in Mexico City shortly after Ginsberg's letter and probably discussed the subject there, making further written correspondence unnecessary. Even if it can't be said with one hundred percent certainty that Ginsberg's anecdote is fictitious, it's very unlikely that weiss had embarked on such an adventure, if one compares the story with her sexual profile, which clearly speaks against such escapades. Although there were occasional one-night stands and brief affairs, outside of relationships—both with men and women—weiss tended to live an almost celibate life despite an excessive nightlife.

A confrontation between Ginsberg and weiss at an event in 1965 is also recorded, which testifies to the now world-famous Beat bard's open hostility towards his colleague. In October, the proto-hippie group Family Dog, formed in Virginia City, Nevada, staged an event entitled "A Tribute to Dr. Strange" at San Francisco's Longshoreman's Hall, which is considered a precursor to the Acid Tests held shortly afterwards, including the Trips Festival in January 1966, which took place at the same venue and was co-organized by Ken Kesey. The Acid Tests in turn gave rise to the Human Be-In in January 1967 and finally the Summer of Love. Bands such as Jefferson Airplane and The Charlatans performed at "A Tribute to Dr. Strange," which was attended by almost a thousand people. Between the music acts, poets such as Ginsberg and McClure recited their work. ruth weiss was also due to perform that day; however, when she wanted to take the stage, Ginsberg prevented her from doing so and pushed her harshly down three steps. McClure prevented the poet from falling, which could have seriously injured her, by grabbing her arm and catching her as if in a dance. "He pulled out a joint and we smoked it in front of a thousand people," says weiss. Years later, she told McClure that he had saved her from ending up being crippled.[6]

A year before Ginsberg's death, weiss and Ginsberg met again at the opening of an exhibition on the Beat Generation at the Whitney Museum in New York. She suddenly felt a piercing gaze at her back, and when she turned around, she looked into Ginsberg's "ice-cold eyes." After staring at each other for a long while, they turned away without exchanging a word. weiss took her revenge elegantly by referring only to "A. GINSBOING" in her autobiographical poem "I Always Thought You Black."

LIST OF WORKS CITED

Agee, Christopher Lowen (2014). *The Streets of San Francisco: Policing and the Creation of a Cosmopolitan Liberal Politics, 1950–1972*. Chicago: University of Chicago Press.

Ginsberg, Allen, and Jack Kerouac (2010). *The Letters*. Ed. Bill Morgan and David Stanford. New York: Viking.

Martinetti, Ron (2005). "To GoGo for Philip: ruth weiss and Friends." American Legends. <http://americanlegends.com/authors/gogo.html> [last access: 2025-08]

Miles, Barry (1998). *Jack Kerouac: King of the Beats*. London: Virgin 1998.

Morgan, Bill (2003). *The Beat Generation in San Francisco: A Literary Tour*. Intr. Lawrence Ferlinghetti. San Francsico: City Lights.

—— (2019, May 13). "Re: ruth weiss." Personal email to Thomas Antonic. Unpublished.

Orlovsky, Peter (2014). *A Life in Words: Intimate Chronicles of a Beat Writer*. Ed. by Bill Morgan. Boulder: Paradigm.

---

6   Again, this is the version often repeated by ruth weiss. Maybe her description was accurate and maybe the proportion of the memories were not entirely reflective of reality after many decades. Without the aim of defending Ginsberg, it could have been an unintentionally hefty shove. Michael McClure was probably too stoned at the event and couldn't remember anything when being asked five decades later.

Peabody, Richard (Ed.) (1997). *A Different Beat: Writings by Women of the Beat Generation.* London and New York: Serpent's Tail.

Schneider, David (2015). *Crowded by Beauty: The Life and Zen of Poet Philip Whalen.* Oakland: University of California Press.

Suiter, John (2003). *Poets on the Peaks: Gary Snyder, Philip Whalen & Jack Kerouac in the North Cascades.* Berkeley: Counterpoint.

weiss, ruth (1953). "Four Small Eruptions At Vesuvio." Unpublished manuscript. ruth weiss Papers, Bancroft Library, University of California in Berkeley, Sign. BANC MSS 2021/139.

—— (2001). "Poetry and All That Jazz: An Interview – Part Two." Interview, conducted by Kevin Ring. *Beat Scene* 39, 26–28.

—— (2011). *Can't Stop the Beat. The Life and Words of a Beat Poet.* Studio City, CA [Los Angeles]: Divine Arts.

—— (2012). "Vienna Never Left My Heart." Interview, conducted by Thomas Antonic. <https://ebsn.eu/scholarship/voices/ruth-weiss-interviewed-by-thomas-antonic/> [last access: 2025–08]

—— (2013). *The Snake Sez Yesssss.* Vienna: Edition Exil.

—— (2016, June 15). *ruth weiss at Monroe.* DVD, produced by the Beat Museum, San Francisco. Unpublished transcript from the audio [Q&A with ruth weiss and Jerry Cimino after ruth weiss' performance].

ENDNOTES

i	"Vienna Never Left My Heart."
ii	*The Beat Generation in San Francisco: A Literary Tour,* p.21
iii	*Can't Stop the Beat,* p.55
iv	"Four Small Eruptions At Vesuvio."
v	*The Snake Sez Yesssss,* p.210
vi	*A Different Beat,* p.231
vii	ibid
viii	*The Beat Generation in San Francisco,* p.144
ix	"To GoGo for Philip: ruth weiss and Friends."
x	*The Beat Generation in San Francisco,* p.168
xi	*Allen Ginsberg and Jack Kerouac: The Letters.* p.335
xii	"Re: ruth weiss." Personal email to Thomas Antonic.

MADELINE GLEASON
THE ROMANTIC RHYMING RADICAL

BY RYAN MATHEWS

> Nothing is won, nothing is lost,
> Shapes shift, yet all remains the same;
> Evening by evening toward the coast.
> New birds come as the old ones came.
>   – Madeline Gleason, *Lyrics*, 1944[i]

Madeline Gleason remains one of the most overlooked figures in the histories of modern poetry, California poets, and the Beat movement. She was there in the early days before the Berkeley Renaissance and championed (as we will see even with some private reservations) many important contemporary poets of her time from Robert Duncan through the Beats and beyond.

Perhaps not surprisingly given the misogyny of many Beats—and too many Beat scholars—her name, like those of so many female writers and artists, has been largely eliminated or relegated to, at best, a footnote or one-line reference in the accounts of the time. To greater or lesser degrees the evaluation of Gleason's contributions mirrors the treatment of many of her female contemporaries including Mary and Lili Fabilli Osborne, the painter and writer Virginia Admiral, and even Josephine Miles.

This shrugged dismissal of the talent and value of female poets is perhaps best summarized in Allen Ginsberg's assessment of women writers in the Nov. 20, 1983, issue of *The Sunday Camera*

Magazine: "But then, among the group of people we knew at the time, who were the [women] writers of such power as Kerouac or Burroughs? Were there any? I don't think so," he said. "Were we responsible for the lack of outstanding genius in the women we knew? I don't think so."[iii]

Despite Ginsberg's sweeping rejection of the idea that anyone without a penis could possibly match the stature of the members of the Beat Boys Club, there isn't much doubt that Ronna C. Johnson's placement of Gleason in the first generation of Beat writers is entirely justified.

"Three generations of women Beat Writers are apparent, a structure that clarifies the longevity of the movement and the continuity of its influences," she wrote.[iii] "First generation Beat writers male and female were born in the 1910s and 1920s. Among Beat writings progenitors are Madeline Gleason (1903–1979), Helen Adam (1909–1992), Sheri Martinelli (1918–1996), ruth weiss (1928–), and Carol Bergé (1928–)."[1] That makes Gleason the chronological peer of the Holy Trinity of the Beat World— William S. Burroughs (1914–1997), Jack Kerouac (1922–1969), and Allen Ginsberg (1926–1997).

A fairly "traditional" poet herself, Gleason was an active participant of building a "big tent" community of modern poets. She was an early exponent of performative poetry, believing it could be more impactful than just the written word.

A strong supporter of Robert Duncan, she would go on to read with ruth weiss in bars and coffee houses often accompanied by musicians. She was a pioneer LGBTQ+ artist in an era when many lesbians were firmly ensconced in their closets. Gleason taught very briefly, preferring a simple, long-term blue-collar job.

Madeline (or "Maddy" as Robert Duncan lovingly called her) knew everyone who was anyone in San Francisco poetry, art, and theatre and they all knew and—in the main—liked and respected her.

It's been said, although not without significant debate, that Kenneth Rexroth can be thought of as "the father of the Beat Generation" since he is broadly credited with creating the modern California poetry "scene" and nurturing many of the individuals who later became linked, directly or indirectly, with the "Beat" movement. If that's true, or at least to the degree that's true, it can equally be argued that Madeline Gleason, who provided a "Yin"

---

1   They were both still living when *Breaking The Rule of Cool* was released, but Bergé passed away in 2006 and weiss died in 2020.

counter to Rexroth's decidedly "Yang" influence, is the rightful "mother" of the Beats.

If this comes as a surprise to you, or if you have only vaguely heard of Gleason, don't worry. You aren't alone. On the surface Gleason was, in many respects, about as far away from the stereotypical Beat poet as one can get.

So why should *Beatdom* readers care about a fairly traditional rhyming poet?

Robert Duncan, who admitted to initially feeling "intimidated" by Gleason, went on to become one of her deepest admirers and friends. In an introduction he wrote for a December 1956 reading featuring Gleason and Brother Antoninus, Duncan said, "She is conventional, but ultimately unique, for she has composed her own convictions."[iv]

Over the years that uniqueness and those convictions took many forms. Gleason was a painter and playwright as well as a poet.

Through her associations with Duncan, Jess Collins, William Everson and his second wife the poet and illustrator Mary Fabilli, and other figures who would rise to prominence in the San Francisco Renaissance and the Beat Generation, Gleason was socially and poetically rooted in the Berkeley Renaissance. Those friendships helped her efforts to found the San Francisco Poetry Center. But she had a life before Berkeley.

Considering that, why do so few of us know her?

That's a mystery and to unravel a mystery you often have to start at the beginning, which in Gleason's case is not in California but the Midwest.

THE POET'S EARLY AND FORMATIVE YEARS

Madeline Gleason's pre-California life was nothing remarkable. She was an only child born to Irish Catholic parents on January 26, 1903, in Fargo, North Dakota. Enrolled in a parish school, she was reportedly a bit of a discipline problem.

Following the death of her mother she moved with her father to Portland, Oregon, where she worked in a bookstore and began to write poetry and a series of articles on poetry and poets for a local newspaper.

Her ties to the San Francisco creative scene began following her move there in 1934 to work on a history of California for the Works Progress Administration's (WPA) Federal Writers'

Project. During that period she also worked with the composer John Edmunds organizing music festivals and translating songs by such classical luminaries as Schumann, Schubert, and J. S. Bach and published work in *Poetry* in 1936.

During part of World War II Gleason lived in Phoenix, Arizona where she clerked in the book department of Goldwater's Department Store. Returning to San Francisco she got a job as a runner—delivering securities from one investment house to another—at J. Barth and Co., a brokerage firm on Montgomery Street in the financial district. She held onto that job, resisting promotions since she preferred being outdoors, until 1968. In her later years, Gleason taught creative writing in her home and at San Francisco State University.

In April of 1947, largely to champion the works of the Berkeley Renaissance, she launched and directed the First Festival of Modern Poetry in San Francisco, America's first poetry festival, held at San Francisco's Lucien Labaudt Gallery on Gough Street. Seen by some as the beginning of the San Francisco Renaissance, the Festival predated the more famous 6 Gallery reading by eight years.

Twelve poets read over the course of two evenings—some to musical accompaniment—including Gleason, Brother Antoninus, Muriel Rukeyser, Kenneth Rexroth, James Broughton, Robert Duncan, and Jack Spicer. Admission was fifty cents.

A vibrant poetic community began to emerge around the festivals, which were held until 1952. "Maddy was central in organizing San Francisco poets and getting them to read," Robert Duncan reported. "I don't know how she got me and James [Broughton] to do all the things we did. We were much lazier and unorganized."[v]

Gleason was also an active member of "The Maidens," a smaller poet's cabal that met monthly in 1959 and included Broughton, Duncan, Jess Collins, and Eve Triem, as well as the occasional invitee such as Robin Blaser. All of this activity makes it hard to understand how her pivotal role in the development of San Francisco's poetic "scene" is often largely ignored and/or minimized.

She is only mentioned once, for example, in Warren French's *The San Francisco Poetry Renaissance, 1955-1960*.[vi] Michael Davidson's seminal study, *The San Francisco Renaissance: Poetics and Community at Mid-Century*, references Gleason just five times.[vii]

One of those references notes that "[w]omen are

conspicuously absent from major critical accounts of the period, although Kenneth Rexroth does acknowledge the pioneering work of Ruth Witt Diamant and Madeline Gleason in establishing the San Francisco State Poetry Center."[viii] This is ironic because it cites a passage from Rexroth's *American Poetry in the Twentieth Century* in which Rexroth gives himself credit for at least part of Gleason's accomplishments. Addressing various factors that helped establish the modern San Francisco poetry scene, Rexroth wrote, "Another was the San Francisco Poetry Center, founded by Madeline Gleason with the assistance of Robert Duncan and myself and shortly thereafter housed by San Francisco State College and managed by Ruth Diamant, a woman as dedicated and self-sacrificing as ever was."[ix]

Rexroth wasn't the only contemporary literary figure to minimize Gleason's efforts. In their *Literary San Francisco: A Pictorial History from Its Beginnings to the Present Day*, coauthors Lawrence Ferlinghetti and Nancy J. Peters mention her only once, in a discussion of *Mark In Time*, a 1971 album of photographic portraits of poets by Christa Fleischmann.[x]

The copy accompanying her picture briefly reads, "Madeline Gleason: Poet, playwright, and painter, she presented the first poetry festivals in San Francisco in the late 1940s." Worse still, Ferlinghetti and Peters give Ruth Witt-Diamant exclusive credit for the 1954 founding of the San Francisco State Poetry Center, never mentioning Gleason or her contributions.[xi]

Not everyone overlooked Gleason. She was only one of four women, along with Denise Levertov, Helen Adam, and Barbara Guest, included in Don Allen's *The New American Poetry, 1945–1960*. However, Gleason didn't make the cut for Allen's revised anthology *The Postmoderns*, which included three female poets: Levertov, Anne Waldman, and Diane di Prima.

Why didn't Gleason make *The Postmoderns*?

Perhaps it was because she wasn't all that well known or didn't sell as well as di Prima or Waldman. Maybe it was because by 1994 her style didn't seem as "modern" or "postmodern" as it had 34 years before. Perhaps her previous champions were either gone or more concerned with securing their own poetic legacies. Or maybe Allen just didn't want to include too many women in his new anthology.

The answer may be any of these, combinations of these, or something else altogether. Perhaps the real answer is contained in the work itself.

THE WORK

Her published oeuvre, contained in 266 pages, is neither prolific nor revolutionary. Over 31 years her poetic output included only five collections: *Poems, The Metaphysical Needle, Concerto for Bell and Telephone, Selected Poems, Here Comes Everybody: New & Selected Poems.* Her *Collected Poems* was posthumously published many years later.

Throughout her work Gleason wrestled with themes that would later appear in the poetry of the San Francisco Renaissance and the Beat Generation such as mysticism, an obsession with love, reverence for nature, identity, and the human experience.

Her first collection, *Poems,* was released by Grabhorn Press in 1944. It reflects Gleason's focus on the problem of evil in the world. But *Poems,* published a year before the end of the Second World War, is not so much an apocalyptic assessment of the state of the human condition as it is an affirmation of the possibility of mystical transcendence and the possibility of salvation through community and love.

In "New Colony," for example, she writes:

> Each moves through a dangerous wood
> Wear sharp branches threaten
> Like shapes that frighten children
> In unlighted rooms;
> We move from light into the tombs
> Of our imaginations, and fall among shadows[xii]

Dire as this sounds, "New Colony" ends on a hopeful note:

> Each hopes to come safely through
> Into an open place,
> Into the light again;
> And stand with those
> Made patient in extremity,
> Reborn in heart and mind,
> Who have the courage to find
> Among old ruins the new colony.[xiii]

The notion of mystical solutions is even more pronounced in her second collection, aptly named *The Metaphysical Needle,* which appeared in 1949. The material in *Metaphysical Needle* seems to indicate that Gleason went through a deeply transformative experience in the five years since *Poems*, perhaps not religious, at least in the conventional sense, but spiritual on some critical personal level. In "Man is the Animal," she writes:

> Man is the animal, yes,
> But he is more than this:
> Because he looks through the rosace
> Of spirit and calls the incommensurable thing
> He walks through, Space;
> Because in his prime
> He overlooks and later accepts Time
> As that which divides life from death;
> And because he has given the name Love
> To the incurable pain
> That runs through his breast
> Again, again, again.[xiv]

In "The Other Side Of Glass," Gleason talks about a world the self lives "without name" in "[a] world that is and yet is not."[xv] The idea that love can conquer appears through the collection in poem after poem from "There Should Have Been No Garden" to the title poem, "The Metaphysical Eye."[xvi]

We know from her long-term partner Mary Clarke Greer that "Madeline went to Mass every day, either in church or in her mind. Her God lived. Her evident spirituality made up for the tribulations she faced as a poet and a woman."[xvii]

In 1966, Gleason published her third collection, *Concerto for Bell and Telephone*. Her earlier reliance on rhyme or off-rhymes to carry the narrative is totally gone, replaced by a kind of staccato, disjointed sonic groove. These are poems definitely written to be read out loud. If there is a "red thread" through *Concerto for Bell and Telephone*, it is the need to detach oneself from banal self-interest of external temporal concerns in favor of connection to an internal dialogue with the transcendent.

In "Acting Out" for example she writes:

> Acting out, fancy steps, thunder making;
> are the drunken living. Poor sweetheart!
>   Shout!   Shout!
> Bluff dance steps in your spilled blood.
>   Death knows nothing:
> the straffing maggot, the gaping socket.

> Poor sweetheart!
>   Run!   Run!
> You want out?
> You are out![xviii]

Selected Poems (1973) contains among other poems some revisions of earlier work. With a not-so-subtle nod in the direction of James Joyce, *Here Comes Everybody: New & Selected Poems* appeared in 1975. It was the last book Gleason would publish during her lifetime. She died in 1979 and her *Collected Poems* were published in 1999.

"Here Comes Everybody" acknowledges her poetic peers and affirms her vision of breaking the shackles of venial personal attachment in favor of love and connection with a higher order, again not necessarily religious per se, but clearly a transcendental element that can be connected to this side of the grave.

"Ars Poetica" name checks, among others, James Broughton, Robert Duncan, Ezra Pound, T.S. Elliot, Marianne Moore, W.H. Auden, Yeats, and e.e. cummings.[xix]

Some of the references are kind, some are not. She describes cummings, for example, as a "lyric clown" and "a comic, a sport / a handy sort / with his typographical bang bang." James Broughton is "the Playground Boy," Robert Duncan is "E.P.'s [Ezra Pound] son" with "a long line delivery. / who can sing a boy into a man."

Writing about Auden, Gleason says:

> Auden, Auden,
>   Wystan, Hugh
> how many poets prayed to you,
> and thought they heard an answer.

Apparently she was dismissive of William Carlos Williams, too. In a letter to Denise Levertov, Duncan said, "I never did forgive Madeline Gleason her dismissal of Williams (but it was also a dismissal of me in my adherence)—'I know you are excited by this poem Robert, but do you really think anyone will be reading him ten years from now'."[xx]

As it turned out, history was kinder to Williams than it was to Gleason. Still, although her work is seldom read today and her books are hard to come by, she was admired by her peers. As we have seen, Duncan thought highly of her even if he disagreed with her about Williams.

AND THE BEATS WENT ON

Gleason was reportedly very supportive of the Beats, many of whom she had known from earlier movements, and the idea of a new poetic community expanding the borders of the poetically possible. Perhaps her favorite of the "pure" Beat poets—as opposed to Beat-related writers such as Duncan—was ruth weiss, who was with her until the end.

Friends since the fifties, Gleason was close on both a personal and collaborator level with the "Beat Goddess." Both poets were strong advocates of what was known at the time as poetry's oral tradition, or what today we call spoken-word performances.

In the early 1970s, weiss tended bar at the Wild Side West, a lesbian bar in Bernal Heights where she and Gleason did Sunday afternoon poetry readings.[xxi] Over the years Gleason and weiss also ran poetry/jazz shows at The Cellar, the Old Spaghetti Factory, and a little theater called Surprise Voyage.[xxii]

Interviewed about her relationship with Gleason, weiss told Nancy M. Grace that "we loved reading to each other. We'd go over and have dinner with her and end up drinking Irish Mist. Yeah, she was a good drinker. Well, okay, we have that in common."[xxiii]

weiss admired Gleason's "short words"—her ability to sum up people and situations without going on and on—and her "impish humor." She was also a fan of Gleason's paintings.

"[S]he loved language, but wasn't verbose," weiss continued. She was very lyrical. Her major work, they're really intense love poems, and she really had a lot of wit and humor, but there was a lot of depth to her. 'Love' was a big word for her. I don't know if she went to Mass or not, but she certainly had a deep religious connection, yes, in the way I do without having a form."

Recalling Gleason's final public reading at the Wild Side West, weiss recalled, "I will tell you the last time she ever read, she was very, very ill, and it was just a few weeks before she died… She's very frail, and all those women friends were going to read her poetry. And I said—and I was a little drunk—I said, 'Maddy, will you just go and read your own fucking stuff?' And she looked at me and she smiled.[2]

"She got up, and even though—as frail as she was, you could

---

2   Careful readers may note references to the Wid Side bar and the Wild Side West. Like Gleason, the Wild Side was centered for many years in the heart of San Francisco. Later both the poet and the bar relocated to Bernal Heights at which time "West" was added to the Wild Side's name.

hear, and of course this was in a bar! You could absolutely feel it—hear the poem—I mean, when she did those poems she wasn't frail."

CODA

Summing up Gleason's importance to the San Francisco poetry scene, Dr. Bill Lipsky, the author of *Gay and Lesbian San Francisco*, wrote, "Making poetry so prominently and publicly the center of their lives, Gleason and her colleagues guided tremendous attention to their chosen art. They truly took poetry out of the ivory towers of academia and into the coffee houses—occasionally into the parks and onto the streets—making it available to anyone who wanted to listen to their words and hear their ideas. Because of her own work, and her work on behalf of poetry and the poets of San Francisco, Gleason remains a principal figure in the poetry of modern America."[xxiv]

Lipsky may be right. There is no question of the enormous impact Gleason had on the work of Robert Duncan and, by extension, Jack Spicer. She championed the Beats and actively engaged with a number of them. She moved performative poetry out of the Ivory Tower and into the streets. And, throughout her life in San Francisco she never stopped building a poetic community.

While she hardly holds a monopoly of them, one can also trace her central themes— mysticism, identity, the search for a transcendent truth, a love of the natural world, the redemptive power of love, and a contempt and abhorrence of venial self-interest, conformity, greed, technology and violence—in the work of many of the Beats, through the hippie movement, and beyond.

We may never know how much her work impacted those around her, but there is absolutely no question that her presence and activism had an impact on many of those she came into contact with, which was pretty much every poet in San Francisco. Whether her impact was direct or indirect, it was certainly profound.

Sadly, all of this doesn't help explain why Gleason and so many other female poets and artists seem doomed to ride in the back of the Beat bus. As the years roll by more and more of their work will be lost.

In 1956 Gleason met Mary Clarke Greer, her partner in life and love until her death. In the late 1960s, after years of living in the North Beach area, Gleason and Greer moved away from the center of San Francisco. The move proved fatal as Gleason began to suffer from a deep depression. She died on April 22, 1979, in her adopted home in San Francisco. She was 76 years old.

Eulogizing her fallen partner Greer said, "Madeline died of despair, what all poets die of."[xxv]

ENDNOTES

i Gleason, Madeline, *Collected Poems: 1919 – 1979* (Jersey City, NJ: Talisman House Publishers, 1999) p.9
ii Peabody, Richard, (ed.) *A Different Beat: Writings by Women of the Beat Generation* (London: High Risk, 1997) p.1
iii Grace, Nancy M. and Johnson, Ronna C., *Breaking the Rule of Cool: Interviewing and Reading* Women Beat Writers (Jackson, MS: University Press of Mississippi, 2004) p.8
iv Duncan, Robert, "Afterword," *Gleason, Madeline. Collected Poems: 1919 – 1979* (Jersey City, NJ: Talisman House Publishers, 1999) p.263
v *Breaking the Rule of Cool* p.xiv
vi French, Warren, *The San Francisco Poetry Renaissance, 1955 -1960* (Boston: Twayne Publishers, 1991) p.19
vii Davidson, Michael, *The San Francisco Renaissance: Poetics and Community at Mid-century* (New York: Cambridge University Press, 1989) p.17, 35, 58, 174, 198
viii Ibid. p.198
ix Rexroth, Kenneth, *American Poetry in the Twentieth Century* (New York: Herder and Herder, 1971) p.140
x Ferlinghetti, Lawrence and Peters, Nancy J., *Literary San Francisco: A Pictorial History from Its Beginnings to the Present Day* (San Francisco: City Lights Books, 1980) p. 204- 205
xi Ibid. p.171
xii Collected Poems: 1919 – 1979 p.7
xiii Ibid. p.8
xiv Ibid. p.54
xv Ibid. p.62
xvi Ibid. p.64 and 82
xvii Ibid. p.xiv
xviii Ibid. p.127 – 128
xix Ibid. p.178 – 183
xx Bertholf, Robert J. and Gelpi, Albert (eds.) *The Letters of Robert Duncan and Denise Levertov* (Stanford, CA. Stanford University Press, 2004) p.431
xxi Knight, Brenda, *Women of the Beat Generation: The Writers, Artists, and Muses at the Heart of a Revolution* (Berkeley, CA: Conari Press, 1996) p.246
xxii Bellingham, Bruce. "Beat poet ruth weiss launches new book" in *Northside San Francisco*. May, 2011. Accessed at https://www.northsidesf.com/may11/ae_ruthweiss.html. July 24, 2025

xxiii   *Breaking the Rule of Cool*, p.74 -75.
xxiv   Lipsky, Bill, "Madeline Gleason and the Poetry of San Francisco" in *San Francisco Bay Times*. Accessed at: https://sfbaytimes.com/madeline-gleason-and-the-poetry-of-san-francisco/. January 16, 2025.
xxv   Flanagan, Michael, "Beats, Bohemians and Bars: Jack Spicer, Allen Ginsberg and their circle's San Francisco haunts" in *Bay Area Reporter*. Wednesday, July 25, 2018. Accessed at: https://www.ebar.com/story/39886#:~:text=Upon%20her%20death%20in%201979,what%20all%20poets%20die%20of.%22 on February 17, 2025.

REXROTH AND KEROUAC
AN ANTIDOTE OF SORTS

BY JAMES K. HANNA

> *Oh, East is East, and West is West, and never the twain shall meet,*
> *Till Earth and Sky stand presently at God's great Judgment Seat;*
> *But there is neither East nor West, Border, nor Breed, nor Birth,*
> *When two strong men stand face to face, though they come from the ends of the earth!*

Those lines of Rudyard Kipling's "The Ballad of East and West" remind the present writer of two strong men—Jack Kerouac and Kenneth Rexroth—whose relationship sadly deteriorated into disaffection, and who never reconciled this side of Kipling's great Judgment Seat.

Reading their comments about each other, public and in letters and journals, and the observations of others, causes those of us who admire the two to suffer—and we don't want to suffer; rather, we long for understanding and to make sense of the trouble and estrangement.

We suffer because the two shared—at least in a widely held perception—a common paternity of Beat movement literature. In the headlines for their respective obituaries, the *New York Times* branded Kerouac the "Father of the Beat Generation" and Rexroth a "Father Figure to Beat Poets."

With that shared titular gravity, whether welcomed by the

deceased or not,[1] their disaffection aggrieves us. The legions unfamiliar with the private details but familiar with the discord and the public details have questions likely to remain unanswered, but in the mere search for answers our suffering is assuaged; some may even find an antidote of sorts.

In the beginning, they had at least a minimal respect for the other's work if not personage. Long before meeting Rexroth, Kerouac sought his approval as shown in letters to Allen Ginsberg who arrived in San Francisco in 1954. In this correspondence, Kerouac encouraged Ginsberg to show the West Coast critic his work.[i] (Rexroth wrote reviews for various publications and also reviewed books on his radio show. He read manuscripts for New Directions, too, and so his opinions were widely respected.) In January 1955, Ginsberg gave Rexroth *Visions of Cody* (then titled *Visions of Neal*)[ii] and a few months later Jack wrote asking Allen to show Rexroth *The Subterraneans*, writing, "It's the first of the 'hip' novels and he might go for it."[iii] According to Ginsberg, Rexroth was enthusiastic about *Visions of Cody/Neal* and praised Kerouac's "Jazz of the Beat Generation," recently published in *New World Writing*.[iv] Even after they fell out, Rexroth rose a bit above the fray in a 1957 review of *On the Road*, writing, "It is by a new author, the best prose representative of the San Francisco Renaissance which has created so much hullabaloo lately."[v]

But then the feud—a cold war of words—public, private, and in thinly veiled fiction. The verbal sparring included a 1958 letter from Rexroth to publisher James Laughlin, calling Kerouac a "weed head."[vi] That same year Kerouac published *The Dharma Bums* in which Rexroth was the model for Rheinhold Cacoethes, "a bow-tied, wild-haired old anarchist fud."[vii]

In *Jack's Book: An Oral Biography of Jack Kerouac*, editors Barry Gifford and Jack Lee write, "To those unfamiliar with the private details of the schism it seemed to be an advanced case of regional chauvinism, but its real roots lay in a personal affair, a serious misunderstanding wherein Rexroth resented what he mistakenly considered Jack and Allen's—especially Jack's—adversary participation. From this time on Rexroth reviled Kerouac both privately and publicly, removing himself as defender of the Beats."[viii]

---

1   Bradford Morrow in *Kenneth Rexroth: Selected Poems* (New Directions, 1984) notes, "With his famous statement, 'An entomologist is not a bug,' (Rexroth) severed (though never lived down) his connection with the Beats."

The genesis included three encounters in the autumn of 1955, beginning almost at once after Kerouac's arrival in San Francisco in September. He was there to visit Allen Ginsberg, and he met Rexroth at Kenneth's home, taken by Ginsberg for one of Rexroth's noted Friday-night salons. This was two weeks prior to the 6 Gallery Reading and, as Linda Hamalian writes in *A Life of Kenneth Rexroth*, Kenneth had agreed to look at Jack's manuscripts but "Kerouac was not prepared for the scene at Rexroth's."[ix] Nor was he sober.

The scene he was unprepared for included Gary Snyder and Philip Whalen. Kerouac, Hamalian informs us, was enthralled that Snyder and Whalen knew a good deal about Buddhism. He announced to the room that he was a great Buddhist scholar[x] and Rexroth cooly informed him that everybody in San Francisco was a Buddhist,[xi] challenging him with "Didn't you know that?"[xii] Kerouac then pulled on Rexroth's mustache and kissed him, which according to Hamalian was intended as an act of affection but one that Rexroth mistook for mockery.[xiii] In any event, one never gets a second chance to make a first impression.

At home that night was Rexroth's four-year-old daughter, Mary, and his third wife, Marthe Larsen, pregnant with their second daughter. Ginsberg's memory is that Kerouac "was a little drunk," and Rexroth was afraid "Jack was going to wake his baby and got mad at him, called him a son of a bitch, and ordered him out."[xiv] Rexroth was understandably upset. The nearly-fifty-year-old host had his personal space violated by "a little drunk" thirty-two-year-old Kerouac whose obnoxious and loud behavior threatened the peaceful sleep of his young child.

The second incident was the 6 Gallery Reading in October, emceed by the sober and serious—and possibly nervous—Rexroth, who had brought the writers together. At the reading, Lawrence Ferlinghetti recalled Kerouac "was drinking wine. He had a jug of wine, and he was lying on the floor up near the stage in front."[xv] Again, Hamalian: "Although he was not on the program, Jack Kerouac was both a visible and audible presence that evening."[xvi] Though the setting was casual yet boisterous, and there was much drinking, one can imagine the concern and chagrin of the emcee—another thing to worry about: Jack Kerouac. "Much to Rexroth's annoyance," Gerald Nicosia reports, "Kerouac began to yell 'Go!' and to moan, gurgle, and beat out the rhythms of the poetry on his jug."[xvii]

The third incident followed soon after the reading. Rexroth

hosted a dinner at his Eighth Avenue home, and Kerouac, surprisingly, was among those invited. Less surprisingly, he and his Beat friends arrived drunk and boisterous. "Nobody calmed down. Kerouac called Rexroth a 'boche,' (dirty German)" writes Hamalian, quoting Philip Whalen.[xviii] "Their rough manners were more than he could bear. It was late at night, and he did not want his children's sleep disturbed. He was convinced that Kerouac had frightened Mary."[xix]

These three encounters, Kerouac drinking throughout, provided a foundation for Rexroth's dislike of the visitor from the East. That antipathy worsened soon after when Marthe and Robert Creeley became romantically involved. Creeley had spent a good deal of time with Kerouac and Rexroth believed he was among those to be blamed for the affair. According to Hamalian, in her chapter titled "Rexroth in Misery, 1956-1957," he accused Kerouac and the East Coast gang of Ginsberg, Peter Orlovsky, and Gregory Corso of "having roped Marthe into orgies."

Though Marthe and Kenneth did not divorce until 1961, no forgiveness was in store for Kerouac. The break was complete. And while Kenneth eventually forgave others in the circle of intrigue, no forgiveness was forthcoming for Jack.

Kerouac may have made lukewarm overtures, but not apologies. In January 1958, in a letter to Joyce Glassman, he wrote, "I don't like [Rexroth], and I don't trust him, and I wrote 2 weeks ago and told him I was disassociating myself from his sphere of interests and he didn't reply although the rest of the letter was friendly."[xx]

Rexroth wasn't interested in communicating. He ignored letters from Kerouac and as Hamalian noted, "Over the next few years it became clear to several people that Rexroth was incapable of appreciating neither Kerouac nor his latest work."[xxi] In credit to Rexroth's professionalism, he initially refrained from attacking Kerouac in public, but as Kerouac's popularity grew, Rexroth began to review his books for major publications.

After *Mexico City Blues* was published in 1959, Rexroth wrote a contemptuous review. "Somebody once said of Mr. Kerouac that he was a Columbia freshman who went to a party in the Village twenty years ago and got lost. How true. The naive effrontery of this book is more pitiful than ridiculous. Mr. Kerouac's Buddha is a dime-store incense burner, glowing and glowering sinisterly in the dark corner of a Beatnik pad and just thrilling the wits out of bad little girls." He added: "I've always wondered what ever happened to those wax work figures in the old rubber-neck dives in Chinatown. Now we know; one of them at least writes books."[xxii] He went on to say that Kerouac knew nothing about jazz and compared his attitude towards race to that of the Ku Klux Klan.

Kenneth had a bellyful of resentment and, in his mind, good reason for it. Jack was harboring a king-size grudge which he too felt justified, but his bitterness was a function of denial, never admitting his behavior offended Rexroth. That's what active alcoholics do—it's a subtle and elusive kind of self-righteousness.

So, they never reconciled, the relationship poisoned irrecoverably. For Kerouac, it was the contaminant of alcoholism, and the temperament that goes with it, and it killed him at forty-seven. For Rexroth it was bitter resentment, and resentment is like a stray cat—if you don't feed it, it will go away. Kenneth fed the cat.

It's sad chapter in the story of Beat movement literature. One we wish could be revised and rewritten, reuniting two giants of the written and spoken word, but there is no "Do Over" this side of Kipling's "great Judgment Seat."

For some, though, hope endures; there is an antidote of sorts to consider. Volumes could be written on their religious, spiritual, and mystical meanderings, and much has already been gleaned from their prose and poetry, studied and debated, but one fact endures: both died Roman Catholic—Kerouac from the cradle and Rexroth a recent convert.

Having professed their faith in the resurrection of the body and life everlasting, their mortal remains were interred with the last rites of the Church. Fellow believers then can find comfort in the hope that the "two strong men stand face to face," resurrected, reunited, and reconciled where there is neither East nor West—the poison drained, suffering subdued, respect restored—and solace for the living. Amen.

WORKS CITED

Ball, Gordon (ed.), *Allen Ginsberg Journals, Mid-Fifties 1954-1958* (Harper Collins, 1995)

Bartlett, Lee, ed., *Kenneth Rexroth and James Laughlin, Selected Letters* (Norton, 1991)

Charters, Ann, *Kerouac: A Biography* (St. Martin's Press, 1994)

Charters, Ann (ed.), *Jack Kerouac Selected Letters* 1940-1956 (Viking, 1995)

Charters, Ann (ed.), *Jack Kerouac Selected Letters* 1957-1969 (Penguin, 1999)

Gifford, Barry, and Lee, Lawrence, *Jack's Book: An Oral Biography of Jack Kerouac* (St. Martin's Press, 1978).

Hamalian, Linda, *A Life of Kenneth Rexroth* (Norton, 1991).

Morrow, Bradford, *Kenneteh Rexroth: Selected Poems* (New Directions, 1984).

Nicosia, Gerald, *Memory Babe* (University of California Press, 1994).

ENDNOTES

i   Letter dated early May 1954, Charters, 415.
ii   *Allen Ginsberg Journals*, 102.
iii   Letter dated May 20, 1955, Charters, 484.
iv   Hamalian, 243.
v   https://www.bopsecrets.org/rexroth/essays/kerouac.htm#On%20the%20Road
vi   Bartlett, 221.
vii   Gifford, 330.
viii   Ibid., 221-222.
ix   Hamalian, 243.
x   Charters, *Kerouac, A Biography*, 243.
xi   Hamalian, 243.
xii   Nicosia, 491.
xiii   Ibid.
xiv   Gifford, 197.
xv   Gifford, 194-195.
xvi   Hamalian, 243.
xvii   Ibid., 244.
xviii   Ibid., 246.
xix   Ibid.
xx   *Selected Letters*, 1957-1969, 128.
xxi   Hamalian, 271.
xxii   New York Times, November 29, 1959.

THE MONK IN THE "BEAT-FOLD"

BY JOHN MARSHELL

> "Saw Ferlinghetti in S.F. and drank some expresso with visionaries"
> – Thomas Merton in a letter to W.H. Ferry, May 24, 1968.

In a late afternoon reverie, I imagined two middle-aged, balding writers sitting in a San Francisco coffee shop watching the young coquettes of the sixties' sexual revolution promenade past their window. The air filling with a mild libidinous energy as both men enjoyed the unique kinesis of mini-skirts and tight T-shirts shifting in the fading sunlight, taunting desire and pricking curiosity, souls clinging to youth, yet mature enough to understand the pitfalls of short-lived pleasures. The liberating effects of a city-wide cultural renaissance creating an interesting show. In an effort to maintain the dignity of their years, the conversation turned to books and authors, which despite its substance became an inadequate substitute for unfulfilled cathexis.

The two authors of my reverie are City Lights Books' publisher Lawrence Ferlinghetti and Trappist monk Thomas Merton. But it is not entirely a work of creative fiction. The source of my reflection is an interview with Ferlinghetti for the PBS documentary *Merton: A Film Biography*, where he vividly recalled the incident with unflinching honesty, Merton's ogling the purely natural and human response to beautiful people. Libidinous energy, however, would not be the driving force of Merton's relationship with Ferlinghetti or the Beat movement of whom he was a part. Despite a recent tryst with a nurse, Merton had left the dubious category of "monk in love with a woman"[i] bestowed by his monastic brothers and returned to his vowed canonical state, with his interactions with Beat writers framed by mutually shared spiritual and political interests. Merton's celibacy was no longer a question.

Defining the Beat movement is a little tricky. Its membership can be as fluid as its characteristics. Allen Ginsberg, Jack Kerouac, William Burroughs, and Gregory Corso are consistent pillars of its literary community, but this should not deter us from including the feminine contributions of Carolyn Cassady, Diane di Prima, and Denise Levertov. Other authors such as Gary Snyder and Philip Whalen may not strictly be considered Beat but enjoy a status of association that often labels them as such. There can be some cross-over writers from the San Francisco Renaissance but Kenneth Rexroth ardently refused membership. Even its founders can be fickle, with Jack Kerouac and Gregory Corso disowning it late in life. The Beat movement's emphasis on spontaneity, freedom (particularly sexual freedom), drugs, non-conformist taboo breaking, Asian religions, and non-colonialist attitudes framing a broader worldview establish parameters that are porous. Placing Merton within the "Beat-fold" is entirely possible but largely because of a wide range of parallel concerns. Once common lines are drawn into latticework, Merton can seem an out-of-place branch in a small family of trees.

A recent publication by Bill Morgan has tried to address Merton's place in the Beat-fold. Morgan's *Thomas Merton, Lawrence Ferlinghetti, And The Protection Of All Beings* is a slender volume, examining the friendship between Ferlinghetti and Merton. Despite the size, readers will get a well-informed review of their relationship and the exchanges between the two authors, with Morgan's research focusing on Merton's publication of poems in Ferlinghetti's *Journal for the Protection of All Beings* and his brief visit to San Francisco in 1968. Included between the covers are reprints of Merton's Beat-related works, vintage photographs, and tantalizing tidbits of unfulfilled future projects and his Asian trip. The Merton reader and the Beat fan can be grateful for this handy and convenient book; however, Morgan offers only a congenial and fraternal interpretation of Merton's association with the Beat movement, and in my opinion leaves some dynamics unexamined. This essay will seek a closer reading of the relationship between Ferlinghetti and Merton within a broad range of concerns contemplating fractures and disagreements.

There is something unsettling about placing Merton in the pantheon of Beat writers. Some of it has to do with sex and drugs. The thought of a celibate monk associating with young men and women on the prowl chills imaginations envious of libertine lifestyles. "What is *he* doing in here?" Merton would not have cottoned to sexual license or same-sex romance, seeing both as traps to deeper commitments. Though he had enjoyed a randy youth, Merton later found an antidote to the "tyranny" of his sexuality in ascetical life.[ii] As for the "turn-ons" of Timothy Leary's psychedelic vision, Merton believed it had little to do with Christian personalism and sacramental mystery. Though the Abbey of Gethsemani for a time grew hemp for ropemaking, there is no evidence that Merton ever smoked it.

Certainly, there are elements of Merton's personality that would commend him to the Beat movement, but even in shared embrace there are rubs that can go the wrong way. Merton cherished freedom and spontaneity—the essential preserve of howling Beat life—but he was consistently careful to distinguish between psychological and theological experience in the pursuit of authenticity. In Merton's mind the passions were subject to reason, and the mind's reclamation of a *sensus anima* (divine sense) was the essential catalyst for reading the sign and symbol of the world's veil. The sobriety of Merton's vocation enveloped all his interests, providing a mature reflection to the mirrored concerns of a slightly younger generation whose actions sometimes betrayed their puerility. The peace movement, Asian religions, the beginnings of identity politics, the craft of language and writing, and the effects of technology on the human condition are part of the common ground of concerns. The commonality of interests seems to run on parallel tracks—so how should we see Merton? *What* is he doing in here?

There is a temptation to suggest that Merton's interest in the Beats was a part of his desire to stay current in cutting-edge affairs. In the parlance of the time, we could say Merton wanted to be "hip." His letters to Ferlinghetti are lightly peppered with sixties' slang, employing "cats" and "squares" as descriptors, as well as "zombie" for people who "are not someone else, nor themselves,"[iii] the unthinking people of the work-a-day world. In the youth culture of the 1960s, such language seemed suited but when coming from the pen of a middle-aged man perhaps a little awkward and even unctuous. Merton, however, could be self-policing and a critical eye to his behaviors was expressed in one of his Cold War letters to Czeslaw Milosz: "You are right about the temptation to get lined up with rebels without a cause. There is something attractive and comforting about the young kids that are going off into non-violent resistance with the same kind of enthusiasm I used to have myself in the thirties for left-wing action. But this too can be a great illusion. I trust your experience."[iv] Merton is not besotted by new movements or a need to relive his younger days as "Frank Swift" in a Communist Party cell or a protester at the 1935 Casa Italia riot at Columbia University. However, I would also be keen not to suggest a parental role, as the "Don't trust anyone over 30" crowd and other Jack Weinberg acolytes of the Free Speech Movement would have balked at even the most well-meaning of intrusions. Certainly, Merton would have been savvy not to become a "daddy."

However, arguments for a generational divide suffer somewhat when examined more closely. Ryan Mathews in his article "Go West Young Beats" (*Beatdom #24*) has meticulously provided the birthdates of a generation viewed as young and rebellious and mostly found them to be just rebellious, with few able to mambo beneath Jack Weinberg's bar of safe discourse. Grouping Merton, Ferlinghetti, and various younger Beat writers seriously stretches the definition of "generation." What draws Merton into the Beat family are his political and literary interests with a spiritual cachet. Here the lines begin to intersect, and the rubbing elbows of his relationships are more evident.

Merton's literary relations are cast from a large net and often result from casual circumstance and happenstance. Mark Van Doren, one of Merton's mentors from Columbia, sent his poems to James Laughlin in the mid-1940s, providing Merton with an early publishing opportunity. *Thirty Poems*, while not exactly Laughlin's cup of tea, intrigued the Calvinist-raised publisher, provoking "some feeling, as I had never had before, of what the Catholic faith was about."[v] Laughlin appreciated Merton's "liveliness" and "verbal spriteliness,"[vi] which ran somewhat counter to the other *avant-garde* writers he sought for inclusion in his growing New Directions catalogue. Even in his earliest years, Merton was unique, a slightly out-of-place bohemian voice birthed more from the communes of post-war Dada modernism than the post-modern coffee shops of the Beatdom that followed upon its heels. Nonetheless, Merton's relationships with Laughlin and Van Doren would become his introductions to Ferlinghetti and the Beat Generation, whose matriculations at Columbia were less than a decade from Merton's graduation.

Generationally, Merton and the Beats are not far removed, and his relationship with Ferlinghetti was a natural product of two writers with mutual friends sharing the same age and background with common interests and bohemian appreciations. Merton's massive epistolary output was far-reaching and varied, with his connections to the Beats somewhat determined by the breadth of his letter-writing. Merton's correspondence included William Carlos Williams, Louis Zukofsky, Boris Pasternak, Evelyn Waugh, James Baldwin, Henry Miller, and long-time friends and confidants Ed Rice and Bob Lax. Just as the Beats are hard to define through their wide-ranging interests, Merton is difficult to pigeonhole through his wide-ranging letter writing.

Within these literary associations, Merton seemed to warm to the Beats, seeing them as an almost secular form of religion. A kind of people he could relate to as slightly over-the-hill, non-conformist rebels still wrangling with contemporary happenings. A people living on the margins of society, just as a monk does. Responding to William Carlos William in 1961, in a letter regarding Allen Ginsberg's *Kaddish and Other Poems,* Merton states:

> I think it is great and living poetry and certainly religious in its concerns. In fact, who is more concerned with ultimates than the beats? Why do you think that just because I am a monk I should

> be likely to shrink from beats? Who am I to shrink from anyone, I am a monk, therefore by definition, as I understand it, the chief friend of the beats and one who has no business reproving them.[vii]

The philology of Merton's "Catholicism" was defined by universalism and inclusivity, not as a term of exclusive remonstration as demanded by Leonard Feeney's *extra Ecclesiam nulla salus*, viewing the Beats with the same Perennial-like scrutiny he gave to American Indians, Asian religions, and Cargo Cults. In his later years, Merton had started to pull away from a dogmatism based on cultural accidentals and monastic mystiques that created dualisms and diminished personhood to notions of pneumatologically-based, integrated persons grounded in love. It was a transition richly suited to the age. In a sense, Merton wanted to redefine the monk to anyone living on the margins unwilling to be falsified by social or religious structures, enjoying a truly free identity centered on God. The Beats lived and wrote as "true persons of no rank," to borrow a phrase from Zen master Linji (618-907), and Merton identified with their sentiments.

Though Merton had a respect and appreciation for monasticism (albeit sometimes grudging), he had been schooled at Columbia to understand identity in non-institutional, de-collective terms. The Beats and Merton shared the common mentor, Mark Van Doren, who "professed the then somewhat revolutionary idea that spiritual insight could be experienced beyond dogma and paradigms of religious institutions, pointing seekers towards an exploration of the self in the social order."[viii] It was here that the self, free from conformity and influences, could express itself with a kind of authenticity. In its most radical forms, this experientially based religious humanism ferreted out the spiritual in almost every nook and cranny of the literate world, establishing a "religion of no religion," as promulgated by Wuzhu (714-774). Though Merton appreciated and employed Van Doren's insights, his thinking seldom became rigorously iconoclastic, preferring paradox and the playfulness of spiritual life. Merton's thinking was imbued with dialectic and revelation and his common perceptions dependent upon antithesis and reciprocity, notably manifested in his interest of Nicanor Parra and anti-poetry and *Cables to the Ace*. Merton's love of William Blake underwrote his communion with spirits and prophecy and that "other" was not an enemy but a means of transcendence within the immanent.

Merton never dismissed the monastic life and often referred to it in his talks with novices as the closest to paradise a Christian could find on earth. Monks were already enjoying the fruits of heaven. Merton's playful coaxing out of the other in the secular world often resulted in an enculturation of celebrities that repurposed the ideals of his vocation, in a sense creating an alterego reborn in a humanist paradigm. In this regard, the world was populated by marginal monk-like people: "Christians turned inside out" and "monks in reverse."[ix] In a 1968 convocation of international students that he attended during his visit to California, Merton introduced himself as a monk, provoking a particularly fruitful exchange with a French student who declared himself a monk, too. During his talk, Merton made an impromptu and non-denominational definition of the monastic:

> The monk is essentially someone who takes up a critical attitude toward the world and its structures, just as these students identify themselves essentially as people who have taken up a critical attitude toward the contemporary world and its structures… [The monk] must have, in some way or other, reach some kind of critical conclusion about the validity of certain claims made by secular society and its structures with regard to the end of man's existence. In other words the monk is someone who says, in one way or another, that the claims of the world are fraudulent.[x]

Certainly, Merton could have taken the opportunity to challenge or cavil, but he did not. Merton chose empathy and fraternity, framing monastic paradise to a larger consciousness. So too his interest in the Beats.

Merton, however, was aware of fraudulency everywhere, and the monastery was not an exception. Writing to Clayton Eshelman in 1965, he continued to follow the road laid out by Mark Van Doren: "I assure you that I am not attached in the least to the institutional exterior of the Church."[xi] Merton was quick to assert that he "did not come here for the costume,"[xii] and he would not stay at Gethsemani if he "had not found some kind of life in it."[xiii] In his relationship with other people, Merton recognized that his monastic clothing was a barrier and the monastery a "forced and arbitrary setup,"[xiv] but he reduced these "fictions" for a genuine life in the spirit and likened their reductions to the "burning of Buddhas" in Zen monasteries, a necessary apophasis to embrace true nature and an unbound humanity. Even his clerical status became a reduction: "if you can possibly forget I am a priest, forget it. And I assure you that I have no interest in pulling any professional magic on you. I pray for you to have life and happiness as I pray for all my friends."[xv]

Despite the Anacreon to burning Buddhas, it is unlikely that Merton ever forgot he was a priest. The monk's letters to Ferlinghetti often slip into spiritual direction, sometimes deep and probing in their brief expositions. According to Bill Morgan, Ferlinghetti had considered monastic life in his youth,[xvi] and given Merton's language and ease of expression, he clearly believed Ferlinghetti capable of understanding his occasional waxing on the theological. In an August 2, 1961, letter, Merton writes:

> What is vitally important is that you should be a Christian and as faithful to the truth as you can get. This may mean anything but resembling some of the pious faithful. But I don't have to tell you, because you know, that there is only one thing that is of any importance in your life. Call it fidelity to conscience, or to the inner voice, or to the Holy Spirit: but it involves a lot of struggle and no suppiness and you probably won't get much encouragement from anybody. There is a dimension of Catholicism, mostly French and German, which gives little room for growth like this. But you have to find it as best you can. I can't necessarily tell you where to look, or how much of it you have found already. The start of it all is that none of us have really started to look. But the mercy of God, unknown and caricatured and blasphemed by some of the most reputable squares, is the central reality out which the rest comes and into which all the rest returns.[xvii]

Merton can also sing in another key with passion. In a December 12, 1961, letter:

> But Zen is beyond metaphysics and so, as far as I am concerned, is the kind of Christian experience

that seems to me most relevant, and which is found in Eckhart and the Rhenish mystics and all the mystics for that matter. I agree theoretically that there is a complete division between the two approaches: one personalistic, dualistic, etc., the other non-dualistic. Only trouble is that Suzuki's very distinction between God and Godhead is dualistic, and his line-up of Buddha vs. Christ is also dualistic, and when he starts that he forgets his Zen. So he forgets his Zen. He can forget his Zen too if he wants to or has to, no law saying you have to remember your Zen every minute of the day.[xviii]

The tenor of these passages is both compelling and amusing as well as surprisingly open and honest. His friend D.T. Suzuki was not spared from criticism nor his own Church with its stogy French and German adherents or the blaspheming squares for whom God's mercy was only conceptual. Though not lacking intellectual substance, the semantics of the texts was largely experiential, harmonizing with Van Doren's admonishment to move freely in the world of the spirit.

As with any good spiritual director, guidance was not always affirming. Merton could be critical and downright negative. He appreciated Allen Ginsberg but not to a point of robust enthusiasm, once describing him in a letter as "articulate but somehow he seems to me to be emotionally or spiritually gooey, viscous."[xix] Ginsberg, the recognized point-man for the Beat Generation, seemed to Merton "like someone from another planet."[xx] But again, Merton is self-policing as "telling everyone else off"[xxi] was not his vocation, nor "claiming to have the answer"[xxii] as so many other monks did. Merton is quick to avoid projection in his relationship with others: "And I do wish everyone would stop inferring that I intend my life to be some sort of reflection on theirs."[xxiii] The mirror however did carry some judgments.

Merton's rubbing elbows with the Beats could become sharp jabs, with much of Merton's argument focused on one area of common interest—spirituality. A superficial reading suggests a common empathy within the ecumenical; a closer look suggests an incongruous branch in the latticework of the Beat-fold. Merton's odd place in the Beat Generation was due to the "longsuffering apprenticeship of spirituality"[xxiv] of a seasoned practitioner who embraced *religion*, which was juxtaposed with those who can best be described as "seekers" with all the hallmarks of "spiritual but not religious" dilettantism. Though several of the Beats hailed from Catholic backgrounds (including Ferlinghetti), their lust for experience and capitalization of freedom had drawn them into a near solipsism of personal experience that reduced horizons to the limitations of self-absorbed, drug induced expressions that were more erotic than ecstatic. Merton diagnosed the problem in an early letter to James Laughlin:

> Sure, the pleasures connected to sex are good. God made them and they must be good, because they were supposed to be in the first place. But [William] Everson and Lawerence [Ferlinghetti] and all the rest of them has that silly conviction that all that can be detached from the order of things and can be considered *sui juris* all by itself in some sort of vacuum into which morality cannot enter.[xxv]

Rather than libertine existence, or any effort at a repressive "scouring out of all sexual desire,"[xxvi] Merton engaged in the "long hard job of sublimation,"[xxvii] channeling libido into creative pursuits. This stance provided him with a spiritual and ethical rock to stand on, and any effort to "make a virtue out of going under,"[xxviii] as the Beats seemed to do, appeared ill-advised.

The Beat ethos had succumbed to a "bad joke," confusing new life and the Beatitude with a confused abstraction that separated them from the moral order to the life of the dumb animal.[xxix] Any benefit from an objective order (religion) that would lift them out of subjectivity became a "turn on, tune-in, and drop out" narcissistic campaign of "join us in the revolution."[xxx] Despite claims of Buddhist membership, guru relationships, and Indian retreats, the Beat addictions to drugs and sex meant "burning the Buddhas" of Siddhartha's eight-fold path prohibitions to their own satisfactions, not to deeper commitments of corporate realities. LSD trips, smoking ganja, and the world of Latin American entheogenic-induced dreams lacked metaphysical authority once the truth-feeling had passed.

According to Ron Seitz, Merton could become genuinely annoyed by the "'adolescent excesses' … all the drug-taking, the anti-rational stance, the 'infantile spontaneity' of many of the artists, the attraction to all forms of occult and anything that was 'other than what we have here in this country or the entire western world.'"[xxxi] Merton's annoyance with the Beats seemed to deepen when his interests turned south to Latin America, where his associations and literary ventures produced an acute and keen understanding of the region, harmonizing with John Kennedy's Alliance for Progress initiatives. This stood in sharp contrast to the Beat authors, who approached the region as a parasitic host for self-promotion. In a November 1965 article for *Harpers*, Merton wrote:

> The South American poets who had a meeting in Concepcion, Chile, last winter, considered the two Americans present to be "innocents"—should one say fools? Especially one—who was continually making a huge fuss about how poets needed lots of drugs and sex and was always the first one to go home.[xxxii]

The two "innocents" were Ferlinghetti and Ginsberg—with Ginsberg being the greater offender. Such antics were not unusual for Ginsberg, even provoking the ire of Gary Snyder while traveling with him in Asia. In a letter to Napolean Chow, Merton admonished the whole movement:

> It seems to me that the protest of the beatniks, while having a certain element of sincerity, is largely a delusion. It is a false revolution, sterile and impotent, and its few flashes of originality, its attempts to express compassion, only increase the delusion. I am afraid the beats are to a great extant infantile.[xxxiii]

Such sentiments echo the concern of Pablo Armando Fernandez, who, upon meeting Ferlinghetti in 1960, caused remarked in writing: "he read a lot of Kerouac and others and had dug their weird dissent but has largely gotten disillusioned with them since they won't come far out enough from their private lives to commit themselves (like revolutionary writers for instance)."[xxxiv] Ferlinghetti conceded to nativist criticism, finding in the views of Jack Kerouac and others the "aimless self-indulgence and a conscious embrace of the irresponsible,"[xxxv] forming an informal alliance with Merton and Greenwich Village sage Amiri Baraka,

91

who also found the Beats simplistic and unable to produce thought alien to cliché, the essential act of an artist. [xxxvi]

When Merton first entered Gethsemani Abbey, he was entirely disposed to life enclosed "in the four walls of my new freedom."[xxxvii] But as his readers know, he decidedly abandoned writing as a vocation. Later, when required by his abbot to write, he complained to Laughlin about those same walls: "On the whole I think a monastery is not ordinarily a good place to write verse in. Too much triviality is dictated by the walls."[xxxviii] Merton needed outside contacts not only to interact with the outside world, but imbibe its language, rhetoric, color and tone, even its logic however surreal. He needed to place himself in the whole Mystical Body of Christ to become less trivial with "Christians turned inside-out." For a time, his association with the Beats was a part of his "leaping the wall," but Merton had many friends, including writers in the southern hemisphere. Merton's favorite language was Spanish, and he made a sober and studied examination of Latin American politics, culture, and literature. His polymathic skills applied to translating Pablo Neruda, Cesar Vallejo, and Pablo Antonio Cuadra and making alliances with the region's publishers. Merton admired the affectivity of the Spanish language, writing to Cuadra in 1959: "I am convinced that Latin American poetry has an ambience more pleasing and appropriate for me than that of the United States, which seems a little removed, less spontaneous, less fiery, more cerebral."[xxxix] The region had its own unique flavor for Merton's *sensus anima*.

As the Beats moved into the conventions of Latin American culture, with attitudes underwritten by libertine excess, Merton undoubtedly chose to favor his Latin relations over ne'er-do-well-good-doers acting past their depths. Perhaps ascribing a judgement to them promethean in its assessment, as men living without a center, "little helpless gods, imprisoned within the four walls of their own weakness and fear… so conscious of their weakness that they think they have nothing to give to another, and that they can only subsist by snatching from others the little they have, a little love, a little knowledge, a little power."[xl] Despite their significance in the United States, the Beats in Latin America were trivial.

Lawrence Ferlinghetti's attitudes were a bit different. His experiences in Latin America and Cuba ran counter to the narrative of the media of the United States and suggested a revolution less dogmatic than the narrow Marxist narrative found in the *New York*

Times. Ferlinghetti had a more positive outlook on Latin America and, with Merton, had a broad "Catholic" view of the region believing that its literary milieu could offer the world the benefit of its culture. Perhaps owing to his good common sense as a businessman, doctoral-level education, or the lingering sobriety of a lapsed Catholic, he developed an empathy with the Beats' critics and avoided Merton's condemnation. And the two friends wound up in a San Francisco coffee shop drinking espresso and watching coquettes. Visionaries in the twilight.

BIBLIOGRAPHY
BOOKS AND ARTICLES

Belcastro, David. (2002). "Thomas Merton and the Beat Generation: A Subterranean Monastic Community." Merton Society—Oakham Papers.

Cameron, Leah. (2016). "Their Own Beat: Mark Van Doren & Thomas Merton and the Revolution in Moral and Religious Poetry" in *Thomas Merton and the Counterculture*. (Ron Dart, Editor). Abbotford, BC, Canada: St. Macrina Press.

Cooper, David (Editor). (1997). *Thomas Merton and James Laughlin: Selected Letters*. New York, NY: W.W. Norton & Company.

Mathews, Ryan. (2023). "Go West Young Beats." *Beatdom #24*. Beatdom Books.

Merton, Thomas. (1993). *The Courage for Truth, Letters to Writers*. (Edited, Christine M. Bochen). New York, NY: Farrar, Strauss, and Giroux.

Merton, Thomas. (1948). *The Seven Storey Mountain*. New York, NY: Harcourt, Brace and Company.

Merton, Thomas. (1961). *The New Man*. New York, NY: Farrar, Strauss, and Giroux.

Morgan, Bill. (2022). *Thomas Merton, Lawrence Ferlinghetti, and The Protection of All Beings: The Correspondence*. United Kingdom: Beatdom Books.

Raggio, Marcelo. (2016). "Thomas Merton's Americanism: A Study of His Ideas on America In His Letters To Writers." *Revista de Estudios Norteamericanos* 20, Seville, Spain. ISSN1133-309-X. pp. 87-107.

Seitz, Ron. (1993). *Song for Nobody*. Liguori, Missouri: Triumph Books.

Tietchen, Todd. (2010). *The Cubalogues: Beat Writers in Revolutionary Havanna.* Gainesville, FL: University of Florida Press.

FILMS

Merton: A Film Biography. Retrieved December 1, 2024. https://youtu.be/xvrvBlplBcw?si=JDS8WeQGeYOb7MjR
Bill Morgan Interview. Retrieved November 26, 2024. https://youtu.be/l8ysysa5HuA?si=Irv81BDKjxbug2QW.

ENDNOTES

i   Thomas Merton. *Learning to Love,* p 84.
ii   Thomas Merton. *Learning to Love,* p 67.
iii   Thomas Merton. *The Courage for Truth,* p 269 (paraphrase).
iv   Thomas Merton. *The Courage for Truth,* p 80.
v   David Cooper. *Thomas Merton and James Laughlin,* p 375.
vi   David Cooper. *Thomas Merton and James Laughlin,* p 374.
vii   Thomas Merton. *The Courage for Truth,* p 290.
viii   Leah Cameron. "Their Own Beat: Mark Van Doren & Thomas Merton and the Revolution in Moral and Religious Poetry," p 2.
ix   I am indebted to the article of David Belcastro, "Thomas Merton and the Beat Generation: A Subterranean Monastic Community" for insights in Merton's redefining the monk.
x   Holy Cross Abbey. "The Monk as Marginal Person," retrieved November 26, 2024, https://www.virginiatrappists.org/2015/11/the-monk-as-a-marginal-person-thomas-merton-100th-anniversary-part-1/
xi   Thomas Merton. *The Courage for Truth,* p 258.
xii   Thomas Merton. *The Courage for Truth,* p 258.
xiii   Thomas Merton. *The Courage for Truth,* p 258.
xiv   Thomas Merton. *The Courage for Truth,* p 258.
xv   Thomas Merton. *The Courage for Truth,* p 258.
xvi   Bill Morgan. Interview. Retrieved November 26, 2024. https://youtu.be/l8ysysa5HuA?si=Irv81BDKjxbug2QW.
xvii   Thomas Merton. *The Courage for Truth,* p 269.
xviii   Thomas Merton. *The Courage for Truth,* p 271.
xix   Thomas Merton. *The Courage for Truth,* p 260.
xx   Thomas Merton. *The Courage for Truth,* p 259.
xxi   Thomas Merton. *The Courage for Truth,* p 263.
xxii   Thomas Merton. *The Courage for Truth,* p 263.
xxiii   Thomas Merton. *The Courage for Truth,* p 263.
xxiv   Ron Seitz. *Song for Nobody,* p 144.
xxv   David Cooper. *Thomas Merton and James Laughlin,* p 34.
xxvi   Thomas Merton. *The Courage for Truth,* p 263.

xxvii   Thomas Merton. *The Courage for Truth*, p 263.
xxviii   Thomas Merton. *The Courage for Truth*, p 263.
xxix   David Cooper. *Thomas Merton and James Laughlin*, p 34.
xxx   Spoken by Timothy Leary at the "Human Be-in" at San Francisco Golden State Park in 1966.
xxxi   Ron Seitz. *Song for Nobody*, p 144.
xxxii   David Belcastro. "Thomas Merton and the Beat Generation: A Subterranean Monastic Community," p 82.
xxxiii   Thomas Merton. *The Courage for Truth*, p 170.
xxxiv   Todd F. Tiecthen. *The Cubalogues*, p 42.
xxxv   Todd F. Tiecthen. The *Cubalogues*, p 42.
xxxvi   Todd F. Tiecthen. The *Cubalogues*, p 96.
xxxvii   Thoms Merton. *The Seven Storey Mountain*, p 410.
xxxviii David Cooper. *Thomas Merton and James Laughlin*, p 136.
xxxix   Thomas Merton. *The Courage for Truth*, p 283.
xl   *Thomas Merton. The New Man, p 25.*

POEM FOR RUTH WEISS
BY A.D. WINANS

she shadowboxes with father time
daytime nighttime bebop jazz time
she dances with timeless time
all rhythm no rhyme

birds in flight flap their wings
copulate with the wind
feed off the flesh of the other
in roller coaster freeze stop motion

she sings lifes song
bitch slaps father time
Kaufman son of jazz in her heart
Micheline in her blood

jazz in the Fillmore
jazz on Harlem rooftops
full moon rising
with poems that dig into my bones
lubricate the gears of my mind
lost in a haze of motionless motion

IN SEARCH OF THE GOOD BLONDE

BY BRETT SIGURDSON

Oh splendid butterfly of my imagination,
Flying into reality more real
Than all imagination, the evil
Of the world covets your living flesh.

— Kenneth Rexroth, "Noretorp-Noretsyh"

Her name appears in one of the thousands of pages in dozens of notebooks where Jack Kerouac recorded his life. "The Good Blonde," as Kerouac called her in his titular short story, had just dropped Kerouac off at the South San Francisco train station after a Benzedrine-fueled ride from Santa Barbara. When she left him, Kerouac found himself amid the swirling energy of the San Francisco Renaissance, which, just a few weeks later, would see its hard launch during the 6 Gallery Reading.

We know a lot about what happened afterward. But who was The Good Blonde? Was she as sexy, uninhibited, and knowing as Kerouac describes in the story he would publish nearly ten years later? Or was she simply a real person that Kerouac mythologized for his story, as he so often did?

In the spring of 2025, I set out to find her. Using details from Kerouac's journals and letters, as well as his multiple versions of "The Good Blonde" story, I aimed to track her down and uncover her true identity. Above her name and address in Kerouac's notebook, someone—perhaps her—sketched hearts pierced by

Cupid's arrow. My goal: to penetrate the mystery of the woman who gave Kerouac the most incredible ride of his life.

On October 12, 1955, Kerouac wrote a flurry of letters, including one to John Clellon Holmes about his experience in the Bay Area living with Allen Ginsberg amid the thriving San Francisco Renaissance, a time that saw him "live and talk about 24 hours a day."[i] Kerouac's breathless description of his arrival in San Francisco that fall echoes the first several chapters of *The Dharma Bums*, as if Kerouac were working on a draft of the novel—something he often did through his letters to Holmes and Cassady.

Kerouac recounts standing at the side of a highway near the Santa Barbara railyard with his thumb raised. Just as he's about to give up, he sees a new persimmon-colored Mercury Montclair squeal to a stop in front of him. A blonde woman in a strapless white bathing suit, a gold bracelet on her ankle, is behind the wheel. The woman is so becoming, and Kerouac is so deep into his celibacy, that he is afraid to look at her. She's tired, yawning, been driving straight through from Fort Worth, Texas. Kerouac offers her Mexican Benzedrine from his bag. His clothes spill out as he searches for them. She takes two pills when they stop at a gas station. The car tops out at 100—even 110—as they drive through the Guadalupe Valley to Santa Ana and San Luis Obispo. In Salinas, they pick up money that her boyfriend, a tavern owner, wires her. They arrive in San Francisco blasting jazz on the radio, and she lets him off at the South San Francisco rail yard, where Kerouac once worked. Before he closes the door, Kerouac makes plans to meet her again, and he scribbles an address in his notebook.

Kerouac took a 75-cent room at the Cameo Hotel in San Francisco's skid row, and the next morning listened to a street preacher. "You are telling the truth," he tells her. He then caught the train to Berkeley and walked to Ginsberg's cottage at 1624 Milvia Street. Upon finding the house empty, he played Bach's "St. Matthew's Passion," perhaps losing himself in the chorus, "*Herr, bin ich's?*" "Lord, is it I?"

There is a game that Kerouacians play when we read his work: name that character. To read *On the Road*, *The Dharma Bums*, or any other work inspired by Kerouac's personal experiences is to invite the opportunity to replace the characters' names with their real-life sources of inspiration. We know that Alvah Goldbrook and Carlo Marx are based on Allen Ginsberg, that Neal Cassady inspired Dean Moriarty and Cody Pomeroy. For some of us, knowing Kerouac's characters signifies our dedication to the work and its author. For others—especially new readers—learning about Kerouac's cast of characters is a badge of belonging, like having opinions on which live version of "Dark Star" is most supreme in the Grateful Dead's canon. (And that would be the rendition from the Old Renaissance Faire Grounds in August 1972, of course—face-melting for reasons beyond the day's blistering heat.)

But what about the names of characters who appear in Kerouac's books but are often left unnamed? The two brothers from Minnesota who picked up a hitchhiking Sal Paradise and transported him in the back of a truck to Wyoming, one of many memorable moments Kerouac fictionalized in *On the Road*. Or the taxi driver who imparts instant enlightenment in *Satori in Paris*? What about Beaudry, the truck driver who takes Smith from Arizona to Ohio, or Burnie Byers, the Forest Service ranger, in *The Dharma Bums*? Do these minor characters realize that their interactions with him were frozen like amber in the narrative Kerouac later unfurled? If they do, how might they feel about it? Assuming most are no longer alive, what about their families? What would it be like to have their loved ones' memories preserved in a novel for time immemorial?

I do have some idea. In San Francisco, I once met a woman whose father, the poet Jay Blaise, hung out with Kerouac in North Beach. On one bawdy Thanksgiving night, Kerouac and Blaise were hanging out when Joanne Kyger broke a wine bottle over Blaise's head, a scene that Kerouac recounted in a letter to Gary Snyder. It was his claim to fame and, I gathered, a story his daughter told often. I once interviewed the last surviving relative of someone who appeared in a Kerouac book. He was stunned that his cousin appeared in a book. In both cases, it was as if their loved one was freed from the past, was somehow still alive.

Sometime in the late fall of 1957, Kerouac inserted a long roll of paper into his typewriter and started recounting his 1955 trip from Mexico City, where he had spent the summer writing in a shack at 212 Orizaba, to San Francisco. His aim, it seems, was to find his way into the opening of the book that would become *The Dharma*

Bums. This effort produced two scrolls that Kerouac set aside as potential openings for the book—he even scrawled "Reject" on the scrolls before storing them away. The second scroll, about four and a half feet long, was titled "Good Blonde in Car."[ii]

The story Kerouac shares in this piece, which would later be renamed "The Good Blonde," mostly matches the experience he described to Holmes. The narrative begins with Jack Duluoz talking to a man on the beach in Santa Barbara. They watch a boy and girl come out of the bushes after having sex. Both older men observe them with longing—the man because he reflects on his youth, Duluoz because he has been celibate.

With eagerness and excitement to reunite with his friends in San Francisco, Duluoz walks to a nearby highway heading north and extends his thumb. However, no one stops for him, and he feels disillusioned with drivers. But suddenly a new Lincoln pulls over ahead of him. It is driven by a beautiful young blonde in a swimsuit, and he assumes she just wants directions. However, the blonde is heading to San Francisco and needs someone to help her drive. Excited, Duluoz hops in for what he considers the ride of his life.

For the rest of the day, he and the woman, whom he calls "Pretty," drive through Central California, with the Bennies in Duluoz's bag fueling their journey. They make a few stops for gas and supplies, experience an incident where they run out of gas and need a tow, and have various snippets of conversation. When she finally drops Duluoz off at a train station in South San Francisco, he catches the train to Berkeley to meet his friends.

Sometime afterward, Kerouac put "Good Blonde in Car" away in his files. In 1963, he retrieved the story from his files and sold it to *Playboy*, which published it in 1964 for a much-needed $500. A comparison shows that the published version closely resembles what Kerouac typed on the scroll. There are only minor differences—the color of the Good Blonde's eyes has changed, and she drinks a Pepsi instead of a Coke. In the scroll version, Kerouac used his own name for the narrator, while he used Duluoz for the published story.

However, "The Good Blonde" is an outlier for a significant reason. Unlike many other experiences from this period that Kerouac later fictionalized, he apparently didn't record it in his pocket-sized notebooks, at least based on my survey of available archival materials. That isn't entirely unusual. Kerouac often jotted down sections of stories or memories out of chronological order in his notebooks. Still, considering how memorable the events seem to have been, the Good Blonde story should have been in his notebook from September 1955.

The period around "The Good Blonde" experience was highly productive. During a decade of creative work, this era was probably his most successful. He wrote nonstop, with his prose and poetry reflecting immediate insights from his journals. They led to the completion (or near completion) of books such as *Scripture of the Golden Eternity* and *Old Angel Midnight*.

Moreover, Kerouac was immersing himself in Buddhist study. When he stayed with his sister's family in North Carolina in early 1955, he spent his days helping with chores and his nights deep in meditation, providing the space needed for his Buddhist study and practice. At one point, he considered pursuing a monastic life to further his Buddhist interests, but he chose instead to record his learnings and teachings in his notebooks. He would later refer to the collection as *Some of the Dharma*. He also wrote *"Wake Up"* and his translation, *"Buddha Tells Us."* None of these texts, however, would sell to publishers.

Kerouac found better luck with *On the Road*—then called *The Beat Generation*—which finally sold to Viking Press. Malcolm Cowley, a Viking advisor, also sold "The Mexican Girl," an excerpt from *On the Road*, to the *Paris Review* in July 1955. At that time, he was living at 212 Orizaba, the apartment building where William Burroughs and Bill Garver resided in Mexico City; Kerouac rented a hut on the building's roof. There, sitting on a toilet and perpetually stoned, he wrote *Mexico City Blues* in his notebooks. He experimented with other short stories, such as a follow-up to *The Town and The City*, in which Peter, the protagonist, explains Buddhism. Kerouac also drafted the opening chapters of a novella he would finish a year later called *Tristessa*.

This creative, spiritual ethos infused his life as he left Mexico for San Francisco in late September 1955. His eyes and his heart were fixed on the Berkeley cottage he was to share with Ginsberg upon his arrival.

By the winter of 1957, Kerouac's memories of that trip had undoubtedly faded, obscured by his journeys across the U.S. and a long trip to Europe, not to mention the chaos surrounding the publication of *On the Road* less than a year earlier. Working without his usual detailed notes about his travels, Kerouac seemed to need the freedom to improvise and explore that the margins of the scroll provided. In short, he needed to recall the events of that period before he could figure out the story he wanted to tell. The Good Blonde had faded from his mind.

The first problem I faced while trying to find the Good Blonde was the address in South San Francisco that Kerouac recorded in his notebook. Located in Buri Buri, a neighborhood named after a Native American tribe, the house number she gave Kerouac doesn't exist. In fact, it isn't even near any possible addresses on the small street. So I wonder: did Kerouac simply write down the wrong street? Could she have meant a different street? Did she give him a fake address to ensure she wouldn't see him again?

Her connection to Buri Buri was perhaps telling, though. It had once been a 15,000-acre ranch in the Merced Valley along the San Bruno Mountains, and out of the land grew Redwood City, Millbrae, and South San Francisco. In 1949, a developer named it "Rancho Buri Buri" for a new suburban neighborhood marketed as a country village surrounded by shopping centers, churches, and a new school. It's the kind of place Kerouac described in *Lonesome Traveler*:

> I wish I was a little child in a crib in a little ranchstyle sweet house with my parents sipping in the livingroom with their picture window pointing out on the little backyard of lawning chairs and the fence, the ranchstyle brown pointed full fence, the stars above, the pure dry golden smelling night.[iii]

The car she drove also gives clues about the Good Blonde's identity. The Mercury Montclair, with its 198-horsepower, super-torque V-8 engine—and the smooth Merc-O-Matic Drive—was so powerful that an advertisement showed it pulling an 8,000-pound camper trailer up a San Francisco hill. "Brilliant new acceleration at every speed from 1 mile per hour to whatever the law allows," reads the advertisement. And they were going at high speeds. Mercury called its design the Jet Ahead style.

And yet, given Kerouac's descriptions of her tendencies— "You've had it before?" Duluoz asks about Benzedrine. "Of course man and everything else."—she is clearly not the typical mid-century suburban housewife. It's possible, then, that Pretty was a B-Girl, the beautiful women hired by San Francisco tavern owners to persuade patrons to buy more drinks. They were particularly notorious in the late 1940s and 1950s. The Good Blonde's description as the comely girlfriend of a tavern owner— one who is no doubt wealthy, given the rarity of the model and

color of the convertible—aligns with some of the notorious San Francisco bars at the time, where some of the tavern owners were known to use B-Girls at their establishments. In the *Evergreen Review*, Ralph Gleason described this kind of woman—and the Good Blonde—as a

> high-price call girl, flush from the Republican convention and an automobile dealers conclave and happily looking forward to the influx of 20,000 doctors, 8,000 furniture dealers and divers other convention delegates, put it simply. "San Francisco is the town where everyone comes to ball, baby," she said.[iv]

These gestures toward defining her identity based on her looks, on visible qualities, are all I have to go on. She seems, from everything I can discern about her, to be among the squares who couldn't know about the San Francisco Renaissance because they are so far removed from it. If the San Francisco Renaissance was concerned with disaffiliation, she displays the signs of belonging. Outwardly, she comes from the world that clutches pearls at Allen Ginsberg's alleged obscenities in *Howl & Other Poems*.

But Pretty is so much more.

As I think about it now, my struggles to find traction in the search for the Good Blonde's identity mirrored Kerouac's attempts to begin *The Dharma Bums*. He had been struggling to write the novel for most of the year. Indeed, while living in Tangier with William S. Burroughs, Kerouac indicated he was planning to write a book titled "Dharma Bums in Europe," though he didn't pursue the idea until he returned to the States.[v] Kerouac made good on that vow in May 1957. In a notebook entry, he writes of completing seven chapters and 4,000 words of a story about the travels of "an American Buddhist Dharma Bum."[vi]

However, Kerouac's archives contain a scant record of this effort. What is available differs vastly from the published version of *The Dharma Bums* in style and content. In the two-page sections of "Dharma Bums in Europe" in the New York Public Library's Berg Collection, the writing is akin to Kerouac mimicking William S. Burroughs. Kerouac uses stream-of-consciousness sketching to describe the landscape of Morocco from aboard a ship. Much of the writing is opaque, wild beyond the writing in *Visions of Cody*.[vii] It reads more like a writing exercise than an attempt to weave a narrative inspired by his time in the Bay Area in the prior year.

By the summer of 1957, a period that found him back in Mexico, Kerouac had given up on the "Dharma Bums in Europe" idea, indicating he was instead going to incorporate it into another novel he was planning: *Desolation Angels*. "Have abandoned Dharma Bums in Europe to make it 2nd part of Desolation Angels," he writes in a notebook that July. "DAngels will thus be a huge novel, almost 1,000 pages, I will raise it to a climax..."[viii] Kerouac, though, would shift his focus again that summer to another long-gestating project, "Memory Babe," a narrative inspired by his youth in Lowell, Massachusetts.

Everything changed after Gilbert Millstein's *New York Times* review of *On the Road* on September 5, 1957–including Kerouac's writing plans. Amidst the notes about meetings, phone numbers, and debts to repay that fill the notebook he kept at the time, Kerouac reflected on his need to tell Malcolm Cowley he would write about Snyder and "the shack gang" for his next book.

That fall, Kerouac wrote the *Dharma Bums* on a new Royal Standard typewriter in the Orlando apartment he shared with his mother. In a December 9, 1957, letter to Cowley, Kerouac boasts of finishing the manuscript on a 100-foot roll of paper filled end-to-end with single-space sentences.[ix] Yet, his celebratory remarks belied the difficulty he experienced in beginning the narrative, as evidenced by the two aborted openings he clearly cut from the roll of paper.[x]

Something Kerouac recorded in a notebook lingers with me, contextualizing in some ways his struggles to write *The Dharma Bums*, its intro, and—well—most of his oeuvre: "I cant [sic] write anything but what burns at the time it burns."

Since Kerouac's writing style was inspired by such commitment, I figured I should take a cue from him as I set out to find the Good Blonde.

Even after signing up for an Ancestry account, I had an impossible time finding anything about her in Fort Worth, Los Angeles, San Francisco, or anywhere mentioned in Kerouac's story. The only women with similar names were in the wedding announcements—women who hadn't really left Texas, hadn't traveled, and were, in fact, homemakers who, one imagines, longed for wedded bliss all their lives. This portrait, though, is based almost solely on the way these women smiled so gleefully in their wedding pictures. It seems fitting that Pretty's identity doesn't stand out on a website as plain as Ancestry. Maybe she shouldn't be so easy to define. After all, the story shows she isn't tied to a place or a man—she seems to have a sugar daddy, not a boyfriend—and she appears to be focused on living in the moment, as Duluoz tries to do.

And what about that title? *The Good Blonde*. It feels so strange and compelling. The most important word is, of course, "good." The apparent implication is her appearance. She is beautiful, according to Kerouac's description of her and the slack-jawed men at service stations. Indeed: instead of a name, she is called "Pretty." Her looks are clearly the reason for the "good" label, although it's a word that's objectifying, similar to the drooling-dog comments made by men in the 1950s. It's a perspective that aligns with criticism of Kerouac as a chauvinist. Scholar Nancy M. Grace deemed Pretty a "white goddess," one of the three character archetypes that Kerouac used (fellaheen and grotesque are the others). The White American Woman, as Grace calls her, is "[p]ure and beautiful, a trophy wife or girlfriend signifying economic, social, and spiritual success."[xi]

To deeply analyze "The Good Blonde" in this contemporary moment is to grapple with the economies of Kerouac's conflicting meaning. On one side, Pretty represents two common criticisms of Kerouac: his tendency to objectify women and to create one-dimensional female characters. In "The Good Blonde," she barely speaks. Almost everything we learn about her is through Duluoz's perspective and the people he encounters at gas stations. We never discover her backstory, why she's in Texas, or what she truly desires. The slack-jawed, horn-dog attitude that she seems to elicit from gas station attendants highlights a typical complaint against Kerouac's male characters—that they can be predatory.

And yet Kerouac seems to acknowledge the male-centered focus of his Duluoz Legend. Throughout, Duluoz undergoes an inner journey colored by emotions that range from lust to shame, anger, abstinence, admiration, and awe. He wonders why she picked him up and what her intentions are. A beautiful young woman with a slightly older male stranger picked up on the side of the road? It's a recipe for sexual encounters—maybe a dangerous one. But Pretty is unfazed. She is clearly experienced in ways other women Duluoz has met or not. She's taken all the drugs. She knows all the jazz musicians, enough that Shelley Manne has a theme song for her. And she's beautiful, confident, and completely free.

The radicalness of Kerouac's conception of her becomes clearer when viewed within the context of the San Francisco Renaissance. According to Michael Davidson, author of *The San Francisco Renaissance: Poetics and Community at Mid-century*, the movement's apparent populism didn't include women, even those female poets who played a key role in the scene: Kyger, di Prima, Helen Adams, Denise Levertov. Hardly artistic equals, these writers were depicted by San Francisco Renaissance writers as, writes Davidson, "Sexual surrogate, muse, or mom." Female writers in the 1950s and '60s lacked the support network needed to gain the recognition they sought, Davidson argues. Instead, they were defined by their relationships with their male counterparts. "Writing about women of and in the San Francisco Renaissance is difficult not because there were so few of them but because the standard definition of the movement has no way of including them," writes Davidson.

This fact, then, makes Kerouac's portrayal of Pretty more radical than it initially seems. While she is a sexual surrogate and muse, Kerouac challenges this trope by placing her at the forefront of the story, giving her the power to drive the narrative—literally. As such, there is an argument that Kerouac adds depth to Pretty as a female character, though the reader needs familiarity with both the San Francisco Renaissance and Kerouac's oeuvre to appreciate it.

After all, the women of the San Francisco Renaissance adopted the discourse of their male counterparts, argues Davidson. That is especially true of the Good Blonde, for Kerouac infuses her with the Virgil-like qualities he admires in Dean Moriarty, Cody Pomeray, and Japhy Ryder. She seems to know who she is, her place in the world, and how to navigate through it—literally, as when the Lincoln/Mercury runs out of gas, and she shifts back and forth to keep fuel in the carburetor. Pretty controls her life, unlike Jack Duluoz. She is experienced, present, confident, unafraid. All these qualities Duluoz admires are reflected in her smooth, confident handling of the car. She possesses a wisdom that Duluoz might see as pedagogical, similar to how Dean might view Sal or Japhy as Ray.

Pretty is *good*. She is the Beat ideal.

The episode with the Good Blonde is only briefly mentioned at the beginning of *The Dharma Bums*, as Japhy Ryder is being introduced. Did Kerouac fear that the energy between them would overshadow the story? Maybe he was worried she might steal some of Japhy's spotlight. After all, when Kerouac conceived of *The Dharma Bums*, he planned to focus on his experiences with Gary Snyder, Japhy's inspiration.

In the first typescript roll that Kerouac wrote, titled "God's Wisdom"—it seems to have been cut at the bottom margin from the top of the "Good Blonde in Car" roll—Kerouac introduces his main character in a manner similar to *On the Road*'s Dean Moriarty: "It all started from meeting Gary Snyder." It's no surprise, as—much like he did with Neal Cassady in *Visions of Cody* and his brother in *Visions of Gerard*—Kerouac's notebooks from this era contain scattered entries about his desire to author a book about Snyder, titled "Visions of Gary." as was his tendency when using the scroll approach, Kerouac used real names, such as Snyder, in the narrative. It seems he needed a way to revisit the memories, a move reminiscent of a journal entry from 1948: "If my hand could only 'keep up with my soul'... so as I say, if my hand could *capture it*."[xii]

In a move he would rarely make in his novels, Kerouac begins "God's Wisdom" where *The Dharma Bums* would eventually end: atop Desolation Peak, where he recalls how he started every morning building a fire to heat a fresh pot of coffee to drink among the panoramic views of the High Cascades—all skills,

Kerouac writes, that he learned from Snyder during the previous year. But what starts as a setup for Kerouac's reminisces of Snyder quickly turns into a detailed retelling of his journey from Mexico City to Ciudad Juarez, El Paso, to L.A. and San Francisco in late September 1955.

The content of the "God's Wisdom" scroll recalls some of Kerouac's best writing from *Lonesome Traveler*, those moments where his galloping syntax overlaps with his love of Western panoramas and his sociological interest in the idiosyncrasies of railroad cars, bus depots, and hobo jungles. Arriving in El Paso, Kerouac writes,

> A [short] survey of our gear by border inspectors, and over the little bridge [over] the Rio Grand [into] El Paso, where suddenly I saw again the well fed rich looking wristwatched American sailors waiting for the westbound L.A. doubledecker airconditioned bus that would sway them to the west coast ['cause] they read pocketbooks bought on racks in bus stations [and] drugstores, the endless Luke [Short] westerns and Mickey Spillane mysteries they red [sic], under the soft glow of seat lights, as the bus balls across the dry sage flats of their ancestors.[xiii]

Only when Kerouac arrives in L.A. at the end of the "God's Wisdom" roll does the reader find anything that appears in *The Dharma Bums*: the St. Therese Bum, whom Kerouac depicts with more depth and tenderness than in the published novel. After the old hobo climbs into the gondola with Kerouac, the man tells him about his bleak life after leaving Ohio to join the WWI effort, how he hoboed across America for twenty years afterward, returning home so bedraggled that his own sister didn't recognize him when he stepped onto the front yard. He decided to move on.

The St. Therese Bum lived in a cardboard shack along the railyard in Santa Barbara, where both he and Kerouac jumped the gondola. Contrary to the image of a kindly bum who inspires Ray to feel deep empathy, Kerouac lies to him about his plans to sleep on the beach to keep his solitude. In the morning, Kerouac wakes up on the beach and encounters an elderly man walking along the shoreline, the "Greek" of the title. Their interaction is brief, ending with the old Greek indicating he doesn't smoke or drink, that he just likes to perambulate.

Here, Kerouac cut off this segment of the paper roll, though it's not clear why, since the next part of the roll would continue right where he left off, with the events that would become "The Good Blonde."

Without Kerouac's customary notes about his novels, though, it's difficult to determine his rationale for beginning *The Dharma Bums*. As I've searched for the Good Blonde, I've imagined what *The Dharma Bums* would have been like had Kerouac used this story as the opening of the novel, as Kerouac seems to have briefly considered. Pretty would have represented Smith's first temptation in the book. All of the qualities she embodies are traits he tries to resist in the pursuit of enlightenment. Therefore, it makes sense that he described Pretty's tempting charms so that she could serve as a foil for the character who became Ray Smith. In chapter five, Smith describes his year-long celibacy as a reaction to his feeling that life brings suffering because sex is the act through which life is created. Lust is, according to Smith, "offensive and even cruel."[xiv] Without lust driving his desires, he had become peaceful, content. Smith's lack of sexual activity had made him even more self-conscious about removing his clothes in front of others. Pretty represents the temptation Smith must forgo to learn the Dharma. Perhaps, then, it is possible to interpret the "good" in "The Good Blonde" as Duluoz/Smith's attempt to resist his carnal desires for spiritual conquests instead.

Kerouac had been focused on controlling his own lustful thoughts. In "On the Path," written two months before Kerouac arrived in San Francisco in 1955, he captures the level of celibacy he practiced before his experience with the Good Blonde. In doing so, he shows the misogyny that sometimes appears in his work. "[A]ll women are essential Napoleons," he writes. The motivation is clear: women conquer and colonize men, taking control over their hearts, souls, and independence. But, as so often happens with Kerouac, he softens the initial sharpness of his claim, as if a scolded child admitting fault. In this case, he vows to "grab no more at pretty girls." That choice of language—*grabbing at women*—shows Kerouac's awareness of his own predatory tendencies. Celibacy seems like an attempt to cool his desires.[1]

---

1 At the close of "On the Path," Duluoz becomes stuck in Sanford, North Carolina. He's resentful of all the people who drive past him, the young and the old. He lashes out at a woman who drives past him: "Oh, you bitch—all the women in America have the cars now" (206). Obviously, it's a strange irony that Kerouac is picked up by the Good Blonde only months later.

Given the Good Blonde's potential role, opening *The Dharma Bums* with the St. Therese Bum encounter seems like a missed opportunity. He is the opposite of the Good Blonde: meek, unassuming, easy to overlook. The St. Therese Bum is almost a model for how Smith wants to be, yes, but this opening doesn't leave an impression the way the Good Blonde might have. She is the quintessential symbol, somehow both tangible and not, as ravishing as the sun and as difficult to pin down as the wind.

In the months before *On the Road's* publication, Kerouac wrote of how he sought to write novels about the American prophets in his circle: Cassady, Ginsberg, Lucien Carr, Gary Snyder. These books were his "vision" books, defined as "full-length prose works concentrating on the character of one individual, with no other form than that, including verse and any thing, even pictures."[xv] These narratives represented Kerouac's mythologizing of his friends, his attempt to exaggerate or idealize them. Like the Duluoz Legend that contextualizes novels like *Visions of Cody*, *Lucien Midnight*, and *The Dharma Bums*, real people and actual occurrences intermingle with Kerouac's fictive fancies. In short, these stories are real and imagined.

The woman who inspired "The Good Blonde" is perhaps also a manifestation of Kerouac's concept of "vision" novels: both legend and not. Or so I think. In my experience searching for the tangible person behind the story, I've come up empty, as if trying to grasp air. The weight of myths, after all, is heavy until one tries to hold them.

Is it any surprise, then, that I haven't been able to track down the Good Blonde? Like so many trips Kerouac took, my best intentions were waylaid by all manner of roadblocks. At this point in the essay, I wanted to reveal the Good Blonde's name, share how I had successfully tracked her down, and interview her about her unique role in Kerouac's work mythos. I imagined writing something noteworthy about the way Kerouac turned their freewheeling encounter into a compelling short story that embodies the essence of his appeal.

But, as of this writing, my thoughts about the Good Blonde mirror Duluoz's as he thinks of *Tristessa*: "I feel we are two empty phantoms of light or like ghosts in old haunted-house stories diaphanous and precious and white and not-there."[xvi]

It may seem forced, but my as-yet-unsuccessful search for

the Good Blonde reveals something essential about the San Francisco Renaissance: it is not all it seems. What we know as the San Francisco Renaissance is really, according to Davidson, a loose confederation of poetic scenes, styles, and stances united by a search for community among separate but similar San Francisco tribes.[xvii] The movement, such as it was, only came to formation posthumously, after it was mostly concluded. "What began as a series of loosely organized readings, publications, and meetings has been read as a unified narrative of the literary and artistic life of the San Francisco Bay Area during the late 1950s and early 1960s," he writes.[xviii] The label is convenient shorthand for the spirit of the times, if not a largely inaccurate one.

Take the poets of the 6 Gallery reading, always credited as the San Francisco Renaissance's founding moment. Despite the event's semblance of a unified movement, the poets who participated had vastly different styles, agendas, and aesthetic beliefs. Two of the poets who read, Gary Snyder and Phil Whalen, were absent from the movement during its height. Kerouac and Ginsberg didn't stay in San Francisco long enough to contribute to the scene. Established San Francisco poets like Jack Spicer, who didn't participate in the 6 Gallery reading, also felt distant from the social concerns associated with the Beat movement and other San Francisco Renaissance poets. "Sectarian rivalries among persons, manifestoes, and subgroups within the city fragmented the scene," writes Davidson, "and when journalists attempted to define some kind of common ground, they had to fall back on vague references to exotic religions and anti-establishment attitudes."[xix]

Of course, San Francisco is a place that has long cultivated the ingredients of allegory. It is a magical landscape at the end of the American West—inhabited by bohemians, radical politicians, and new ways of thinking—that has long represented a place for rebirth. Like the nineteenth-century flaneurs who celebrated the city, the story of San Francisco embodies how the geography of the self and the city can become intertwined.

It is this very self-created mythmaking that Kerouac began exploring soon after the Good Blonde events in fall 1955. Only a few pages after her name is recorded, Kerouac writes of his plan to author the Duluoz Legend, starting with *Dr. Sax*, *Mary Cassidy*, and on through *Tristessa*, intermingled with his books of dreams, blues poems, and Dharma writings. These texts we know as the myth he constructed of his own life: some facts, a lot of fiction.

Nearly sixty years after his death, the degrees of this balance are still being determined. And so I find something compelling in my inability to locate the Good Blonde—yet. The mystery that still surrounds her real identity embodies how there's so much more to discover about Kerouac and his world. With time, perhaps she will be found and the mystery of her identity revealed. Or, as Kerouac wrote near her name in his notebook:

Can time crack rock?
Marble'll chip,
Diamond die.[xx]

ENDNOTES

i   Kerouac, Jack. *Selected Letters, Volume 1*, 1940-1956. Ed. by Ann Charters, New York: Viking, 1996. p. 521.
ii   Kerouac, Jack. "Dharma Bums Reject Good Blonde in Car. Typescript 'Bums reject (good).' Typed by Kerouac." Jack Kerouac Papers, Henry W. and Albert A. Berg Collection of English and
American Literature, The New York Public Library.
iii   Kerouac, Jack. *Lonesome Traveler*. New York: Grove, 2007. p. 56.
iv   Gleason, Ralph J. *San Francisco Jazz Scene*. *Evergreen Review*, vol. 1, no. 2, 1957. pp. 59–63. p. 59.
v   Kerouac, Jack. "Diary # 3. Holograph diary 'Feb. - May '57.' February 25, 1957–May 27, 1957." Jack Kerouac Papers. 56.3. Henry W. and Albert A. Berg Collection of English and American Literature.
vi   ibid.
vii   Kerouac, Jack. "Typescript story with holograph notes. "'Dharma Bum in Europe.' With holograph note: 'This is original official beginning of prose story about my 1957 trip to Morocco and Europe' - JK." Jack Kerouac Papers. 19. 9. Henry W. and Albert A. Berg Collection of English and American Literature.
viii   Kerouac, Jack. "Diary # 4. Holograph diary 1957 ['Berkeley Way 1957'] June 19, 1957–July 5, 1957." Jack Kerouac Papers. 56. 4. Henry W. and Albert A. Berg Collection of English and American Literature.
ix   Kerouac, Jack. "Letter to Malcolm Cowley (December 9, 1957)." Box 35, Folder 2100. Malcolm Cowley Papers, The Newberry Library, Chicago.
x   Another example of his struggle to write the introduction: he attempted to write the introduction longhand, as he sometimes did when he sought to experiment. In the six-page holograph in his archives, Kerouac writes of what happened when he (or the Ray Smith/Jack Duluoz character) arrived in the L.A. train yards, how he couldn't land a ride hitchhiking, so a "Mexican Sex Fiend" in the nearby hobo jungle told him what train to catch north. "When the Saint Therese Bum arrives, Kerouac describes him as slightly menacing and intimidating—quite the opposite of the meek hobo he describes in *The Dharma Bums*. See Kerouac, Jack. "Holograph draft 'The Dharma Bums. Chapter One.

L.A. Yards.' (Begins:' Because I had worked on the railroads before.')." Jack Kerouac Papers. 19. 7. Henry W. and Albert A. Berg Collection of English and American Literature.

xi   Grace, Nancy. "A White Man in Love: A Study of Race, Gender, Class, and Ethnicity in Jack Kerouac's Maggie Cassidy, "The Subterraneans, and Tristessa"." *College Literature*, vol. 27, no. 1, 2000, pp. 39-62. p. 41

xii   Kerouac, Jack. *Windblown World: The Journals of Jack Kerouac 1947-1954*. ed. by Douglas Brinkley, Viking, 2004. p.94–95.

xiii   Kerouac, Jack. "Typescript 'God's Wisdom.' Titled in Kerouac's hand on verso 'Dharma Bums 'Greek' / Reject.' Typed by Kerouac." Jack Kerouac Papers, Henry W. and Albert A. Berg Collection of English and American Literature, The New York Public Library.

xiv   Kerouac, Jack. *The Dharma Bums*. Penguin, 1958. p. 29.

xv   Kerouac, Jack. *Some of the Dharma*. Penguin Books, 1999. p. 342

xvi   Kerouac, Jack. *Tristessa*. New York: Penguin, 1992. p. 57.

xvii   Davidson, Michael. *The San Francisco Renaissance: Poetics and Community At Mid-Century*. Cambridge University Press, 1991. p. 216.

xviii   *ibid*. p. 1.

xix   *ibid*. p. 3

xx   Because my research into the Good Blonde's identity remains ongoing, I have deliberately withheld the citation for the notebook in which her name appears.

ADVERT

In late 2025, Beatdom Books will publish two new titles. One is about the 6 Gallery reading and the other is about William S. Burroughs and his Bunker residence in New York.

A Remarkable Collection of Angels: A History of the 6 Gallery Reading is the first book-length study of this pivotal moment in Beat history. It looks not only at the actual reading but explores how it was organised and what happened in the weeks and months that followed.

The Bunker Diaries is a memoir by Stewart Meyer, who was a friend and associate of William S. Burroughs in the late seventies and early eighties. He recalls a period when he was learning to write whilst helping Burroughs score for dope on the streets of New York.

THE SAN FRANCISCO RENAISSANCE AND FAR EASTERN RELIGIONS

BY PETER OEHLER

The San Francisco Renaissance is typically said to have begun at the 6 Gallery reading of October 1955. Ann Charters, for example, described this reading as "the inauguration of the San Francisco Poetry Renaissance"[i] and Rick Fields, author of a book about the history of Buddhism in America, said that "The Six Gallery Reading became, in retrospect, the beginning of what journalists would soon call the San Francisco Renaissance."[ii]

An interest in Buddhism was common among the writers associated with the San Francisco Renaissance and also the related movement known as the Beat Generation. At the 6 Gallery reading, the "introducer," Kenneth Rexroth, was quite well versed in the religion and claimed to speak several Asian languages, and all the other poets on stage would later become Buddhists except for Lamantia. Some of the people in the audience were also interested, including Jack Kerouac. The reading and the weeks before and after it were recounted in Kerouac's 1958 novel, *The Dharma Bums*, which as the name suggests was infused with Buddhist ideas.

Five months later, the poets from the 6 Gallery—with the exception of Lamantia—gathered for a repeat performance at the Berkely Town Hall Theater. This time, Snyder's friend Alan Watts attended. Watts was or would become an associate of the poets and although he was not a poet himself, he was a writer. He was also a priest, religious philosopher, and lecturer, which gave him a completely different focus from the poets. While Far Eastern religions, especially (Zen) Buddhism, were of interest to them to varying degrees, Watts had already converted years before. Spirituality, mysticism, and religion had been his primary interests for some time, and not only in a literary sense but also didactically, as a teacher and lecturer/academic concerned with imparting knowledge.

This essay will look at each of the aforementioned writers and discuss their interest in Buddhism. It will also look at a few key events or organizations associated with the San Francisco Renaissance and Eastern religions.

KENNETH REXROTH (1905–1982)

Kenneth Rexroth, by far the oldest of the authors considered here, was a poet, translator, painter, critic, pacifist, and anarchist. He is considered one of the first to have popularized Asian literature and culture in California, particularly through his translations. William Everson said, "Rexroth is a profoundly religious man [...] Rexroth caught the awakening religious vibration and espoused it—the first time I ever heard the name of Martin Buber was from Kenneth's lips. Also San Francisco is the gateway to the Orient and Rexroth extolled Pacific Basin culture, translating Chinese and Japanese poetry into the vital American verse idiom."[iii] Regarding the book *Written On The Sky: Poems from the Japanese*, translated by Kenneth Rexroth, edited by Eliot Weinberger, the New Directions website states: "Over the years, thousands of readers have discovered the beauty of classic Japanese poetry through the superb English versions by the great American poet Kenneth Rexroth. Mostly haiku, these poems range from the classical and medieval to modern poetry, with an emphasis on folk songs and love lyrics."[iv] In doing so, he also strongly appealed to and influenced other poets. Ann Charters said, "In particular, Rexroth's interest in Asian literature and philosophy contributed to the Beat writers' study of what Ginsberg later called 'Buddha consciousness.' Rexroth's translations of Asian poetry published by New Directions were a seminal influence on Gary Snyder and other young poets."[v]

Jack Kerouac sketches Rexroth in his role of M.C. at the 6 Gallery Reading in *The Dharma Bums*: "old Rheinhold Cacoethes the father of the Frisco poetry scene was wiping his tears in gladness. [...] Between poets, Rheinhold Cacoethes, in his bow tie and shabby old coat, would get up and make a little funny speech in his snide funny voice and introduce the next reader."[vi]

GARY SNYDER (BORN 1930)

Gary Snyder can be described as a nature lover who feels a strong attraction to the wilderness. In terms of his poetry, he can be counted among the nature writers, but his interests and themes are more diverse. In addition to nature and ecology/environmental protection, he is very interested in the indigenous peoples of North America. He feels particularly drawn to Zen Buddhism. Gary Snyder and Philip Whalen met in 1946 at Reed College in Portland, Oregon. They shared an interest in Buddhism and Asian studies. Snyder was introduced to Buddhism at Reed College by his professors David H. French and Lloyd Snyder, while Whalen had already encountered it through the esoteric teachings of Russian-American spiritualist Helena Petrovna Blavatsky, known as Theosophy.[vii] Snyder became interested in Zen after finding a book about it during an early trip to San Francisco, and this was partially responsible for his decision to study in the Bay Area and prepare for an extended stay in Japan. From 1956 to 1968, with some interruptions, he lived in Japan, where he studied Zen Buddhism at Daitoku-ji and other monasteries.

Jack Kerouac gave Snyder the leading role in his Zen-obsessed novel *The Dharma Bums* in 1958 under the name Japhy Ryder. He described his friend as follows: "Japhy Ryder was a kid from eastern Oregon brought up in a log cabin deep in the woods with his father and mother and sister, from the beginning a woods boy, an axman, farmer, interested in animals and Indian lore [...] Finally he learned Chinese and Japanese and became an Oriental scholar and discovered the greatest Dharma Bums of them all, the Zen Lunatics of China and Japan."[viii] In addition to poetry (his most successful poetry collection, *Turtle Island*, was published in 1974 and won the Pulitzer Prize in 1975) Snyder also writes prose and essays. For good reason, the authors Bill Devall and George Sessions of *Deep Ecology: Living as if Nature Mattered* mentioned Gary Snyder as one of the pioneers of "deep ecology" and even dedicated this book to him as the sole representative of the San Francisco Renaissance and the Beat Generation.[ix]

PHILIP WHALEN (1923-2002)

After serving in the United States Army Air Corps during World War II, Whalen went on to study at Reed College, where he met Gary Snyder and Lew Welch, with whom he shared a room. At that time (1946) he had already been practicing Zazen meditation (a sitting Zen meditation where the awareness of breath is important) for four years.[x] Inspired by Snyder, both Kerouac (once) and Whalen (several times) worked as fire lookouts at Mount Baker National Forest in the North Cascades in order to study Zen and meditate. Kerouac also immortalized him in *The Dharma Bums* as "booboo big old goodhearted Warren Coughlin a hundred and eighty pounds of poet meat."[xi] During extended stays in Kyoto in the 1960s, Whalen studied Zen Buddhism intensively, and in 1972 he moved to the San Francisco Zen Center, where he became a Zen monk in 1973 and was ordained as a Zen priest in 1976. In 1984, he moved to Santa Fe, New Mexico, where he became head monk of Dharma Sangha. In 1987, he returned to San Francisco to become the abbot for the Hartford Street Zen Center. Later on, his ill health forced him to retire at the Zen Center until he died in June 2002. He wrote and published a lot of poetry and prose which was related to Buddhism. In his "Zen Talks," for example, he reflects on his experience with Zazen: "The business of 'just sitting' is very difficult. Zen wants you to rip yourself to pieces. We sit down, fold our legs and watch breath. Sit on a cushion being bored stiff. Then our minds start flashing ugly pictures, sad feelings, weird ideas, and our knees hurt. We are attacking the structure of the personality, the casing, so we get distracted from what practice is about."[xii]

MICHAEL MCCLURE (1932–2020)

Michael McClure was a poet, playwright, essayist, and novelist. Beat writers of the 1950s and 1960s pursued various approaches to reconnecting with the natural world. To this end, they drew on older models such as Buddhism, Native American religion and myth, and Romantic traditions. Gary Snyder referred to these as "the old ways." Michael McClure shared this interest in "the old ways," although Rod Phillips comments: "More often, however, the primary vehicle in McClure's nature poetry is not seventh century Buddhism or nineteenth century Romanticism, but instead the twentieth century scientific disciplines of biology and ecology."[xiii] Buddhism also played an important role for him.

According to the Poetry Foundation, "McClure's poetry combined spontaneity, typographical experimentation, Buddhist practice, and 'body language' to merge the ecstatic and the corporeal."[xiv] One reporter said, "In the early 1970s, McClure was one of the first writers to popularize the movement to Save the Whales, and his poems and activism have been important to ecology movements ever since. A noted American Buddhist, McClure has written some of the most beautiful and profound poems in that genre."[xv] Another added, "McClure's work as a poet, playwright, essayist, novelist, and artist establishes him as one of the most important Western Buddhist figures of the long 20th century."[xvi] Kerouac also introduces Michael McClure in *The Dharma Bums* with a minimum of words, namely as "delicate pale handsome poet [...] Ike O'Shay (in a suit)."[xvii]

ALLEN GINSBERG (1926-1997)

Allen Ginsberg was the most famous American poet for a time. With his commitment to social and environmental issues, he can certainly be described as a political and environmental activist. He became interested in Buddhism in 1953 on the recommendation of Raymond Weaver, one of his professors at Columbia University. He then visited the New York Public Library and the First Zen Institute to study Buddhism, Chinese painting, and philosophy, including *An Introduction to Zen Buddhism* by D.T. Suzuki.[xviii] He became far more interested in Buddhism later in life and studied and practiced it seriously. Later, he was also interested in Indian Hinduism as another Far Eastern religion and traveled throughout India, together with Gary Snyder, Joanne Kyger, and Peter Orlovsky. After that he often sung matras as part of his readings and performances.

He was not only one of the "founding members" of the Beat Generation and involved in the San Francisco Renaissance, but later also one of the (unofficial) leaders of the hippies and the flower power movement. He allegedly coined the term "flower power,"[xix] by which he meant that people should approach police officers and the military, etc. with flowers, for example during demonstrations or sit-ins. Allen Ginsberg is also briefly but precisely and brilliantly portrayed by Kerouac in *The Dharma Bums*, namely as "hornrimmed intellectual hepcat [...] with wild black hair [...] Alvah Goldbook."[xx]

JACK KEROUAC (1922-1969)

Ginsberg recommended Buddhism to his friend Jack Kerouac, who studied it intensively from the winter of 1953/54 onwards. This had a considerable influence on Kerouac's writing. His best-known testimony to Zen Buddhism is undoubtedly *The Dharma Bums* (1958), in which he discusses his friendship with Gary Snyder, from whom he received much instruction in Buddhism. Kerouac had met Snyder in 1955 and the two had long discussions about Buddhism. They did not always agree. According to Ann Charters, "The two of them disagreed on most points of Buddhist thought, though their disagreements were primarily differences of emphasis, with Jack a Hinayana Buddhist, hostile to the intellectual effetism, as he called it, of Snyder's Zen Mahayana Buddhism."[xxi] Some of their bickering, for example the Mahayana versus Hinayana debate, Kerouac inserted into *The Dharma Bums*: "'Lissen Japhy,' I said, 'I'm not a Zen Buddhist, I'm a serious Buddhist, I'm an oldfashioned dreamy Hinayana coward of later Mahayanism,'"[xxii] Beside *The Dharma Bums*, Kerouac also wrote other books influenced by Buddhism: *The Scripture of Golden Eternity*, *Some of the Dharma*, *Book of Haikus*, and *Wake Up: A Life of the Buddha*. Yet more of Kerouac's Buddhist-inspired writings are collected in *Jack Kerouac: The Buddhist Years* (2025), edited by Charles Shuttleworth. Excerpts can be found at www.beatdom.com/kerouac-buddhism/

ALAN WATTS (1915–1973)

The authors discussed so far have contributed to a certain degree of popularity for Buddhism in the US and worldwide. This is partly due to translations of Far Eastern texts and partly due to their own Buddhist-influenced poems. Probably the most popular was *The Dharma Bums*, which has been referred to as "the bible of the backpack revolution." But Alan Watts was even more intensely involved in communicating Buddhist ideas. His deep commitment to the cause and his charisma certainly contributed to this. One website explained his popularity as being due to "his witty, sometimes provocative speaking style [which] captivated audiences, helping philosophical ideas feel alive and relevant."[xxiii]

Watts is also mentioned by Kerouac in *The Dharma Bums*: "I went out to the bonfire to hear Cacoethes' latest witticisms. Arthur Whane [Alan Watts] was sitting on a log, well dressed, necktie and suit, and I went over and asked him 'Well what is Buddhism? Is it fantastic imagination magic of the lightning flash, is it plays, dreams, not even plays, dreams?' 'No, to me Buddhism is getting to know as many people as possible.' And there he was going around the party real affable shaking hands with everybody and chatting, a regular cocktail party."[xxiv]

Watts' work was about bringing spirituality (or mysticism) closer to his audience or readers. In his autobiography, he compared this attempt to that of poets, thereby distancing himself from them in a certain way, but on the other hand, he saw his own writing as a kind of poetry: "My own work […] is basically an attempt to describe mystical experience […] In this I set myself the same impossible task as the poet: to say what cannot be said. Indeed, much of my work is poetry described as prose (with margins adjusted) so that people will read it."[xxv]

"BEAT ZEN, SQUARE ZEN, AND ZEN" BY ALAN WATTS

In Watts' legendary article, "Beat Zen, Square Zen, and Zen," which was first published in the *Chicago Review* in the summer of 1958[xxvi] and later appeared in expanded form as a pamphlet from City Lights Books and reprinted many times since, he distinguishes between "Beat Zen," "Square Zen," and (true) Zen. He said that the Westerner who is attracted by Zen "must be free of the itch to justify himself. Lacking this, his Zen will be either 'beat' or 'square,' either a revolt from the culture and social order or a new form of stuffiness and respectability. For Zen is above all the liberation of the mind from conventional thought, and this is something utterly different from rebellion against convention, on the one hand, or adopting foreign conventions, on the other."[xxvii] At the end of this article, however, Watts shows a sympathetic understanding of both Beat Zen and Square Zen:

> The old Chinese Zen masters were steeped in Taoism. […] They didn't […] set themselves apart as rather special. On the contrary, their Zen was wu-shih, which means approximately 'nothing special' or 'no fuss.' But Zen is 'fuss' when it is mixed up with Bohemian affectations […] And I will admit that the very hullabaloo about Zen, even in such an article as this, is also fuss - but a little less

so. Having said this, I would like to say something for all Zen fussers, beat or square. Fuss is all right, too. If you are hung on Zen, there's no need to try to pretend that you are not.[xxviii]

There is definitely a hint of self-criticism there, and he even half-admits that his Zen Buddhism, as taught in the West, is (partly) responsible for Beat Zen. Fields wrote, "as he [Watts] would write in his autobiography, 'it had often been said, perhaps with truth,' that his easy and freefloating attitude to Zen was largely responsible for the notorious 'Zen Boom' which flourished among artists and pseudointellectuals in the late 1950's, and led on to the frivolous 'beat Zen' of Kerouac's *Dharma Bums*, of Franz Kline's black and white abstractions, and John Cage's silent concerts.'"[xxix]

And others see it the same way. In *The Zen of Anarchy*, James Brown writes: "Although Alan Watts was critical of 'lifestyle' Beats with shallow interests in Eastern philosophy, his Sinocentric criticism of Western life, along with Suzuki's sharp criticism of Western rationalism, shaped the counterculture in ways that Watts tentatively accepted."[xxx]

The following sections briefly discuss some of Watts' most important activities: his teaching at the American Academy of Asian Studies, his contributions to radio and television, and two significant events that took place during the hippie era, which could be seen as growing out of the San Francisco Renaissance. They clearly show that most of the writers considered in this paper were still very active and concerned with Far Eastern religions.

AMERICAN ACADEMY OF ASIAN STUDIES

From 1951 onwards, Watts was a teacher at the newly founded American Academy of Asian Studies in San Francisco. Watts said, "I followed [Frederic Spiegelberg] again when, in 1951, he designed the American Academy of Asian Studies in San Francisco, and invited me to join the faculty."[xxxi] In the fall of 1952, Spiegelberg stepped down as director of the Academy, and Watts took over the position. He remained director and teacher there until the spring of 1957: "For six years I was to be absorbed—for sometimes as much as fourteen hours a day—in teaching, and later in administration as well, at the American Academy of Asian Studies."[xxxii] He saw the Academy as an important part of the San Francisco Renaissance:

"The American Academy of Asian Studies was one of the principal roots of what later came to be known, in the early sixties, as the San Francisco Renaissance."[xxxiii] But the Academy itself, which later changed its name to California Institute of Integral Studies (CIIS), still sees its roots in the San Francisco Renaissance. On their website, it is explained that:

> Our university emerged from the San Francisco Renaissance as Asian wisdom traditions mingled with the avant-garde poetry of the Beats and the progressive spiritual values of the hippie counterculture. CIIS's institutional progenitor, American Academy of Asian Studies, was established in 1951 with funding from businessman Louis Gainsborough. Gainsborough strove valiantly to bring his vision to reality with a board comprised of representatives of Asian consulates and a distinguished faculty that included Frederic Spiegelberg, professor of Sanskrit and comparative religions at Stanford; Alan Watts, one of the first and most effective teachers of Taoism and Buddhism; and Ernest Wood, an expert on yoga.[xxxiv]

Incidentally, Gary Snyder was also a student at the Academy for a time, where he became close friends with Watts.

KPFA UND KQED

Watts was also heavily involved in local radio and television in San Francisco. On the one hand, he was active at the non-commercial radio station KPFA in Berkeley, where he also met Kenneth Rexroth, one of the station's founders. Brown wrote that "Rexroth was the dominant force in the cultural life of San Francisco for more than half a century. He was one of the founders of KPFA, the local radio station in Berkeley, where he had weekly programs discussing books and various cultural topics."[xxxv] Watts hosted the weekly program "Way Beyond the West" from 1953 to 1962. During this time, he attracted "a legion of regular listeners," according KPFA Folio.[xxxvi] Brown said that "Watts's reach and popularity resulted largely from the left libertarian KPFA, which broadcast Watts's weekly show, 'Way Beyond the West,' adjacent to

Rexroth's broadcasts on the same station."[xxxvii]

Watts was also active in local non-commercial television. According to Brown, "As a result of our ways of knowing in the West, Watts stated in the opening minutes of a 1949 series of lectures for San Francisco's public TV station, KQED, 'Our whole culture, our whole civilization . . . is nuts. It's not all here. We are not awake. We are not completely alive now.'"[xxxviii] However, Brown is mistaken here because Watts hosted the series "Eastern Wisdom and Modern Life" in 21 episodes from 1959 to 1960. (Watts did not move from New York to California until early 1951). These 21 episodes of "Eastern Wisdom and Modern Life," as well as several episodes of the radio series "Way Beyond the West" on KPFA, can be viewed or listened to at https://www.organism.earth/library/author/alan-watts. Many more of his talks and videos can now be found on the internet.

In his autobiography, Watts described his activities at KPFA and KQED as follows:

> At the same time [the early 1950s] I became involved with Lewis Hill, Richard Moore, and Wallace Hamilton of the Pacifica Foundation, which was then sponsoring radio station KPFA in Berkeley [...] to create a style of broadcasting superior in quality and freer in speech than even the BBC in England, and without commercial advertising. Later I worked also, with Richard Moore, on San Francisco's educational television station KQED - an equally imaginative and intelligent project, which even today is still gasping for adequate funds.[xxxix]

HUMAN BE-IN

The Human Be-In took place on January 14, 1967, under the motto "A Gathering of the Tribes" in Golden Gate Park in San Francisco, marking the beginning of the "Summer of Love." Approximately 20-30,000 people attended. The poster announced Timothy Leary, Richard Alpert (known as "Ram Dass"), Dick Gregory, Allen Ginsberg, Jerry Rubin, and "all of San Francisco's rock bands, including Santana and the Steve Miller Band." Alan Watts was not widely advertised, but he was there. Gary Snyder and Michael McClure were also present. Monica Furlong writes: "On the morning of January 14, Snyder, Ginsberg, Watts, and others performed pradakshina, a Hindu rite of circumambulation at the polo field. [...] At sunset Gary Snyder blew on conch shell, Allen Ginsberg led a chant, and the crowd drifted away, some of them to build fires, chant, and pray on Ocean Beach."[xl]

HOUSEBOAT SUMMIT

Shortly after the Human Be-In, a panel discussion called "The Houseboat Summit" took place on Alan Watts' houseboat (the ferryboat S.S. Vallejo). In addition to Watts, Allen Ginsberg, Timothy Leary, and Gary Snyder were on the panel. The conversation was then published in the *San Francisco Oracle* in February 1967 and reprinted in *Notes from the New Underground: An Anthology*, edited by Jesse Kornbluth. The introduction to this conversation states: "To assemble Ginsberg, Leary, Snyder, and Watts in one room is to convene a summit conference of hip, a colloquium of those who have somehow assumed leadership roles in the underground subculture."[xli]

CONCLUSION

Even today, Alan Watts is still quite well known in some circles. Many of his books are still available, including translations into numerous languages. However, it should not be forgotten that he (alongside D. T. Suzuki) was very well known in relation to Buddhism in the US and worldwide during the counterculture era (the 1960s and early 1970s). As early as 1969, Theodore Roszak wrote: "Along with D. T. Suzuki, Watts, through his televised lectures, books, and private classes, was to become America's foremost popularizer of Zen."[xlii] Suzuki probably did more than any other person to make Buddhism popular throughout US society, but in the countercultural circles of the US—from the Beat Generation through the San Francisco Renaissance to the hippies—Watts was probably the better known and more influential of the two. Of course, Suzuki also had an influence on counterculture (and on Watts himself). According to Brown, "Zen's foremost philosopher to the West, D. T. Suzuki, whose writings introduced Gary Snyder to Zen, who influenced Philip Whalen's poetic/meditative practice, and who had an immeasurable influence on the counterculture's understanding of Buddhism, especially as related by Alan Watts."[xliii] In summary, it can be said that Far Eastern religions gained a strong foothold in the 1950s, '60s, and '70s, not only in the US but also in the rest of the Western world. They were particularly embraced by the counterculture, with some poets and authors of the San Francisco Renaissance and the Beat Generation (alongside D. T. Suzuki) playing a key role in this development.

ENDNOTES

i   Charters, Ann, "Constantly Risking Absurdity: Some San Francisco Renaissance Poets" in *The Penguin Book of the Beats*, edited by Ann Charters (Penguin Books: London, 1993) p.227

ii   Fields, Rick. *How the Swans Came to the Sea: A Narrative History of Buddhism in America* (Shambala Publications: Boston, 1992) p.212

iii   Everson, William. "REXROTH: Shaker and Maker" in *The Penguin Book of the Beats*, edited by Ann Charters (Penguin Books: London, 1993) p.243

iv   "Written on the Sky, Kenneth Rexroth," https://www.ndbooks.com/book/written-on-the-sky.

v   Charters, Ann, "Kenneth Rexroth" in *The Penguin Book of the Beats*, edited by Ann Charters (Penguin Books: London, 1993) p.232

vi   Kerouac, Jack, *The Dharma Bums* (Viking Press, New York, 1958) p.14-16

vii   Negus, Sean. "The Intersection of Buddhism and the Beat Generation" in *Beatdom #18*, May 2017.

viii   Kerouac, *The Dharma Bums*, p.9

ix   Devall, Bill, and George Sessions. *Deep Ecology: Living as if Nature Mattered* (Gibbs M. Smith: Salt Lake City, 1985) frontmatter

x   Negus, "The Intersection of Buddhism and the Beat Generation" in *Beatdom #18*, May 2017.

xi   Kerouac, *The Dharma Bums*, p.12

xii   Whalen, Philip, "Zen Talks," in *Hartford Street Zen Center Newsletter*, San Francisco, 1997.

xiii   Phillips, Rod, *"Forest Beatniks" and "Urban Thoreaus": Gary Snyder, Jack Kerouac, Lew Welch, and Michael McClure* (Peter Lang Publishing: New York, 2000) p.103

xiv   "Michael McClure", https://www.poetryfoundation.org/poets/michael-mcclure.

xv   "Beat Legend Michael McClure Comes to Las Vegas!" https://poetrypromise.org/michael-mcclure-43016.

xvi   "Legendary Zen Poets to Read at SF Zen Center" https://blogs.sfzc.org/blog/2012/03/22/legendary-zen-poets-to-read-at-sf-zen-center.

xvii   Kerouac, *The Dharma Bums*, p.11

xviii   Schumacher, Michael, *Allen Ginsberg - Eine kritische Biographie*. German translation of *Dharma Lion: A critical Biography of Allen Ginsberg* (Hannibal Verlag, St. Andrä-Wördern, 1999) p.156

xix   Mandeville-Gamble Steven. "Guide to the Allen Ginsberg Papers: Biography/Administrative History." The Online Archive of California, Stanford University, Stanford, 2007, https://cdn.calisphere.org/data/13030/hb/tf5c6004hb/files/tf5c6004hb.pdf.

xx	Kerouac, *The Dharma Bums*, p.12
xxi	Charters, Ann, *Kerouac: A Biography* (St. Martin's Press: New York, 1994) p.243-244
xxii	Kerouac, *The Dharma Bums*, p.13
xxiii	"Alan Watts: A 5-Minute Overview of His Life and Main Ideas," https://conspicuousbourgeois.com/2024/11/13/alan-watts-a-5-minute-overview-of-his-life-and-main-ideas.
xxiv	Kerouac, *The Dharma Bums*, p.195
xxv	Watts, Alan, *In My Own Way: An Autobiography*, Random House (Pantheon Books: New York, 1972) p.5
xxvi	Watts, Alan, "Beat Zen, Square Zen, and Zen" in *Chicago Review*, Vol. 12, No. 2, Summer 1958, The University of Chicago Press, Chicago, 1958, p.3-11
xxvii	Watts, Alan, "Beat Zen, Square Zen, and Zen" in *The Penguin Book of the Beats*, edited by Ann Charters, (Penguin Books: London, 1993) p.610
xxviii	Watts, Alan, "Beat Zen, Square Zen, and Zen" in *The Penguin Book of the Beats*, 614
xxix	Fields, Rick. *How the Swans Came to the Sea: A Narrative History of Buddhism in America*, p.221
xxx	Brown, James, "The Zen of Anarchy: Japanese Exceptionalism and the Anarchist Roots of the San Francisco Poetry Renaissance" in *Religion and American Culture: A Journal of Interpretation, Vol. 19, No. 2*, Summer 2009, published by Cambridge University Press on behalf of the Center for the Study of Religion and American Culture, 2009, http://www.thezensite.com/ZenEssays/Miscellaneous/The_Zen_of_Anarchy.pdf, p.222
xxxi	Watts, Alan, *In My Own Way: An Autobiography*, p.110
xxxii	Watts, Alan, *In My Own Way: An Autobiography*, p.232
xxxiii	Ibid
xxxiv	McDermott, Robert. "A Brief History of California Institute of Integral Studies". CIIS Today, 2017, https://www.ciis.edu/discover-ciis/our-history.
xxxv	Brown, James, "The Zen of Anarchy," p.229
xxxvi	*KPFA Folio April 8-21, 1963*, Pacifica Foundation, p.19
xxxvii	Brown, James, "The Zen of Anarchy," p.220
xxxviii	Brown, James, "The Zen of Anarchy," p.221
xxxix	Watts, Alan, *In My Own Way: An Autobiography*, p.231
xl	Furlong, Monica, *Zen Effects: The Life of Alan Watts* (Skylight Path Publishing: Woodstock, Vermont, 2001) p.181-182
xli	Ginsberg, Allen, et al, "Changes" in *Notes from the New Underground: An Anthology*, edited by Jesse Kornbluth (Viking Press: New York, 1968)
xlii	Roszak, Theodore, *The Making of a Counter Culture: Reflections on the Technocratic Society and Its Youthful Opposition* (Doubleday & Company: New York, 1969) p.132
xliii	Brown, James, "The Zen of Anarchy," p.214

REMEMBERING BOB KAUFMAN
BY A.D. WINANS

He walked the streets of North Beach
An ancient warrior with blinking eyes
Forced to carry decades
Of heavy sorrow on his back
Like a bent-over hunchback
Burdened with the rust of time
Flesh stripped to the marrow
The mirror of his eyes
Doing a slow dance
Up and down Grant Avenue

He rode the clouds of "Ancient Rain"
His life measured in hot jazz and verse
A surreal mirage where hip cats
In streets and bars
Rode Be-bop rhythms
To the end of the line

He walked imaginary zoos
Looked for tigers to talk too
Runaway poems blaring in his ears
Like a stuck car horn
The Ancient Rain falling
    Falling
        Falling
            Washing away his wounds

BEGINNER'S MIND
A REREADING OF ALLEN GINSBERG'S REVOLUTIONARY "HOWL"

BY JONAH RASKIN

I

On the cusp of the 70th anniversary of Allen Ginsberg's first public reading of "Howl," I vowed to explore and map it with "Beginner's Mind," or *Shosin*, a Zen Buddhist practice familiar to the Beats and to several generations of spiritually minded Americans thanks to Shunryū Suzuki's landmark book, *Zen Mind, Beginner's Mind* (1970). But rereading "Howl" as though for the first time presented a challenge. After all, I was no longer a beginner when it came to Ginsberg's life and his work. In addition to the biographies, I had read and reread "Howl" a few dozen times, beginning in the 1950s, when I was a teenage beatnik, then on and off through the 20th century as a student, a teacher, and scholar.

A rereading of "Howl"—a revolutionary poem in both form and content—struck me as a kind of adventure in the realm of poetry. No poem has meant more to me. An account of my decades-long engagement with it might prompt others to recall their relationship with a poem that has been translated into dozens of languages and has sparked the imaginations of writers around the world.

With a few exceptions, such as "Paterson" (1949), no poem that Ginsberg wrote in the decade before he composed "Howl" boasts the originality of "Howl." Not surprisingly, "Paterson" contains some of the same pivotal words as "Howl": Golgotha, Eternity, peyote, marijuana, and more. Like "Howl," "Paterson" has long lines and compressed phrases: "cloakrooms of the smiling gods of psychiatry." Like "Howl," it travels across America: to Denver and Chicago and to Mexico. Like "Howl," it offers alliteration: "Wrath/ and rumor of wrath to wrath-weary man," and like "Howl" it offers lists: "employment bureaus, magazine hallways, statistical cubicles, factory/ stairways." It also surfaces madness—one of the main themes of "Howl"—in the pivotal phrase, "I would rather go mad."

But "Paterson" is a short poem that has no hipsters, doesn't address a generation, doesn't offer obscenities (except for the word "shit," used only once), and lacks the cadence of the epic he wrote in San Francisco and Berkeley. "Howl" marks a qualitative change, a real breakthrough, in Ginsberg's work. "Paterson" doesn't have a beginning or an ending that matches the start and the crescendo of "Howl." It hints at work ahead. Surely, I thought, Ginsberg wrote "Howl" with Beginner's Mind: openness, freedom from the past and liberation from his own mental habits.

Of course I didn't know any of the above when, at 15, I could recite the opening lines from memory and quote key phrases, such as "the crack of doom on the hydrogen jukebox" and "drunken taxicabs of absolute reality." My passion for and engagement with the poem culminated in 2005 at a public reading with Beat scholar, Ann Douglas, and four of her Columbia College students. Also, in 2005, I hosted with Kerouac biographer, Gerald Nicosia, at the San Francisco Public Library a celebration of the 6 Gallery reading. I persuaded the city's board of supervisors to declare June 3, the day Ginsberg was born in 1926, "Allen Ginsberg Day."

Over 700 people attended the event with Ann Douglas and her students, which took place in a bar and restaurant on Broadway in New York, where the Beats once congregated and caroused. I imagined Kerouac in the audience, chanting, cheering, and applauding as he had done at the 6 Gallery in 1955, an occasion memorialized in chapter two of *The Dharma Bums*.

In 2005, I published *American Scream: Allen Ginsberg's "Howl" and the Making of the Beat Generation*, which was inspired by my love for the poem and by an astute comment from poet laureate, Robert Pinsky, who wrote, "Allen Ginsberg's genius for public life should not obscure his genius as an artist or the study of his art." No one has heralded Ginsberg's talents as succinctly or as enthusiastically as Pinsky.

To write *American Scream*, I conducted research at Ginsberg's archive at Stanford, scrutinized Lawrence Ferlinghetti's papers at the Bancroft Library in Berkeley, and pored over Kerouac's letters at the Ransom in Austin, Texas. Plus, I conducted interviews with Beat luminaries, including Ginsberg, Michael McClure, and Gary Snyder, all of whom read at the 6. *American Scream* evolved gradually as a biography of the poem, not as the biography of the poet who howled on October 7, 1955. I thought I could say everything I wanted to say about Ginsberg by focusing on "Howl."

In a long interview, Dr. Philip Hicks—Ginsberg's therapist at Langley Porter Psychiatric Hospital—told me that his patient had arrived for therapy sessions complaining about writer's block and troubled about his own homosexuality. According to Hicks, Ginsberg shared a manuscript version of "Howl" written in his own handwriting that predated the typewritten versions which Barry Miles published in *Howl: Original Draft Facsimile, Transcript & Variant Version*. That volume is as essential for an understanding of the poem as *The Waste Land: A Facsimile and Transcript of the Original* is for an understanding of T. S. Eliot's modernist masterpiece.

I had no reason to doubt Dr. Hicks' account of "Howl." The more I thought about it, the more I doubted Ginsberg's own stories of the genesis and the evolution of his poem: his insistence, for example, that he had not revised it, and that the phrase "First Thought, Best Thought" expressed his aesthetic. It was clear that he had indeed revised "Howl" again and again, changed words and added crucial phrases. He even inserted whole lines which enhanced the poem, such as "angelheaded hipsters burning for the ancient heavenly connection / to the starry dynamo in the machinery of night."

The text of "Howl" seems to provide clues about Ginsberg's thought process. Take, for example, the stanza that begins "Peyote solidities of halls." Free association and a kind of structured improvisation are at work. "Halls" lead the poet to "backyard" and "backyard" leads to "rooftops," which leads in turn to "storefront." "Green tree cemetery" leads to "tree vibrations" and "dawns" to "winter dusks." Also, "drunkness" seems to lead to "rantings." Ginsberg paints a fractured portrait of a time and a place—winter in Brooklyn—and a state of mind perhaps shaped by peyote, which he used in San Francisco. "Peyote solidities" sounds like a paradox or contradiction. Under the influence of peyote, things often seem blurred. Nothing is solid.

I gave up hoping to find the lost manuscript Hicks had seen, but I came to believe what many writers and critics have said: that the author of a work is the least qualified person to judge it. Ginsberg was too close, emotionally and intellectually, to "Howl" to see it clearly; moreover, when it came to the poem, his memory was faulty. The title didn't come from Kerouac, as he sometimes claimed. Also, at times he used poetic license and even altered facts. In "Howl" he wrote of an unnamed person "who jumped off the Brooklyn Bridge this actually happened and walked away unknown and forgotten." In fact, Tuli Kupferberg didn't jump from the iconic Brooklyn Bridge, but from the less dramatic Manhattan Bridge. Kupferberg wasn't forgotten and unknown, but a legendary New York hipster and later one of the members, along with poet Ed Sanders, of The Fugs, the Beat rock band.

After the publication of *American Scream*, I initiated new projects, including a study about the wilderness in American literature published as *A Terrible Beauty*. "Howl" faded from my mind and my memory; the work of Emily Dickinson took its place at the innermost part of my poetic heart.

II

For the 70th anniversary of the 6 Gallery reading, as I approached "Howl" with Beginner's Mind, I told myself I would hold back judgments. Or at least make the effort. I would think and speak for myself, not for the "common reader," as Virginia Woolf called her, or for all fans of the Beats, and I would compare and contrast "Howl" with "America," a short poem Ginsberg wrote and revised around the same time.

I knew that I was not the same person I had been in the fall of 1957 when I boarded a Long Island railroad train bound for Penn Station in Manhattan. I took a subway downtown to Greenwich Village and bought for 75 cents a copy of the City Lights paperback, *Howl and Other Poems*, which fit neatly into a back pocket. It made me feel very cool and a member of the "subterraneans," as Kerouac would call them.

The next school day I took the paperback with its black-and-white cover to show my classmates and read aloud some of the capitalized words and the cool phrases that leapt out from the pages: "Absolute Reality," "Eternity," "endless ride," "motionless world of Time," and "Time & Space." They hinted at something mystical, unseen and timeless, which figure in the neo-symbolist poems he wrote in the 1940s.

"Dig it!" I heard myself say. Something big, important, interesting and complicated had to be going on in the poem, though I didn't know exactly what it was. Years later, I would come to appreciate the notion that I first heard from Lawrence Ferlinghetti, Ginsberg's publisher, that difficult poems mean more to readers than easily understood poems. They demand a commitment of time and energy that can be rewarding. After all these years, "Howl" is still as difficult as any long poem I have ever encountered. Rereading it has yielded a sense of profound satisfaction about the poem, the author and myself.

III

Ginsberg's "America" was much easier to grasp than his surrealist, post-modern epic about his own generation. "America" seemed to spring from another side of the author's imagination. It is comedic, close to stand-up comedy at times, and sometimes even silly, while "Howl" is melodramatic and tragic. "America" is angry, defiant, and self-mocking, too. "Howl" is mournful and soulful; a kind of elegy for a generation. "Howl" mimics T.S. Eliot's "The Waste Land." "America" springs from the verse of Walt Whitman, who is acknowledged in "A Supermarket in California" (1955) as "lonely old courage-teacher." Like Eliot's "grouse" about civilization, "Howl" is made up of "objective correlatives." One example is: "Who cowered in unshaven rooms in underwear, burning their money in waste baskets and listening to the Terror through the wall." The poet doesn't tell readers how to feel. Rather, he provides vivid details, sets the stage and allows us to conjure our own feelings. In "America" he howls his feelings.

"America" is based in part on the poet's memories of childhood and boyhood in the company of his mother, Naomi, who took him to lefty political gatherings, where he heard about Scott Nearing and Mother Bloom. "Howl" springs from Ginsberg's observations of New York in the 1940s and from his own adventures on the road to Denver, Mexico, and on "ship to Africa."

"America" features historical figures and organizations: the Wobblies, Henry Ford, Sacco & Vanzetti, and the "Scottsboro boys." "Howl" is mythical. "America" is addressed to the nation, "Howl" to a generation that endures wars both hot and cold.

After I read "America" in 1957, I made the fourth line—"Go fuck yourself with your atom bomb"— a part of my vocabulary, along with the final line, "I'm putting my queer shoulder to the wheel." At 15, I wasn't sure what "queer" meant, though I associated it with something subversive. To be queer was to be a misfit in a society that demanded conformity. Not just the last line, but the whole poem struck me as a kind of coming out of the closet, sexually and politically. "I used to be a communist when I was a kid I'm not sorry," the speaker boasts. The line, "I'm putting my queer shoulder to the wheel" is more effective than "I'm queer." To say "shoulder" rather than, say, "my whole body" is also more effective because it's more precise, more tangible, and less abstract. The reader visualizes the shoulder leaning into the wheel.

IV

I went back to "Howl" with apprehension and anxiety. I knew that I would never be able to approach it with the same measure of innocence and curiosity I had in 1957. Still, decades later I had the eyes and ears of an experienced literary critic. Along with Beginner's Mind, I vowed to pay close attention to the text, closer than ever before, read slowly and deliberately, savoring and interrogating every single word. I could appreciate the improvisation within the framework.

I found that the obscenities—"fucked" and "cunt" for example—and the explicit sexual passages were far less explosive than they were when I first saw them on the page in the 1950s. Then, too, the overtly political parts of "Howl", including the stanzas about the F.B.I., "the narcotic tobacco haze of Capitalism," plus the phrase "the fascist national Golgotha," seemed less potent than they had seemed in the 1960s.

I threw myself into my "Howl" project and set out from my apartment near San Francisco's Japantown to find the 6 Gallery, which I thought of as Beat ground zero. At 3119 Fillmore there was a plaque to commemorate the reading although I did not notice it when I first arrived and surveyed the scene. Installed by the city of San Francisco on October 7, 2005—50 years after the initial event— the marker sits on a platform raised about three feet above the sidewalk. It features an engraving of Ginsberg's face and the words, "San Francisco salutes the Beat Generation poets Jack Kerouac, Philip Lamantia, Michael McClure, Kenneth Rexroth, Gary Snyder, and Philip Whalen."

Had the plaque been at eye-level and bolted to the outside wall of a building it would have been far more visible. Still, the inconspicuous plaque was better than nothing at all to honor an event I thought of as the perfect storm to launch the San Francisco

Poetry Renaissance and the Beat Generation, and that marked a tipping point for Ginsberg and his fellow poets, with Ferlinghetti, Rexroth, Kerouac, and other members of the audience playing significant roles at the start of a cultural revolution that swept across the globe.

I taught a class on guerrilla marketing at Sonoma State University and required students to read Malcolm Gladwell's *The Tipping Point: How Little Things Can Make a Big Difference*. From then on, I saw October 7 at the 6 through Gladwell's eyes. I adopted his terms—"the tipping point," "sticky messages," "early adopters," "mavens," and "salesmen"—and applied them to the event. A little thing that made a big difference was the postcard that Ginsberg mailed to publicize the reading; so was the jug of red wine that was passed ritualistically from hand-to-hand and mouth-to-mouth.

I regarded Ginsberg as the author of the poem's "sticky messages"—the memorable phrases that lodged themselves in the mind. In the 1990s, when I invited Ginsberg to lecture and read at Sonoma State University, he gave a workshop in which he invited students to write phrases similar to "hydrogen jukebox," which, he explained, combined two things not normally connected and thereby make something new and different and hopefully wonderful. He knew that he'd created memorable messages and wanted the student to do the same.

At the 6, Kerouac, with his enthusiasm and active participation—his shouts of "Go, go, go"—served as a salesman who helped to persuade readers to dig "Howl." Rexroth and Ferlinghetti emerged as the connectors and mavens who brought the poem to the public by publishing it and writing about the Beats, Ginsberg, and the 1957 obscenity trial that I read about in the pages of *Life* magazine and that introduced me to "Howl."

Gladwell also emphasizes the importance of the context for a tipping point. The freewheeling social and cultural milieu in San Francisco helped to give birth to "Howl." It could not have been written anywhere else in the world.

V

In *American Scream* I interpreted parts of "Howl," but I was more interested in writing about the Beats, Ginsberg's family and friends, the year 1955, and San Francisco in the 1950s than I was in the poem itself. Now, on the 70th anniversary of the reading, I wanted to dive headfirst into the poem. Right away, I realized I had to use the City Lights edition of "Howl," not the version of "Howl" in Ginsberg's *Collected Poems*, nor the version of "Howl" on the Poetry Foundation's website, and not any of the online versions of "Howl" that come with extensive footnotes emphasizing the poet's biography over the language of the poem. Still, I knew that a biographical approach was understandable and perhaps even necessary; few 20th-century American poems are more personal and subjective than "Howl," though the emphasis on the author's own experiences can flatten the work and skirt ambivalences and contradictions.

Like Walt Whitman, Ginsberg might have said in a conversational tone of voice: "Do I contradict myself? Very well then I contradict myself, (I am large, I contain multitudes.)" No poem in his oeuvre exudes more contradictions.

In addition to the versions of "Howl" that can be found online, there are the literal "translations" of the poem also online that strip it of its mystery and make it all too prosaic. LitCharts AI turns the marvelous third stanza into something trite: "Poor, ragged, sunken-eyed, and stoned, they sat smoking in the mystical-seeming darkness of cheap apartments, feeling like they were floating above their cities while thinking about jazz music." These words rob the poem of its electrifying and energizing power.

Perhaps, I thought, it was also time to recycle the New Criticism, which was popular in the 1940s and 1950s and in the early 1960s, when I was an English major at Columbia College and where Ginsberg had been a student after the end of World War II. Professor Edward Taylor practiced the New Criticism and required me and my fellow students to use it to analyze and interpret John Donne's metaphysical poetry.

It was cruel and unusual punishment to ask undergrads to grapple with Donne's sonnets without a knowledge of 17th-century history, theology, biography, and without a dictionary or a thesaurus. Even experts don't know for sure if "Batter my heart, three-person'd God" is an octave or a sestet. They also debate the meaning of the last line, "Nor ever chaste, except you ravish me," which to my ear sounded pornographic. When I wrote provocatively in an essay for Professor Taylor that those words of Donne's reminded me of Ginsberg's "fucked in the ass by saintly motorcyclist and screamed with joy" he assigned me a C-.

Now, decades later I thought I might adopt the New Criticism I scorned in Taylor's course. I would use the methodology known as "explication de texte." I would be as objective, apolitical, and non-judgmental as possible, and examine the language, the imagery, and the structure of the poem, though at times it seems to have no obvious structure and to be governed by randomness. But the more time I spent with the poem, the more I could appreciate the force of continuity that ties together loose threads, connects the beginning to the end and comes full circle. The phrase "saxophone cry" and the word "jazz" that appear at the end of the poem connect to "jazz" and "the negro street" at its start.

Unlike the version of "Howl" in the *Collected Poems*, the City Lights version of "Howl" offers William Carlos Williams' stunning introduction, which suggests that the poem is organized as a journey through a modern inferno ("Hold back the edges of your gowns, Ladies, we are going through hell").

Williams also offers biographical information about the author as a "young poet living in Paterson, New Jersey... son of a well-known poet" that would have introduced the largely unknown author to his audience. Without Ginsberg's "Dedication," and without Williams' introduction, the poem lacks two essential parts of the whole.

Beginner's Mind suggested that Ginsberg's "Dedication" to Jack Kerouac, William Burroughs, and Neal Cassady serves as a love letter to his friends, an advertisement for their work and offers a series of clues about the characters in "Howl." (Carr was originally included but objected and had his name removed from the second printing onwards.) The phrase "best minds" in the first line surely refers to the author's three closest friends: Kerouac, "the new Buddha of America prose"; William Burroughs, "the author of *Naked Lunch*, an endless novel which will drive everybody mad"; and Neal Cassady, author of *The First Third*, an "autobiography which enlightened Buddha." All their books, he added playfully, "are published in Heaven." Indeed, they were not yet in print.

"N.C., secret hero of these poems" had to be the Neal Cassady mentioned in the "Dedication." No secret there. Surely, too, when the poet describes *Naked Lunch* as a novel that would "drive everyone mad," he meant the word "mad" to be praiseworthy, as in Emily Dickinson's line: "much madness is divinest sense." Ginsberg's characters can be "destroyed by madness" or they can use madness to infuse and sustain creativity. The words "mad" and "madness" reflect the author's ambivalence about his own expressive albeit self-destructive generation.

When I wrote about "Howl" in *American Scream* I focused my attention on the first line, the section about "the three old shrews of fate," the part about Neal Cassady's sexual prowess and his identity as a Don Juan. I also emphasized the sense of apocalypse that informs the poem, in part through the phrase "the crack of doom," and the repetition of the word "last": "last fantastic book," "last door, "last telephone," and "last furnished room." Now, I saw those phrases as a kind of flashing neon sign that told me I was fast approaching the last part of the poem.

VI

With Beginner's Mind and a close and slow reading of the text, I savored every word and noticed the key themes and the variations on them. The poem's coherence rested, obviously, on the prominence of the ordinary word "who," which is repeated dozens of times. Coherence and structure also derived from the incantatory power of certain select words that provide a kind of musical subtext. They extend and amplify the opening lines. Those words include: "jazz," "mind," "angels," "night," "mad," "naked," "burning" and its offspring "burned." Plus, the musicality derives from the poet's riffs on the word "lonesome," which appears twice, once as a noun and once as an adjective. The word "lonesome" links to the words "loned," "jail-solitude," and "midnight solitude-bench."

Clearly, the angelheaded hipsters were lonely, and so it made sense that they "followed the brilliant Spaniard to converse about America and Eternity," and "sat up smoking in the supernatural darkness of cold-water flats... contemplating jazz." Clearly, too, the hipsters craved community, conversation, a spiritual kind of sex with motorcyclists who are "saintly." They needed emotional nourishment, too, and not just or only "borsht & tortillas," "the lamb stew of the imagination," and the "meat for the Synagogue." Food for thought ranged all over the poem.

Beginner's Mind led me step by step to appreciate the poem in new and exhilarating ways. I saw the first part of "Howl" as self-contained, with a clear beginning that introduced the overarching themes (destruction, insanity, hunger, and transparency), an ambiguous middle, and a clear, resounding crescendo.

As a prime candidate for the poem's vital center I choose the vivid line, "who walked all night with their shoes full of blood on the snow-bank docks waiting for a door in the East River to open full of steamheat and opium."

That image made me think of Herbert Huncke, who introduced Ginsberg to the New York Beat world of the 1940s that offered the young poet a kind of subterranean sanctuary away from "the academies" and away from "the scholars of war." Steam heat and opium provided a space where "hallucinating Arkansas and Blake-light tragedy" was not only permitted but also encouraged.

Yes, the first section of "Howl" is self-contained and complete in and of itself. Ginsberg wasn't obliged to write another word. Still, the first part also demanded an extension and an addition which Ginsberg wisely provided. The second section, which is more akin to William Blake (think "The Garden of Love" and "The Chimney Sweeper") than to Whitman or Eliot, points an accusing finger at Moloch. The monster, borrowed from the Old Testament, bashes open the skulls of the hipsters and devours their brains and imaginations.

Ginsberg offers a bleak picture of the social and economic environment that spawns the madness, the hunger, the solitude, and the hysteria endemic in the best minds. Kerouac, Burroughs, Cassady, and the angelheaded hipsters, Ginsberg suggests, are the authors of their own fate and not passive victims. They're condemned and damned by the choices they make, but they're also capable of redemption and sanctification. The poem seems Christian, a notion buttressed by the next-to-the-last line, "eli eli lamma lamma sabactani," supposedly some of Christ's last words on the cross.

The third section of "Howl" extends the narrative about Solomon which is introduced in Part I. It adds a sense of solidarity and brotherhood. The poem ends on a note of joy and optimism first sounded in Part II in which a glimmer of Heaven begins to replace the spectacle of Hell. The fallen city of the damned, which is depicted in snapshots in Part I, is resurrected in Part III. "Miracles" and "ecstasies" replace nightmares, screams and suicides. "Holy the groaning saxophone! Holy the bop apocalypse! Holy the jazzbands marijuana hipsters peace & junk and drums," Ginsberg chants. He turns the "Howl" narrative inside out and outside down; the mention of marijuana and peace almost make the poet sound like a New Age hippie.

The last section offers as bold and as marvelous an ending to an epic poem as any in modern literature, including "The Waste Land." Had Beginner's Mind, I asked myself, enabled me to reinterpret the poem anew? I thought that it had and hoped that it would do the same for others. "Howl" had grown on me and I had grown on it. The poem that resonated in my own boyhood resonated again in my 80s.

ADVERT

Earlier this year, Beatdom Books published *The Burroughs-Warhol Connection* by Victor Bockris.

Filled with journal entries, recorded conversations, photographs, and illustrations, this is an incredible collection that charts the fraught relationship between two of the twentieth century's most influential artists. Bockris knew both men and brought them together on several occasions, hoping for artistic collaboration.

Learn more at www.beatdom.com.

THE BEAT POET SPILLS IT OUT

BY HENRI BENSUSSEN

In 1955, Allen Ginsberg was 28 and felt "saddled" with himself. He was about to perform "Howl" at the 6 Gallery in San Francisco, a poem still in its early stages. I was ten years younger, about to saddle up for the rodeo called "my future," which the next year would have been U.C. Berkeley, chosen by Dad, my bankroller, when I fell into the arms of a boy. We'd met at a party in May, and a week later he drove four of us to Palm Springs. We got back late. My girlfriend and I made pancakes for dinner, which the boys laughed at. *Don't marry him!* my brain telegraphed, having been totally silent up to this point. A week later he asked me to my first date, a movie, *Rock Around the Clock*, but I was more smitten by his collection of folk music records, and then it was graduation night, and we were suddenly alone, friends and family melted away. "Let's take a drive," he said. To drive away from the homes full of drama, to escape into the purity of freedom—this was L.A., the San Fernando Valley, and it became our fallback thing, these late-night rides up and down the coast. *Let's take a drive.*

His car was a used Willys 4-door, green and white, our route was Hwy. 99, the Grapevine. The moon was full, but I couldn't see it, and then he said he loved me, and we turned around, down, down to the homes we knew, my brain, stunned, switching a college girl future for sober matron role in a new movie. I'd trade Berkeley for L.A. City College and get a part-time job, escape the parents to live with a husband, who was Jewish and had a job, the basic criteria required by this family. All my problems with Dad over a budget for college, and with Mom over my lack of marriage prospects: solved. No longer the wallflower who wrote morbid poems, I was suddenly the bride who could iron shirts. The children came later, tying up the last of the requirements for the good daughter. Like Carolyn Cassady, I was stuck at home with the kids in San Jose, after we moved there in 1962. Soon we would give up Woody and Pete for Bob Dylan. Bob's sweet voice, turning harsh, turning prophetic.

The husband didn't read *On the Road*. Instead he was often on the road himself chasing construction jobs far and wide, while I fell for Jack, reading *The Subterraneans*, *The Dharma Bums*, *Big Sur*, and even *The Town and the City*. I needed Jack's words if not his typewriter to daydream my way into the writer's world, or maybe I needed the freedom to grab whatever car my husband passed on to me, to step on the gas, speed into the night, though that wasn't possible till the children came, when he said I too needed a car. After the Willys he traded for a VW bug for a VW van for a Citroën with 300,000 miles already on the clock for a Nash Rambler with car seats for a Ford 150 pick-up with a gun rack, which, by then, the 1970s, I would drive back and forth to my job, while he drove the sedan de jour, having graduated from construction worker to shop teacher.

Where would I drive if I wasn't caring for kids, house, dog, and getting the husband to wake up and get to work on time, carrying the lunch box I had lovingly stuffed with his favorite sandwiches, the thermos full of juice? I was juiced with energy, flitting to and fro from one task to another, at home, at work, full-time now, my own private outings on weekends, after the laundry and vacuuming, cooking and grocery shopping, paying the bills, and overseeing the kids as they grew into fraught teenagers, handling their problems, keeping up the façade of the perfect marriage, surviving on coffee and short *affaires de coeur*, with absolutely no time for long rants like this one, as I sped down the freeways, radio tuned to the songs that spoke to me, Carly Simon's "You're so Vain" vying with Joan Baez's "Diamonds and Rust" and Elton John's "Rocket Man."

Carolyn and I, both of us marrying too young, both moving from San Jose to more rural areas, to homes that could be bought for little cash, and fifty years later would sell in the millions as tear-downs, like our marriages in a way, even like our own lives— bought cheap, worn down, torn apart, freeing us to rebuild our lives our way. She fought her husband over his love affairs, while my husband tried to ignore mine. In the town of Los Gatos, where they had moved a few years earlier, we found a little house on a big lot. Our dog would have a place to run, and I could make a garden. I found a job dealing food stamps to migrant farm workers, smoked pot at weekend parties, and saved enough money to go back to college to study biology, how we were made, and of what, all that bacteria and fungi, us and the apes.

1974. A two-year break from working to study genes, plants, ecology, but first we learned the meaning of paradigms. U.C. Santa Cruz, still new, and me, an "older returning student," tramping up and down mountains to inspect manzanitas, how they hybridized, freely exchanging pollen hither and thither high above the Pacific. William Everson/Brother Antoninus lived in Swanton, above Santa Cruz, dressed in buckskin, writing about ways to cherish a woman and to live for Eros rather than Ego with its always correct answers. One day, walking to my next class, I looked up to behold Everson in burly buckskin form, striding past me in sandals laced up muscular calves, smiling through his beard at my rapturous, surprised gaze.

Richard Brautigan, living farther north, a fisher of trout, touting the pleasures of watermelon and women, everyone sampling love and smoking weed. There was *Mountains and Rivers, Big Sur*, Esalen, red wine and redwoods. All things, things we love, things we hate, things we never understood, they all come to an end, in a slow erosion of molecular webbing, like Dylan's voice, fragments kept in sacred crypts by guardians of history. I was a wannabe Beat, born too late, yet the Beat goes on, breaking up paradigms in its need for deeper truths, subject to chance and altered by scribes.

The dog died, too soon, then the marriage, as the kids left one by one. I was 48, I had a future to construct, discarding the past of marriage for the other side of the sex/gender divide. I took the latest car, left the truck for him, along with the house, the garden, the Dylan LPs. I took my books, a frying pan, a few plates. Much later I'd buy my own pick-up, a smaller version, churn through lovers and relationships, discover Thoreau and meet him in Concord, a life-long love with one more complicated person. I'd write poems, stories, a few essays, get some published, a very late-blooming, miming Beat who hadn't been beaten down, who would cross more rivers than Gary Snyder, rack up the miles like Kerouac, and who gave up the Shalt Nots for an inner voice that seemed smarter than my own crippled version.

Later, moving to the Mendocino Coast, I wrote about the sea and sea birds, about dying parents and aging lovers, the passion of sex and its connection to empathy, for oneself as well as others, from fungal mycelia to overstories, making a garden of lavender, rosemary, apples, and plums in which to dream an absence of boundaries. Studied poetry from the Carmel coast to Walden Pond to the Sierras to New Mexico, Montana and Oregon, to the Mayacamas mountains of Napa, and now, at 88, to be here, in the Beats' San Francisco, their anchor and now mine, the 6 Gallery and its address permanently fogged and almost forgotten, yet Ginsberg's words live on as marker of place. To look up, up at buildings cemented to their patterns, while insisting on the uniqueness of self, maintaining grace while falling apart inside, the cracked sidewalks at our feet homes for drugged bodies arranged in an operatic chorus singing of The Fall of Rome.

"These are my rivers..." wrote Ungaretti, words reclaimed by Ferlinghetti for his rivers, we each had our own, diving into the watery rush, bravely facing the resident demons, dog-paddling to stay afloat, as we were swept to the welcoming ocean that had birthed us. After a life of moving back and forth and up and down the Golden State, staving off Freud's death wish by tapping letters into words, maintaining hope through the power of impulse-impulsiveness, I am helpless against this yearning to write about what I have come to know, about why we would drive ourselves into the sun or straight down into a deep canyon, this fatal urge for more than what we're given, to spill oneself out, to find a way through, even when feeling there's no way out but out.

A.D. WINANS ON THE COUNTERCULTURE

I grew up in the 1950s when you were expected to be a logically thinking, level-headed individual whose purpose was to work hard, raise a family, and be patriotic to your country. It was a society of rules, order, and materialism. There was little if any room for individualistic behavior.

As the fifties progressed, the Beat movement began to emerge. It had its roots in New York (Greenwich Village) and San Francisco (North Beach). The Beats openly challenged and defied the established order. They spoke out in opposition to what America represented as they rebelled against everything the establishment stood for: the repression of dissent in the name of militarism, racism, materialism, and conformity.

Bob Kaufman personifies the true meaning of the Beat spirit. He was one of the original Beat poets to come out of the fifties and is rightfully considered by many to be the most influential black poet of his era, although his poetry transcends race identification. Like many of the Beats, he started out in New York and later found his way to San Francisco's North Beach but while Ginsberg was reading his poetry to large audiences, Kaufman chose another path, becoming the undisputed street poet. He frequented the Co-existence Bagel Shop, located on Grant and Green.

By the late fifties, the Beats had cemented their role in the New American Counterculture, but much to their dismay, it was their lifestyle rather than their art that began to take center stage. What distinguished them from ordinarily malcontents was their talent and inner conviction. They represented a large contingency of youths around the world, but it was also a time when the media began to mass-produce the "ideal" America. The media began to turn a revolution into a cultural fad. The word "Beat" began to lose its significance as part of a sub-culture and became instead a label for anyone living as a bohemian or acting out rebelliously. In 1958, the word "beatnik" was coined by *San Francisco Chronicle* columnist Herb Caen to characterize the physical allure of the Beats instead of their social and intellectual radicalism.

When I returned home from Panama in 1958 after serving four years in the Air Force the Beats were already beginning to move out of San Francisco's North Beach, migrating to places like Mexico and Venice Beach, California. The term "beatnik" made them the brunt of jokes rather than a serious revolution. The media had exploited the only two things they could understand about the Beats: their image and lifestyle.

The North Beach creative hub took place in a six-block radius from lower Grant Street to upper Grant, centered around a large number of bars, cafés, and coffee houses, frequented by poets, artists, and jazz musicians. While Grant Avenue was the center stage of creativity, the bevy of cafés and bars extended from Broadway and Columbus, all the way to the produce district, where the self-proclaimed King of the Beats, Eric "Big Daddy" Nord, held court in a large warehouse called Eric's Pad, which remained open 24/7. You could walk in any night of the week and see blacks and whites freely mingling and dancing to the music of bongo and conga drums. On the roof, there was a string of mattresses with couples fornicating in full view of interested and disinterested onlookers.

However, two decades earlier, San Francisco was already thriving with creative energy. Kenneth Rexroth, often referred to as the "Father of the Beats," was a prominent second-generation modernist poet who corresponded with Ezra Pound and William Carlos Williams. He came to the city from Chicago, where he had hung out at a jazz and poetry tearoom known as the Green Mask, which housed an upstairs brothel, right in line with San Francisco's bawdy history.

Rexroth held regular readings in his apartment located over a record store in the Fillmore District. Among the many poets who frequented the meetings was Philip Whalen, who later appeared in Kerouac's novels as Ben Fagin and Warren Coughlin. The poets who attended the meetings represented a wide range of writing styles, from the ballads of Helen Adams to the bawdy rhymes of poet and filmmaker James Broughton. The readings were a haven for both young and old poets as well as visiting luminaries.

If Rexroth was the father of the Beats (and this is something he very much denied) then Madeline Gleason was the founding mother. During the 1940s, both she and Rexroth befriended a group of younger Berkeley poets including Jack Spicer and Robert Duncan.

In 1952, Dylan Thomas came to the city and captivated a standing-room audience who came to see the Welshman drunkenly read his work. A year later Lawrence Ferlinghetti and Peter D. Martin opened City Lights Bookstore, partly to finance *City Lights Journal*, which at the time was publishing the Surrealist poet Philip Lamantia.

When Ginsberg came to the city in the mid-50s, it was only natural he would find his way to Rexroth's weekly gatherings. In 1954, he had not yet come to accept his homosexuality, but this same year he met Peter Orlovsky and the two became life partners. In August 1955, Ginsberg began writing the first lines of his epic poem "Howl." He began searching for a place to showcase the poem and with Rexroth's help he set up a reading at the 6 Gallery, located at 3119 Fillmore Street. The reading featured Ginsberg, Snyder, Whalen, Michael McClure, and Philip Lamantia, with Rexroth serving as the Master of Ceremonies.

Kerouac was not on the bill but did attend the event. The reading drew a large crowd with Kerouac drunkenly passing large jugs of red wine through the audience. Ginsberg was the last poet to read and, urged on by Kerouac, gave a passionate reading that helped launch him on his way to fame.

The most important thing Kerouac, Ginsberg, and Cassady did was to make rebellious young people throughout the land aware there were others out there who felt the same way. This was expressed by Diane di Prima, who is quoted as saying that "Howl" encouraged her and others to step forward and make their voices heard.

The single most important event that helped the Beats gain notoriety occurred on March 25, 1957, when the U.S. Customs Bureau seized a shipment of *Howl and Other Poems* and declared the book to be obscene. Ferlinghetti and Shig Muro (manager of City Lights) were charged with selling obscene literature. The American Civil Liberties Union intervened, providing free legal assistance. Writers and critics testified in court on behalf of City Lights and Judge Clayton Horn set a precedent by ruling that if a book has "the slightest redeeming social importance, it is protected under the First and Fourteenth Amendments to the U.S. and California Constitutions, and therefore can not be declared obscene." This legal precedent allowed D.H. Lawrence's *Lady Chatterley's Lover* and

Henry Miller's *Tropic of Cancer* to be published by Grove Press.

It's equally important to note the influence of jazz on the work of the Beats. Charlie Parker and Charles Mingus were among the many jazz musicians to whom the Beats were drawn. In the late '50s and into the '60s jazz was central to what was happening. Wes Montgomery and Cal Tjader were active participants of the scene. The Fillmore District, a largely black community, was known as Bop City, a hangout for musicians like Ella Fitzgerald and Sarah Vaughan. It was common to see New York jazz musicians visiting San Francisco's Fillmore District, and it was here that musicians and lovers of jazz gathered in the early hours of the morning.

The Beats and bebop were like twins. Carter Monroe points out, "When discussing the bebop movement in terms of Beat Literature, you are talking about the freedom it represents. A great deal of Beat Literature in terms of influence is all about content and challenging social mores." Bebop challenged the existing parameters of music. You can see this influence in the work of Jack Kerouac and perhaps even more so in the work of the poet Bob Kaufman. In North Beach, Kaufman was regarded as the bebop poet, and much of his poetry is infused with jazz. Rexroth and Ferlinghetti would both read their poems accompanied by jazz musicians at The Cellar.

Today, both literary critics and academics recognize the Beats as legitimate poets, writers, and artists, but the legitimacy did not come without a cost. As is often the case, success comes with a price tag. Many of the Beat poets were co-opted into the system. Ginsberg applied for and received not one but three NEA writing grants and sold his archives to Stanford University for over a million dollars. Burroughs made a commercial and had a small role in a movie. Ferlinghetti's once avant-garde bookstore cannot be distinguished today from other commercial bookstores. As the years passed, Ferlinghetti was second to Ginsberg in marketing himself, commanding thousands of dollars for a reading.

It was poets like Jack Micheline, Bob Kaufman, Gregory Corso, Charles Plymell, and Ray Bremser who remained true to the Beat spirit. While today's youth remains intrigued if not directly influenced by the Beat Generation, there hasn't been a real counterculture revolution since the Hippie Generation, which was a youth movement that began in the U.S. during the early 1960s and like the Beats soon spread around the world. The word "hippie" was derived from the word hipster and was initially used to describe beatniks who had moved into San Francisco's Haight-Ashbury district. These people embraced the counterculture values of the Beat Generation, forming their own communities, listening to psychedelic rock, embracing sexual revolution, and experimenting with drugs like LSD, grass and peyote to explore alternate states of consciousness. I had the privilege of living and experiencing both generations.

LIFTING THE LIGHT FROM THE JADE GREEN WAVES BELOW
PAUL W. JACOB (JAKE)

(An homage to old San Francisco and my late mentor and comrade Neeli Cherkovski)

ONE

I want the lushness,
strange hands groping
fleshy, colorful fruit,

long green vegetables
sticking out of bamboo baskets
like pagan phalluses.

I want to bask
in the jazz
of a language
that drifts through me
i n t u i t i v e l y.

I want to float
unaware of anything
but the stench of the air,
the ping of wind chimes,
the swerve of dragons,
and the punch of drums.

I want to pick a hanging duck
from the window of a Hong Kong barbecue shop
and watch the butcher lop its head off.

I want the stale rotten American fruit of my mind
to blossom once more,
        like when I was young.

TWO

Afternoon calamari
at Enrico's sidewalk café,

    slick tech professionals,
        guys on iPhones,
          women with Chromebooks,
sashay up and down Broadway
 unaware of their infinite loveliness,

        such loveliness in the afternoon
on this noisy city street
 full of strip bars and strippers, porn shops and johns,
forever leaning towards the sun.

THREE

Where is the real North Beach,
those astral bohemians
and word strumming vagrants/seraphim
skipping arm-in-arm into psilocybin alleys.

Where are the vanguard citizens
of the new world, never found,
always searching, hoping
for the gold to rush in
off the dusty mountains
and snow-capped peaks
of our forlorn existence.

FOUR

There is nothing
I long for anymore
besides the dying,
that slow infantile crawl
to the living source.

Spent tea leaves
at the bottom
of a porcelain teacup.

FIVE

When I hang-out in San Francisco long enough
the writing comes,
it's not that it flows
but gushes straight out of the sewer of my soul:
all the waste, stench, abominations I flush down inside
spew up and out of my loins, my mind,
my dharma smacking me in the salty mouth,
waves and sea spray crashing over the half-drowned boulders
plunging from the Pacific Ocean,

    and the Golden Gate Bridge,
        swaying oxidized fog breath Buddha
traversing eternity over the soft flood of karma,
of connected streams and rivers and bays,

                my consciousness sun-
            soaked and liminal,
                  lifting the light
                  from the jade
              green waves below.

FESTIVALS OF POETRY, 1947-1952

BY TOM CANTRELL

On the San Francisco Poetry Center's website, there is a two-part video entitled "Poets of the Forties" and it shows nine poets reading at an event from May 1974. The lineup includes Robert Duncan, Thomas Parkinson, William Everson, and Madeline Gleason. The title refers not to the fact that these poets were active in the 1940s, but rather that the reading was a re-enactment of an extremely successful event held by Madeline Gleason's San Francisco Poetry Guild in April 1947. This was called "The Festival of Poetry" and it proved so popular that it became an annual event, repeated between 1947 and 1952.

In the book *Robert Duncan: A Descriptive Bibliography* by Robert J. Bertholf, on page A46 there is a reproduction of a page from a program for the 1974 re-enactment. It is a six-paragraph essay written by Duncan that recalls the two-night Festival of Modern Poetry, which was organized by Madeline Gleason and featured twelve poets reading to an audience at the Laubaudt Gallery in San Francisco. Duncan mentions the later San Francisco Renaissance and calls Ginsberg's "Howl" "the watershed" but suggests that April 1947 was the *real* beginning. "We had been told that modern poetry had no readers," he wrote. "That was the decisive message writ large in the 1930s." However, the event was extremely successful. Gleason's approach was to model it on music festivals and Duncan says this made them "the first such Readings presented in the contemporary world. [...] Certainly, it was in San Francisco that the first audience [for modern poetry] began."

Kenneth Rexroth read at the 1947 festival and in describing

the San Francisco poetry scene that developed after WWII, Duncan wrote, "Kenneth Rexroth was its Prophet." He describes the scene as emerging post-WWII with Rexroth at the center, but says it was Gleason who brought them all together. He writes: "I sought out Madeline Gleason after friends had given me her first book, *POEMS*, which had been printed by Grabhorn Press. When William Everson emerged for the [Conscientious Objector] camp, I took him to meet her." Everson would read at the poetry festival, along with Duncan, Gleason, Rexroth, James Broughton, Robin Blaser, Rosalind Moore Brown, Robert Horan, Janet Lewis, Thomas Parkinson, Richard Brown, and Jack Spicer.

What Duncan does not mention here is that the first Festival of Poetry was successful enough not just to be repeated a year later, but to be repeated later that same month. The following announcement appeared in the *San Francisco Examiner* on April 28, 1947:

> Poetry Fete Tomorrow—Festival Session Due for Repeat. A repeat performance of the second session in the Fesrival of Modern Poetry, held last week at the Lucien Labaudt Art Gallery, will be given at 8 p.m. tomorrow at the Gallery 1407 Gough Street.
>
> Under the direction of poetess Madeline Gleason, the festival presented 12 San Francisco poets reading their own works on two evening programs last week.
>
> Tomorrow's program will present Kenneth Rexroth, Madeline Gleason, Leonard Wolf, Robert Duncan, Jack Spicer and George Elliot.
>
> The admission is fifty cents.

The San Francisco Renaissance is often said to have begun with Allen Ginsberg's reading of "Howl" at the 6 Gallery on October 7, 1955, but as we can see here, not only was there an active poetry scene before that moment, but there were popular festivals of poetry being held as long as eight years before that night.

"IT'S NOT MY SCENE"
THE EVOLVING POETS AND POETICS OF THE BERKELEY AND SAN FRANCISCO RENAISSANCES AND THE BEAT GENERATION

BY RYAN MATHEWS

> I met an angel
> Who said he was a beatnik
> He didn't drink brandy or honey water
> Just pure vowels.
> Vowels are the pauses between things
> Silence is what we fight against, I told him
> But his wings
> Were paused to beat against the pure air.
>   – Jack Spicer. *Notes and fragments*[i]

The Northern California poetry scene that preceded it defined the Beat Generation as we now think of it. Without the influence of the San Francisco scene the Beats would be all but unrecognizable to us today.

Wait! How can I spout such heresy?

After all, didn't Ginsberg's reading at the 6 Gallery transform the California poetry scene forever? Well, yes and no. When it comes to modern poetry, hindsight is not only not 20/20—it's downright myopic.

In this essay, I will argue that the many of the characteristics we have come to think of as primarily associated with the Beats were in fact already present before the 6 Gallery reading and that what happened in San Francisco in the 1940s and early 1950s (and even earlier) had more influence on the Beats than the Beats had on the San Francisco poets of the 1960s and beyond.

To support this hypothesis, it's necessary to set aside most of the academic treatments that tend to stress the discontinuities between generations of poets and focus instead on the common threads running through almost a half century of San Francisco poets and poetics from the arrival of Kenneth Rexroth and his wife in the 1920s to the Summer of Love and beyond.

The truth is that there isn't enough space in a full issue of *Beatdom* to begin to do justice to all the poets we should discuss. We are talking about roughly half a century and upwards of 100 key figures.

So, acknowledging the unforgiving limitations of space, biographical details and extensive sampling of work have been condensed. One could argue against the wisdom of letting one or two individuals stand for an entire movement, and I would agree, but the space limitations are what they are.

This doesn't mean that Josephine Miles or Madeline Gleason, or for that matter Charles Olson, Robert Creeley, Denise Levertov, William Everson, Robin Blaser, or Robinson Jeffers weren't critical characters in our story and couldn't be used to support our premise. It just means this is an essay, not a book.

THE ORIGINAL MISSION TURNED OUT TO BE MUCH LIKE ORIGINAL SIN, JUST LESS FUN

The original aim of this essay was to determine what, from an aesthetic and structural point of view, separates the work of the poets of the Berkely Renaissance, the San Francisco Renaissance, and the Beat Generation.

Turns out it's not as simple an exercise as it seems and not even a particularly useful one. But please don't stop reading. The search for one set of superficial insights surfaced volumes of deeper, more compelling ones, some of which we will explore here.

Unlike Dada and Surrealism, this is less a story about who

adhered to which aesthetic dogma and who was allowed to participate in which movement and more a story about people just living their lives—individually and together—growing and sharing their art and not paying any attention to the labels other people insisted on attaching to them.

Did Jack Spicer hate Lawrence Ferlinghetti? Probably.

Did Robert Duncan change the object of his poetic affections multiple times? Yes he did.

Did Kenneth Rexroth go from being a promoter of the Beats to a major critic of the movement. No doubt about it.

All that said, I'll argue that we have been thinking about the major post-World War II California poetry movements all wrong for decades and that all the complex literary scholarship has actually taken away from our understanding of the evolution of modernism and postmodernism, not increased it.

Our reevaluation starts, perhaps appropriately enough, with a touch of poetic license regarding the word elision. Linguists use the term to describe the moment in the juncture of two phrases where—simultaneously—one phrase ends and another begins. In music elision refers to the point in a song where different sections overlap one another. And, in poetry, elision refers to the omission of a normally pronounced sound or letter to decrease the number of syllables in a word or phrase in order to conform to meter or structure requirements and/or improve word flow. A slightly broader definition of elision provides a key to understanding the California poetry milieu from the 1920s through the post-Beat period.

What we now tend to describe as a series of discrete, hermetic, and unrelated literary movements, specifically the Berkeley and San Francisco Renaissances and the Beat Generation, weren't separate at all but "historical elisions"—points along a continuum where people, ideas, and activity overlapped in ways that blurred the borders of their work so that it becomes hard to determine where one set of ideas stopped and another began.

Along with Michael Davidson's *The San Francisco Renaissance: Poetics and Community at Mid-century*, Warren French's *The San Francisco Poetry Renaissance* stands as one of the handful of books attempting to take a comprehensive academic look at poetry scene from the 1940s through 1960.

In his preface, French readily concedes, "Since key terms like 'Beat,' 'Beat Generation,' 'beats and beatniks,' 'San Francisco Renaissance,' have been used indiscriminately and interchangeably for three decades, there is no generally agreed upon meaning for them."[ii]

In fact as we will see shortly, there really isn't much that's "generally agreed" about these three movements period, starting with when or if they existed and how to date them.

The one thing everyone seems to agree about is that whatever actually happened, it could have only happened in California, and more specifically the San Francisco Bay area.

CALIFORNIA HERE THEY WERE, OR CAME, TO "THE OTHER SIDE OF THE RABBIT HOLE"

> There was a whole new school of poets brewing, and there were pioneering artists around the School of Fine Arts who later became famous as San Francisco Figurative painters and abstract expressionists. It was the last frontier, and they were dancing on the edge of the world.
>
> – Lawrence Ferlinghetti, "The Poetic City That Was"[iii]

When do a few friends become a scene, and beyond that, when does a scene become a school, a school become a movement, and a movement become an institution of the establishment? And when does one movement stop and another start if the people that defined the former are still present in the latter?

The writers and artists of the Berkeley Renaissance, the San Francisco Renaissance, and the Beat Generation shocked public sensibilities and morality with lurid tales of sex, drugs, and jazz; joyously flaunted interracial and same-sex relationships; and popularized and promoted what up to then had largely been seen as esoteric Eastern religions.

Fueled by gallon jugs of Mar-Vista and Belle Wine muscatel, iced bottles of Anchor Steam beer, Benzedrine, smack, grass, and various hallucinogens, the poets of these movements served as ragged volunteers in the vanguard of the "New American Poetry" revolution. Together they stormed forward across all lines of defense, dragging art bodily into the streets while gleefully vomiting on the academic literary establishment, the New York-based publishing industry, and a massed counterinsurgency of cultural critics.

They slept together, sometimes married, often divorced, created petty spats out of nothing, and built common cause in the service of art. The poets associated with the three movements we are looking at often disagreed. They fell out with each other, sometimes for years or decades. But the one thing they always agreed on was that, in those days, San Francisco—the real main character of this essay—was a world unto itself.

"This represents a continued tradition from Ambrose Bierce," Jack Spicer once told *San Francisco Chronicle* reporter Tove Neville, "that the sea coast of California is so different from the rest of the U.S., (in climate, or economic or political interest) that it isn't really part of the rest of the U.S."[iv]

Asked to explain why the state had hosted two poetic "revivals" (the San Francisco Renaissance and the Beat Movement), Spicer told Neville: "It is impossible to say what really happened in San Francisco (poetry) but it is like Alice in Wonderland. It gets curiouser and curiouser, is [sic] the key to how it happened. California is the other side of the rabbit hole. It is because we are so far away from the East Coast that the new American poetry is able to survive."[v]

Kenneth Rexroth concurred. In "San Francisco Letter," which appeared in *Evergreen Review No. 2*, he wrote, "It is easy to see why all this has centered in San Francisco," adding, "I always feel like I ought to get a passport every time I cross the Bay to Oakland or Berkeley."[vi]

This sense of otherness, of separation from the rest of the country, the confines of orthodox academia, the barbs of East Coast critics, and the elitist standards of New York City-based publishing enabled the Northern California poets—native and immigrant—to build a new vision and a new vocabulary based on rejecting limits and limitations, which makes our formal academic view of them all the more comic in retrospect.

In *American Poetry in the Twentieth Century*, Rexroth once again addressed the issue of why San Francisco proved such fertile ground for poets. "In San Francisco," he wrote, "the revolt against the entire culture of the interbellum period [1918-1941] was more widely and solidly based than on the East Coast."[vii]

"It was not just a regional renaissance like the Middle Western, Chicago-centered one of the early years of the century," he added. "It was more like the culture of a different country whose inhabitants happen to speak American."[viii]

San Francisco of the 1920s to 1940s was a culture bouillabaisse made up of anarchist, socialist, and communist politics; a long tradition of outlaw writers like Ambrose Bierce and Jack London; tolerance for "sin" and eccentricity in all its various forms; ethnic enclaves; and several nascent poetic and artistic communities. It was long on ideas and creativity, short on formalism, and tolerant of individuals other communities might find deviant.

It was a place where Eastern and Western thought, religions, languages, and art coexisted and more than occasionally merged together. Somehow, all these disparate and sometimes dissident flavors blended in the end.

MAYBE IT WAS THE WATER ...

Maybe it was war or the dropping of the atomic bombs.

Or maybe it was the fog or the fact that it's as far west as a lost soul can wander without falling into the Pacific, or disappearing without a trace like Lew Welch, who on May 23, 1971 wandered away from Gary Snyder's house on Mount Tamalpais carrying a Smith & Wesson .22 caliber revolver... or Weldon Kees, who vanished on July 19, 1955, leaving his car abandoned on the Marin County side of the Golden Gate Bridge.

Maybe it was magic. Maybe it was madness. Most likely it was a heady and sometimes toxic blend of both.

Maybe it was all these things. Or maybe none.

Whatever the reason, from 1945 through the 1970s the San Francisco Bay area produced poetry, prose, art, music, and theatre that shattered the formalistic chains that had restrained them for generations.

The apparent academic obsession with wrestling sterile order from the jaws of messy historical reality has encouraged many of us to force fit our literary heroes and villains into discrete little boxes with labels like New York School, Black Mountain, Berkeley and San Francisco Renaissances, Second San Francisco Renaissance, Black Arts Movement, Wichita Vortex, Beats, Baby Beats, and my personal least favorite—Beat Adjacent.

Despite our best efforts to impose structure on lives that while they were being lived avoided definition with every fiber of their being, these labels don't help us understand the flesh-and-blood realities of the men and women who produced a staggering amount of revolutionary artistic work in California in the second half of the 20th century.

Who cares if Robert Duncan was a Black Mountain "projectivist" poet, a member of one or two of the Bay Area Renaissances, more closely aligned with Charles Olson and Robert Creeley than Kenneth Rexroth and Jack Spicer, or a Beat as some insist on labeling him?

And what about his fellow travelers like Michael McClure and Gary Snyder? What boxes should we put them in?

Was Kenneth Rexroth really the "father of the Beat movement" and, if so, does that make him, by extension, the grandfather of the hippies or the surrogate poppa of the San Francisco Renaissance or was he just the ring master of his own semi-private poetic circus?

Were Ted Joans and Bob Kaufman Beats, Black poets, surrealists, all of the above, some of the above, or something else altogether?

And what do we do with poets like Lawrence Ferlinghetti, Helen Adam, Madeline Gleason, and William Everson, who roamed from circle to circle, eschewing membership of any of them?

The answer is that not only doesn't any of this actually matter outside the pages of a modernism textbook, but it tends to camouflage simpler and deeper truths that we ought to be paying attention to. The most important of these is that we are largely dealing with the same cast of characters interacting over decades.

What we ought to be focusing on is what they had in common and how they built on what they learned from each other, not how they differed.

The fact we don't traces back to the hero/villain of academic poetic modernism, Donald M. Allen, who got us thinking of the most important poets of the period as beings more or less permanently sequestered in what today amounts to five different universes.

BALL OF CONFUSION: YOU CAN'T TELL THE PLAYERS BECAUSE OF THE SCORECARD

The road to literary taxonomological Hell is paved with good intentions. In this case those intentions belonged to Donald Allen, the editor of *The New American Poetry: 1945-1960*, the first and—with over 100,000 copies sold—perhaps the most successful anthology of the American poets of that era.

To his credit, Allen brought attention to a number of poets who otherwise might have never been recognized, at least as early as 1960 when the first edition of his anthology appeared. But the organizational model he used to present the poets he selected was—to be charitable—a bit capricious, creating a confusion reinforced by critics and commentators for the last 65 years.

"In order to give the reader some sense of the history of the period and the primary alignment of the writers," Allen wrote in the preface, "I have adopted the unusual device of dividing the poets into five large groups, though these divisions are somewhat arbitrary and cannot be taken as rigid categories."[ix]

"Somewhat arbitrary" was putting it mildly.

Allen's first group included, "those poets who were originally closely identified with the two important magazines of the period, *Origins* and *Black Mountain Review*." Those were Charles Olson, Robert Duncan, Robert Creeley, Edward Dorn, Joel Oppenheimer, Johnathon Williams, Paul Blackburn, Paul Carroll, Larry Eigner, and Denise Levertov.

The second, members of the "San Francisco Renaissance" included Helen Adam, Brother Antoninus (William Everson), James Broughton, Madeline Gleason, Lawrence Ferlinghetti, Robin Blaser, Jack Spicer, Lew Welch, Richard Duerden, Philip Lamantia, Bruce Boyd, Kirby Doyle, and Ebbe Borregaard.

Next come the "Beats," apparently limited to Allen Ginsberg, Jack Kerouac, Gregory Corso, and Peter Orlovsky.

The fourth division was labeled the New York Poets, which includes Barbara Guest, James Schuyler, Edward Field, John Ashbery, Kenneth Koch, and Frank O'Hara.

The fifth group Allen said, "has no geographical definition; it includes younger poets who have been associated with and in some cases influenced by the leading writers of the preceding groups, but who have evolved their own original styles and new conceptions of poetry." This group was comprised of Philip Whalen, Gary Snyder, Stuart Z. Perkoff, Michael McClure, Ray Bremser, Ron Loewinsohn, David Meltzer, John Weiners, Ron Loewinsohn, Edward Marshall, David Meltzer, Gilbert Sorrentino, John Wieners, and LeRoi Jones (Amiri Baraka).

There were some obvious problems.

By his own admission Allen saw Robert Duncan belonging

to both his first and second groups. Poets like Snyder, McClure, Meltzer, Wieners, and Jones/Baraka fell into the "all others" category even though, for example, Snyder and McClure were as much a part of the San Francisco Renaissance and Beat scenes as Jones/Baraka was both a New Yorker and a Beat.

Apparently aware of the potential mess he was making, Allen noted, "Occasionally arbitrary and for the most part more historical than actual, these groups can be justified finally only as a means to give the reader some sense of milieu and to make the anthology more a readable book and less still another collection of 'anthology pieces'."[x]

In fairness to Allen, there was no way that in 1960 he could have understood how the alignment he adopted to make his anthology "more readable" would go on to shape the way academics thought about and taught these writers for the next six or seven decades. Sadly, the truth is his well-meaning attempts to provide structure have caused readers ever since to think of these groups as distinct schools and that's a problem.

If Allen is guilty of confusing us in terms of who fit where, confusing us about *when* any of these movements started or stopped has been a team effort.

DATING "THE SCENES"

One could argue, and rightfully so, that the 6 Gallery reading was the first shot in a poetic revolution.

One could also argue that the poetic zeitgeist had been in a revolution since the turn of the 20th century, led by writers including Ezra Pound, H.D., Andre Breton, Tristan Tzara, T.S. Eliot, Gertrude Stein, William Carlos Williams, and James Joyce, who did for language arts what Heisenberg and Einstein did for physics; Freud and Jung did for psychology; and Picasso, Ernst, and Dali did for painting.

In this version of history, the 6 Gallery reading can be seen as the culmination of forces that had been circulating for half a century or so. But whichever version of the truth you prefer, it's pretty hard to dispute that the nexus of poetic activity in the pre-Beat period could be found in Berkeley.

As to dates, it is far less clear when the Berkeley Renaissance started and/or stopped.

It's hard to fix the start date because many of the central

personalities associated with the Berkeley scene such as Robert Duncan, Mary Fabilli, and the painter Virginia Admiral had known each other and lived with each other off and on since the late 1930s. In fact it was in a series of constantly revolving households from February 1938 through November of 1939 that Admiral, Duncan, the Fabilli sisters, and a few friends formed the core of what would later become known as the Berkeley Renaissance.

"I met Robert [Duncan] sometime in February 1938," Admiral recalled. "I had noticed Robert, Mary and Lili Fabilli, and Cecily Kramer earlier having a wonderful time dancing into and out of the small record concerts on the Berkeley campus, laughing hysterically, Lili with sandals and a flower in her hair (she was the original Flower Child). So when I saw my landlady turn Lili away from my rooming house on Bancroft Way I invited her to share my room. Soon after, she took that room and I moved back to the top floor, a sort of garret with huge dormer windows, which Mary shared with me.[xi]

"My first memory of Robert—who was called 'Symmes' [as opposed to Duncan] most of the time—is of him sitting on one of the beds up there reading a long poem, probably his 'Ritual.' Robert wore horn-rimmed glasses, and one eye turned out a little which gave him an earnest, almost owlish look when he was reading his poetry. He had an apartment on the other side of the campus, but we never went there. From time to time, he would mention affairs he was having, but they were episodic except for an instructor named Ned, and, in fact, he spent all of his time with us.

"The YPSL [The Berkeley Young People's Socialist League] mimeograph machine was in the middle of our garret room. There were always a few people around, and Robert had a built-in audience. He was writing a great deal and read it all to us immediately. Sometimes we would go over a poem line by line, and I would ask him to explain every word. That spring Robert was reading Gertrude Stein (often aloud), St. John Perse, *Les Liaisons Dangereuses*, Henry Miller, D. H. Lawrence, and, I think, some Freud. I remember that then, or a little later, he was talking about Melanie Klein and the fact that so few children committed suicide. He mentioned shamans quite a lot but said little of his parents' involvement with the occult.

"Robert and Mary [Fabilli] were dissatisfied with the campus literary magazine, the *Occident*, so we decided to put out our own, having the mimeograph machine right there. Robert and I were both good typists and we did all the work. He wanted to call it *Ritual*; I wanted to call it *Epitaph*. I won. There were no other disagreements. We had no trouble getting it out, also doing whatever political leaflets were necessary. Robert and I took a few magazines with us on campus to sell, but I don't recall that we gave any to stores to carry."

Jack Spicer, along with Duncan—seven years his senior—and Robin Blaser, was one of the three "tentpole" poets of the Berkeley Renaissance. Spicer, who studied poetry with Josephine Miles, met Blaser and Spicer and his lover James Felts shortly after arriving in Berkeley in 1945, living with them briefly and problematically. It was Duncan who provided the foundation for the Berkeley group. So strong was their bond that Spicer once said that his "year of birth" was 1946, the year he met Duncan.[xii]

The poets met at a meeting of the Libertarian Circle, a group of "philosophical anarchists" who met every Wednesday at Kenneth Rexroth's apartment on Steiner Street.[xiii] Addressing the whole notion of a Berkeley Renaissance, Spicer biographers Lewis Ellingham and Kevin Killman wrote, "Duncan, Spicer, and Blaser began to invent their own myth, an insurgence of culture and ease they called—only half-mockingly—'The Berkeley Renaissance.'"

It's equally problematic to precisely date the origin and end point of the Beat Generation. Should we say that it began in 1943, when Allen Ginsberg met Lucien Carr at Columbia University, who would in short order introduce him to Jack Kerouac and William S. Burroughs? Or was it 1944 when Carr, Kerouac, and Ginsberg began to explore "The New Vision" they believed would revolutionize the written world? Or was it later?

Beat legend says Jack Kerouac coined the phrase "Beat Generation" in a 1948 conversation with his friend John Clellon Holmes, who did more than most to introduce it to the square world of 1950s America. But naming a generation and being a generation are two different things.

In a November 16, 1952 article in *The New York Times Magazine* entitled "This is the Beat Generation," Holmes wrote: "Any attempt to label an entire generation is unrewarding, and yet the generation which went through the last war, or at least could get a drink easily once it was over, seems to possess a uniform, general quality which demands an adjective. It was John Kerouac, the author of a fine, neglected novel, *The Town and the City*, who finally came up with it. It was several years ago, when the face was harder to recognize, but he has a sharp, sympathetic eye, and one day he said, 'You know, this is really a beat generation.'"[xiv]

"The origins of the word 'beat' are obscure," he continued, "but the meaning is only too clear to most Americans. More than a mere weariness, it implies the feeling of having been used, of being raw. It involves a sort of nakedness of mind, and, ultimately, of soul; a feeling of being reduced to the bedrock of consciousness. In short, it means being undramatically pushed up against the wall of oneself. A man is beat whenever he goes for broke and wagers the sum of his resources on a single number; and the young generation has done that continually from early youth.

"Its members have an instinctive individuality, needing no bohemianism or imposed eccentricity to express it. Brought up during the collective bad circumstances of a dreary depression, weaned during the collective uprooting of a global war, they distrust collectivity.

"Their own lust for freedom, and the ability to live at a pace that kills (to which the war had adjusted them), led to black markets, bebop, narcotics, sexual promiscuity, hucksterism, and Jean-Paul Sartre. The beatness set in later."

And if the beginning of the generation is tough to pinpoint, its end is impossible. The "Beat Umbrella" has been stretched by a variety of writers to cover such obviously non-Beat folks as Henry Miller, Charles Bukowski, Patti Smith, Denise Levertov, Duncan, Lawrence Ferlinghetti, Hunter S. Thompson, and Johny Depp.

In other words, the Beats have apparently never ended or stopped their recruitment drive. There are "Beat" writers who weren't born for a decade or two after Kerouac's death. There's probably one being born right now. And that brings us down to building a timeline for the San Francisco Renaissance.

Here there is some general agreement regarding the dates, if not the precise membership roster.

In *The San Francisco Poetry Renaissance*, Warren French dates the movement as lasting from 1955 to 1960. Michael Davidson, the other well-known scholar of the period is a bit more precise telling us, "According to most commentators, the San Francisco Renaissance 'began' on October 13, 1955 at the Six Gallery, a small cooperative artspace run by painters associated with the San Francisco Art Institute and located in the Marina district."[xv]

As to an end date Davidson, like French, settles on 1965— somewhere between the Berkeley Poetry Conference held on July 21 and Jack Spicer's death on August 17.

It has frequently been observed that the 6 Gallery reading was not attended by some of the city's most prominent poets—

Duncan, Spicer, and Blaser included—but of course its most prominent poet was not just in attendance; he was on the stage.

KENNETH REXROTH: POSTER CHILD FOR POETIC REVOLUTION OR REACTIONARY PAPER TIGER?

> A poem is a perspective on a person and a person is a totalized perspective on all other sentiment beings.
> – Kenneth Rexroth, *American Poetry in the Twentieth Century*[xvi]

The powder for what became the modern and postmodern California poetry movements had been carefully assembled and packed since the 1920s. All that it needed to explode were a fuse and an ignition device. Oh... and an anarchist willing to light the fuse never hurts. So, we could say the Northern California modernism poetry revolution really dates back to 1927, when Kenneth Rexroth and his wife, the painter Andrée Rexroth, arrived in San Francisco after hitchhiking and camping their way across the country.

Rexroth, the 6 Gallery reading's emcee, stands adjacent to every pre- and post-World War II California poetic movement as either a poetic *pater familias*, engaged participant, vocal advocate and promotor, or equally vocal critic. Understanding Rexroth's evolving relationship to the various "movements" helps us understand how fluid and interchangeable their casts of characters really were.

"Rexroth was a magnificent poet. In a real sense, he was the father of all these guys," according to Jack Hirschman, the Bronx-born poet, translator, painter, and lifelong political activist who arrived in San Francisco in 1973, staying on to become its second poet laureate.[xvii]

"He was the man who wrote the first major political poem after the Second World War, outside of the communists who were writing poems against McCarthyism published in newspapers," Hirschman said in an interview with *American Legends*. "Rexroth's poem, on the death of Dylan Thomas, was one of the great lyrical poems by a North American poet. He was also one of the great translators from Chinese and Japanese. A marvelous figure, of real international importance. People in other countries know that Kenneth Rexroth was the father of the Beats, and, if you ask Lawrence Ferlinghetti, he'll tell you, too."

In some ways Rexroth can be seen as the Allen Ginsberg of his generation, tirelessly promoting the work of his friends. One of those friends, William Everson, recalled how he, Robert Duncan, and Gary Snyder all came to be published by New Directions.

In an interview with Lee Bartlett, Everson said "[It was] through Kenneth Rexroth. He fostered the San Francisco movement which was an entering wedge. He had a strong connection with James Laughlin before we ever met him. My book was published by New Directions in the forties, and I can honestly say Rexroth discovered me. He sold Laughlin on me, and I owe him a great debt for that. Jeffers was my ideal; Rexroth was my mentor, my manager. Eventually, because of a personal problem we had a falling out which never did get straightened out properly. It has been painful for me. I was committed to his program, but I couldn't fulfill what he expected of me. I should have taken more care, but it was impossible."[xviii]

Asked if he thought Rexroth was "pretty much single-handedly responsible for the San Francisco Renaissance," Everson said, "Sure. Duncan of course labored hard at it, but he was too young. He just didn't have Rexroth's stature. He was not a polemicist, which was one of Rexroth's greatest strengths. Ginsberg also, whereas both Kerouac and Duncan were the writers. Rexroth got the thing started in San Francisco, then Ginsberg took it back east and sold it to *Time*. Kerouac and his group wrote for ten years before the Beat Generation emerged, and it was Rexroth who made the difference."

Rexroth's ability to organize and promote, or attack, is a "red thread" through all three of the movements we're discussing. He organized everything—radio programming and reading on KPFA, jazz and poetry recitals (either alone or with other poets like Lawrence Ferlinghetti), political groups such as the local John Reed Club, his Anarchist Circle, the San Francisco Artists and Writers union, and... well, you get the idea. As Rexroth saw it, San Francisco had what he called "pretty relentless organizational activity."[xix] Rexroth was also a great matchmaker. As we have seen, it was at his salons in the 1940s that Robert Duncan and Jack Spicer met, and he later welcomed Snyder, Ginsberg, Whalen, and other Beat poets into his circle.

We could write volumes on Rexroth's years as the nurturing

rabbi and bête noire of generations of poets, but what is important here are the shallowly planted seeds that eventually shaped the San Francisco scene. These included the idea of personal freedom in the form of the "rucksack revolution" people often associate with Kerouac. He was an early advocate for ecological causes, a thread later picked up by Snyder and McClure among others.

And like Snyder and Philip Whalen, he was a devoted student of oriental languages, literature, art, and religions.

His own poetry is free form and dominated by images of love and eroticism, themes carried on with a vengeance by poets from Robert Duncan and William Everson to Allen Ginsberg and Lenore Kandel.

Look for any of the themes associated with any of the San Francisco movements and you are likely to find their roots somewhere in Rexroth's collected works.

Now let's turn our attention to these movements starting in Berkeley.

THE BERKELEY RENAISSANCE: 1944-1950 (?): THE THREE-PLUS HORSEMEN OF THE POETIC APOCALYPSE

> What have I lost? When shall I start to sing
>   A loud and idiotic song that makes
>   The heart rise frightened into poetry
>   Like birds disturbed?[xx]
>
>   – Jack Spicer, "A Postscript to the
>   Berkeley Renaissance"

The Berkeley Renaissance may have been the most Californian of all California's literary movements. Three of its four principles—Robert Duncan (born in Oakland on January 7, 1919), Jack Spicer (born in Los Angeles on January 30, 1925), and Landis Everson (born in Coronado on October 5, 1926)—were all natives. Robin Blaser, the only non-Californian, was born in Denver on May 18, 1925.

Blaser was also the only one of the four not to die in California.

On August 1, 1965, after 16 days in a coma, Spicer died a tragic alcohol-related death at 40 in San Francisco. Duncan died on

February 3, 1988, at the age of 69 following a prolonged battle with kidney disease. Everson, who many scholars somehow manage to overlook, took his own life at 81 in Mill Valley on November 17, 2007. Blaser outlived them all, dying of a cancerous brain tumor at 82 in Vancouver, British Columbia on May 7, 2009.

Don't feel bad if you've never heard of the Berkeley Renaissance. It might have been lost to the shadows of literary history if it wasn't for the work of Ben Mazer's masterful 2004 essay "The Berkeley Renaissance," which appeared in the journal *Fulcrum*.

As Mazer freely admits, the actual origin of the phrase "Berkeley Renaissance" may be lost to history. "According to Robin Blaser it was Kenneth Rexroth on KPFA radio who first spoke of a 'Berkeley Renaissance' in describing the exciting new poetry that was being created by Robert Duncan and Jack Spicer," he wrote.[xxi] Landis Everson, a key member of the group, thought "the Berkeley Renaissance was spearheaded and thought up by Spicer, and abetted by Robert Duncan and Robin [Blaser]."[xxii]

"Duncan used the term as if he had coined it," Mazer wrote in *Fulcrum*, "indicating that the word 'renaissance' was a reference to the group's preoccupation with medieval and Renaissance studies."[xxiii]

Like other authorities, Michael Davidson agrees on who made up the Berkeley circle but is a little hazy on why it was called the Berkeley Renaissance. "Another important group in Berkeley was that surrounding Robert Duncan, Jack Spicer, and Robin Blaser, who, as students of English literature and medieval historiography, formed a circle of sectarian adepts."[xxiv]

Duncan himself offers yet another perspective. In his elegy to his friend Jack Spicer originally published in *Manroot 10*, he wrote, "In the late 1940s, Jack Spicer, Robin Blaser, and I hoped for what we called a Berkeley Renaissance. We wanted a learned poetry, learned not in terms of the literary world but in the lore of a magic tradition and of a spiritual experience we believed to be the key to the art."[xxv] He might have added that the magic and spiritual experience often came with a large helping of gay eroticism.

According to the author of a book about Spicer, "[t]he 'Berkeley Renaissance'—to use the half-ironic term favored by the poets themselves—which coalesced principally around Duncan, Spicer, and Blaser was also to a very large extent a gay renaissance; sexuality, gender, homosexuality, and queer poetry and poetics were at its core."[xxvi]

Duncan had "come out" in 1944, generations ahead of his time. "[M]y article 'The Homosexual in Society' appeared in Dwight Macdonald's *Politics*, in the Nov-Sept issue 1944, and made a stir in the intellectual community," he told Robert Peters in an interview with the *Chicago Review*.[xxvii] "I was thinking of Charles Henri Ford's *View Magazine*, and the idea that the ambience of many poets was a kind of advertisement for their homosexuality, a covert advertisement. I called for overtness, for declaration. My premise was that if a poet like Auden had finally declared himself, choosing not to continue redundantly giving hints and providing innuendoes of self advertisement, others of us should."

By the time of the Berkeley Renaissance, Duncan was what by Northern California standards could pass as an established poet. In 1938, with Virginia Admiral, he brought out a single edition of *Epitaph*, a forerunner of the mimeograph revolution carried on by Edward Sanders and d. a. levy decades later. His second mimeographed "magazine," *Ritual*, produced with Ned C. Fahs, also only had one edition although between 1940-41 it morphed—again with Admiral's help—into two full issues and one supplemental issue of *Experimental Review*.

An editorial in *Experimental Review*'s first issue, jointly written with the poet Sanders Russell, proclaimed: "The experiment is not to foster an eccentricity or a novelty of language, nor to create a new literature: it is to extend the understanding, to bring everything into consciousness, to develop the artist's awareness in the field of observations—in the world of objects, values, dreams, in tensions within the social and economic order as well as in more involved states of consciousness—the way of the primitive, the saint, or the mystic."[xxviii]

If all this talk of a new literature, consciousness, dreams, states of consciousness, saints, and mystics sounds familiar in a Beat sort of way it's not accidental. Duncan's neo-Romanticism was apparently as contagious as his fondness for longline poetry.

If Robert Duncan mimicked Rexroth's notions of poetic community and collaborative art, Jack Spicer prefigured the darker side of his life.

Spicer once told an interviewer, "I think that anyone's a fool to become a junkie or a poet." He added a grim warning to fledgling poets: "I don't know if it's tragic or not, but I just know that you better make certain that you don't get in on the things unless you really want to pay the price for them."[xxix]

Spicer's poetic profile was significantly raised by the inclusion

171

of his poem "Imaginary Elegies, I -IV (for Robin Blaser)" in *The New American Poetry*. Written between 1950 and 1955, the poem traces the arc from an idealism captured one of Spicer's most famous lines, "Poet, Be like God," to the more melancholy note:

> Yes, be like God. I wonder what I thought
> When I wrote that. The dreamers sag a bit
> As if five years had thickened on their flesh
> Or on my eyes. Wake them with what?
> Should I throw rocks at them
> To make their naked private bodies bleed?
> No. Let them sleep. This much I've learned
> In these five years in what I spent and earned:
> Time does not finish a poem.[xxx]

"Imaginary Elegies" has plenty of references to some of the "magic" elements Duncan mentioned including dreamers, God, and Tarot cards. But it also shows that the academic medievalism of the early days in Berkeley were giving way to the drunken bitterness that would cause Spicer's early demise.

Spicer knew how to work the system. He just chose not to. He published very little during his lifetime and refused to deal with major publishing houses, preferring small presses like White Rabbit, which he seemed to be able to marginally tolerate. He also had ideas that were either elaborate put-ons or one step beyond eccentric. For example, Spicer was obsessed with the idea that poets were "catchers" of messages sent to them by forces he called "Martians."

His poem "Golem," written on October 1, 1962, both anticipates his own death and the sad state of modern poetry as he saw it. In an obvious slap at Allen Ginsberg, he wrote:

> I have seen the best poets and baseball players of
> our
> generation caught in the complete and
> contemptible
> whoredom of capitalist society[xxxi]

Spicer doesn't spare himself. He prophetically ends the poem:

> He died from killing himself.
> His public mask was broken

> because
> He no longer had a public mask.
> People retrieved his poems
> from wastebaskets. They had
> Long hearts.
> Oh, what a pain and shame was
> his passing
> People returned to their
> Businesses somewhat saddened.

In 1975, Richard Ellman wrote in *The New York Times*, "Jack Spicer's poems are always poised just on the face side of language, dipping all the way over toward that sudden flip, as if an effort were being made through feeling strongly in simple words to sneak up on the event of a man ruminating about something, or celebrating something, without rhetorical formulae, in his own beautiful inept awkwardness. It's that poised ineptitude and awkwardness of the anti-academic teacher, the scholar of linguistics who can't say what he knows in formal language, and has chosen to be very naive and look and hear and do."[xxxii]

"Spicer was not a very happy poet," he added. He was obsessed with possibilities he could only occasionally realize, and too aware of contemporary life to settle for anything less in his work than what he probably could not achieve. He must have been a great spirit."

He may have been a great spirit but he was a violently unhappy man. A chronic alcoholic who could never subdue his demons, no matter how hard or how many times he tried to drown them, his last words whispered to Robin Blaser captured his dark humor. They were: "My vocabulary did this to me. Your love will let you go on."[xxxiii]

Spicer died but the Beats went on. In fact, some are still going.

THE 6 GALLERY READING: THE GHOST OF NORTH BEACH PAST, PRESENT AND FUTURE

I'm not going to dwell too much on the Beats, and especially not on the 6 Gallery reading. That has been covered in depth and better than I could hope to do, most recently in *Beatdom* editor David S. Wills' new *A Remarkable Collection of Angels: A History of the Six Gallery Reading*.

Asked by an interviewer in 2020 whether he saw the 6 Gallery reading as the start of a movement, the then 90-year-old Snyder replied, "There was already a movement. I was very much a student of the poet and essayist Kenneth Rexroth. He had an open seminar twice a month in his apartment out in the Avenues district of San Francisco. I got over there and listened to what Kenneth had to say. It was from Kenneth that I first heard discussion of labor unions, the anarchist movement, the history of West Coast Communism. The circle of people around Kenneth were part of my continuous education in the history of the West Coast left."[xxxiv]

"The first time I met Allen Ginsberg was at Rexroth's house," Snyder added.[1] "Allen had just come up from Mexico. The first time I saw Kerouac was when Allen brought him to Rexroth's place. Because Allen was living in Berkeley, I saw more and more of him. Kenneth thought of both Jack and Allen as 'talented jerks.'"

Rexroth, who had mentored Snyder, saw him as "probably the most influential—on the young poets of his generation—influential as a poet on new poets, that is."[xxxv] He described Snyder as "an accomplished technician who has learned from the poetry of several languages and who has developed a sure and flexible style capable of handling any material he wishes."

Philip Whalen stood outside the pack that night. As the late Steve Silberman wrote, "In many ways, Whalen was not like the others. In a group of wiry, strikingly handsome young men, he was decidedly pear-shaped and already seemed middle-aged, though he was still in his early thirties. The other poets had aspirations to be alpha males, but Whalen could seem nearly feminine or maternal, as if he was channeling the female muses whom he frequently called to his aid in his work. 'Straightforward' was not quite the word for his writing; instead, his poems rambled affably among disparate kinds of material, often in multiple languages. While Kerouac and Ginsberg cultivated very public voices, Whalen's language was so personal, idiosyncratic, and even cranky that it could seem hermetic."[xxxvi]

"He was a poet's poet," Gary Snyder said in his friend's obituary in the *Los Angeles Times*. "People looking for subtlety, nuance and beautiful turns of language looked to Philip. He had a wonderfully dry sense of humor—ironic, cutting, mocking."[xxxvii]

---

1   Snyder misremembered his first meeting with Ginsberg, whom he actually met at home in Berkeley. They later attended a few of Rexroth's Friday-night salons together but had somehow not met at these events prior to September 1955.

The other Philip reading that night, Philip Lamantia, didn't read his own poetry and is usually, and more correctly, associated with the Surrealists than the Beats.

For his part Michael McClure seemed nonplussed by the attention generated from that poetry reading, not shunning it but not letting himself get defined by one October night. In a November 21, 1999, interview with Michael Hibblen, he was asked how he saw the Beat movement.

"I would say that it was about going for the deepest level of the imagination possible," he told Hibblen. "We discovered it was inevitable to speak out against the cold, gray, fascist American way politics of the '50s and also to begin speaking out in favor of the environment. That's not quite the way it's pictured with people sitting around with spaghetti in their beard playing bongo drums and wearing splotchy berets."[xxxviii]

If the 6 Gallery reading did anything, it was to bring all of the elements of the earlier North Beach movements together—spirituality, mysticism, ecology, love, rebellion, an emphasis on public performance, etc. McClure, it could be argued, moved the ecological theme closer to science than romance. Lamantia kept the flame of surrealism alive, which opened the door to Bob Kaufman and Ted Jones. And Ginsberg brought a new vocabulary to public poetry, at least once "Howl" was found to not be obscene.

In one sense very little "new" happened that night outside of the supposedly shocking language in "Howl." But what was new was the fusion of poetry and lifestyle, the crystallization of a countercultural revolution that had been brewing for decades. That was new … and dangerous.

And after the 6 came the deluge as Beats were replaced by beatniks and a period when everyone who could afford a beret thought they were a poet.

THE SAN FRANCISCO RENAISSANCE

In the same way that "Beat" has become a "Big Tent" idea, the San Francisco Renaissance better describes the survivors of the 6 Gallery and their friends who chose to stay in the city and keep writing poetry.

As an identifier of poetic form, it is even less useful than the word "Beat," covering everyone who owned a pen and was breathing San Francisco's air from Helen Adam to Bob Kaufman, whose work had little in common beyond being poetry.

However you choose to label them, the ranks of the post-6 Gallery poets thinned as the scene shifted to the San Francisco Renaissance, eventually flowing into the halcyon days of the 1960s. In May, 1956, Gary Snyder left to study in Japan. Later that year, Ginsberg also left and Duncan decamped for Black Mountain College. Whalen left San Francisco in 1957 and then moved to Japan in 1967, the "Summer of Love." A year after that, Kenneth Rexroth—credited and/or blamed for so much of what happen in San Francisco poetics from the 1930s on—left the city to teach in Santa Barbara.

Jazz gave way to rock and roll. The black-clad Beats were replaced by the tie-dyed hippies. Meanwhile, the tribe of North Beach poets kept doing what they always had done no matter what you called them—living and writing and, with a few exceptions, doing their best to ignore the labels people put on them, choosing to remain focused on the issues that had been important in the California arts community since the 1920s.

Time for two last voices. The first belongs to Gerald Nicosia, whose *Memory Babe* remains the preeminent biography of Jack Kerouac. While best known to some for his nonfiction work, Nicosia was also an active poet who moved to San Francisco in 1979, where he remained off and on for the better part of 40 years. He has sometimes been lumped in the "Post-Beat" bucket along with others like David Meltzer, Jack Micheline, Harold Norse, Howard Hart, and dozens of other writers.

"For the most part, we did not talk about movements," Nicosia told *Beatdom,* "other than specialized ones, like the Language Poets, whom the writers I hung around with all thought were pretentious assholes looking to make academic money by creating something that was not worth existing—i.e., an artificially created poetic category."[xxxix]

"We were all just doing our work," he continued. "Duncan did not seem part of a movement to us, though we all knew he had been part of an intellectual and avant-garde post-war movement that had included Spicer, Robin Blaser, and some others. Duncan kept to himself a lot, did not come out much, though occasionally he would show up at a reading. He was always very private, shy maybe, cards close to his vest. We all had great respect for him, not just as a poet but because he was a very kind and humble man, seemed to have extremely decent values, and showed a sense of dignity always, as if he felt being a poet was a dignified profession, which

I think we all felt but most of us couldn't manage to demonstrate!

"We all had great respect for the Beats as the pioneers they were, and many of us were proud to wear the label post-Beat," Nicosia added. "Micheline, Kaufman, Corso, Norse, Kirby Doyle, and many others I knew had no problem with the label Beat. What we disliked were the hypocrites, those like Ferlinghetti, McClure, and others who disdained the label Beat, but made money off of it wherever they could. Ferlinghetti was often snide about Beat, talked about it as if it were a joke—but he too accepted big money to go to Beat conferences. For most of the poets my age, Beat was a serious matter—a powerful breakthrough in modern American consciousness that we were always striving to live up to."

Asked about the whole idea of a "San Francisco Renaissance," Nicosia told *Beatdom*, "[The] San Franciso Renaissance was not a movement that we recognized. For us it was just an event, the Six Gallery and the poets that gathered around it—a piece of recent SF literary history, but not something anyone 'belonged' to.

"None of us wanted to be categorized, but Beat and post-Beat were labels with recognizable meanings to us, and most of us accepted those meanings and wore them—if someone wanted to call us that—with pride.

"Many of the writers I knew also wore multiple caps. Norse considered himself not just a Beat poet, but also a gay poet, and also a poet of the American idiom, in the mode of W.C. Williams. Neeli Cherkovski accepted not only the label of post-Beat, but also gay poet, surrealist, 'California pastoral' in the mode of Robinson Jeffers, humorist poet a la Bukowski, and probably others. We all understood labels as just an indication of the different areas we were working in, and not something that would limit us or ultimately define our work. Kerouac, of course, initially felt proprietary about Beat, because he had named it, and later extended it to beatific, but then began to detest and shun it when Herb Caen modified it to the diminutive and pejorative 'beatnik.' Because that latter label was used as part of the vicious assault on both Kerouac's person and his work, it became a very sore spot with him and ultimately he tried to get away from it. But for most of us in San Francisco, Beat was an honored label—because we understood the power of the breakthroughs, the honesty, universal compassion, ecumenical embrace, etc., that it represented."

Summarizing his thinking, Nicosia added this last note: "We were too excited about the work we were all doing, reading each other our new works, going to readings to see what others were doing. We did have a sense of being part of an ongoing revolution—which also devolved in part from the New Age revolution of the Sixties—but it was part of the larger American revolution, the freedom of spirit, the universal love and tolerance, the expansion of consciousness, that we considered America represented and embodied—or at least, ideally, should represent and embody."

Our final voice belongs to A.D. "Al" Winans, who is to me the living embodiment of this article's hypothesis. A native San Franciscan—born there on January 12, 1936, not far from the building that housed the 6 Gallery reading—Winans has lived in his hometown his entire life with the exception of three years of military service which ended in 1958. Technically, Gary Snyder is the oldest of the well-known native San Francisco poets but, as Winans once reminded me, "he was born here, but he left when he was a kid."

He is the founder of Second Coming Press, the editor of *Second Coming Magazine* from 1972 to 1989, a poet with around 70 collections of his own work, an author of two prose volumes, whose work has appeared in over 1,500 magazines and anthologies, and the recipient of multiple awards. More critically for our purposes, he was the publisher, friend, co-reader, and drinking companion of many Beats including Bob Kaufman and Jack Micheline. In short, Winans has had a ringside seat to the ebb and flow of poets and poetry in and out of North Beach for almost seventy years.

Asked what separated the Beats from the poets that preceded them or their other San Francisco contemporaries, Winans said, "The Beats did not subscribe to any particular school of poetry. They were anti-academic, deliberately rejecting formal structure and traditions of academic poets. They rejected the formal verse that dominated poetry after World War Two."[xl]

"By and large, their writing was driven through spontaneous composition that Jack Kerouac referred to as 'spontaneous bop prosody,' influenced by bebop jazz, capturing the immediacy of thought and experience" he continued. "Their writing ranged from the subject matter of alienation to spirituality, drug use, and sexual freedom. Much of it could also be described as Confessional Poetry."

Conceding that "Ginsberg was influenced to some degree by the 'Black Mountain' poet Charles Olson," Winans added, "None of them that I knew belonged to any school of poetry. It would have been against their very nature and core beliefs."

While Winans' analysis is spot on, it does draw us back to the idea of elision, which is to say the point where sounds or ideas meet in such a way that it is impossible to say where one stops and another starts.

The most visible original Beats—William S. Burroughs, Allen Ginsberg, and Jack Kerouac—may have started out as East Coast-based, Ivy League-educated men, but the Beat Generation was transformed when Ginsberg, in particular, and Kerouac discovered the streets of Berkeley and North Beach.

Part of the problem Donald Allen faced when he sat down to organize *The New American Poetry* was that the poets themselves, and by extension their work, were all products of an artistic sensibility that had been evolving and maturing since before the Second World War.

Were Snyder and McClure concerned with nature and environment? Of course, but Kenneth Rexroth and William Everson had been wrestling with these same issues for decades before the 6 Gallery reading.

Were Philip Whalen, Diane di Prima, Ginsberg, and Kerouac passionate about Buddhism and other Eastern faiths? Yes, but again so was Rexroth well before them.

Did writers like Lawrence Ferlinghetti move from being leftists to anarchists? Yes, but once again not really before Rexroth.

Did Bob Kaufman and Jack Micheline take poetry "to the streets" by reciting in bars, coffee houses, galleries, and street corners rather than salons, the drawing rooms of the rich and cultures, or the halls of academe? No doubt, just like ruth weiss and Madeline Gleason had already done.

I want to avoid the sadly predictable arguments around who did what first. The point is that the themes floating around Northern California for decades became amplified by the media attention that surrounded the Beats and—depending how you define them—the first and/or second San Francisco Renaissances and/or the "Baby Beat" movements.

CONCLUSION

> We have seen the best minds of our generation destroyed by boredom at poetry readings
> – Lawrence Ferlinghetti, *Wild Dreams of a New Beginning*[xli]

In 1971, looking back on the men and women of the Berkeley and San Francisco Renaissances and the Beat movement who stormed the ivy-covered barricades of academically centered poetry and dragged it kicking and screaming into the bars, coffee houses, and streetcorners of North Beach, Kenneth Rexroth wrote, "Today these people are established if not members of a new Establishment. Most of them in their turn are teaching at a university, although some have remained preternaturally inassimilable and they have a half generation of accomplishment or more behind them."[xlii]

Ironically, Rexroth, who saw himself as a permanent fixture of the San Francisco political and artistic avant-garde, had been mocked as part of the establishment 14 years earlier by a group of young, rebellious writers.

In "An Open Letter To Kenneth Rexroth," which appeared in the Summer-Autumn 1957 issue of *Mainstream*, Ron Offen, who later became a distinguished Chicago-based poet, playwright, critic, editor, and theatre producer, wrote (tongue I assume firmly planted in cheek):

> Pops,
> You're right, you are too old for the scene, like the old man who joins the session and who we got to put down because he keeps talking like [Louis] Armstrong about those nasty boppers ...
> The trouble is you're starting to take the whole gig too seriously ...
> Like you keep yelling like that and we begin to wonder if you're straight like your boy Ginsberg, that's old stuff, we made that scene years ago with Patchen and Miller and just because Ginsberg blows louder don't necessarily make him the greatest ...
> We got to play it cool and if that means freezing you out what you going to do?[xliii]

To liberally paraphrase Jacques Mallet du Pan's 1873 observation, the poetic revolution always devours its parents. It always has. It always will and rightly so.

The last line of the *Los Angeles Times'* obituary for Berkeley Renaissance poet Landis Everson read, "Everson has no known survivors."[xliv]

Nothing could be further from the truth. While Landis

Everson, Jack Spicer, William Everson, Madeline Gleason, Robin Blaser, Robert Duncan, and Allen Ginsberg may not have left any biological children, their spiritual descendants not only survive, but prosper and, over time and space, their song of creative liberation has birthed generations of outlaw poets and artists, true rebels with a cause.

The voices first which began as whispers in Berkeley between Everson, Blaser, Duncan, Spicer, and others eventually migrated to San Francisco, where they joined a poetic chorus including Gary Snyder, Kenneth Rexroth, Michael McClure, Lawrence Ferlinghetti, Bob Kaufman, and countless others.

Like the blare of the ancient Israelite horns toppling the walls of Jericho, having marched around academe's Ivory Towers and ivied walls, the sound of those voices—amplified now by the hundreds and thousands—parades ever forward, bringing down the walls of institutional formalism that always seeks to constrain them.

I started this saying that we should be paying attention to how the people we now associate with these artistic movements evolved and honed their craft, not whether or not their poetry rhymed.

The story of the community is, was, and hopefully always will be the chronicle of people's search for freedom of expression. If Jack Spicer had survived his demons, who knows if he would have written more like Robert Creeley or Mother Goose?

As Winans points out, North Beach has always been about breaking rules, not formalizing them.

ENDNOTES

i   Spicer, Jack, *Untitled fragment. be brave to things: The Uncollected Poetry and Plays of Jack Spicer* (Middleton, CT: Wesleyan University Press, 2021) p.177

ii   French, Warren, *The San Francisco Poetry Renaissance* (Boston: Twayne Publishers, 1991) p.ix

iii   Ferlinghetti, Lawrence, *"The Poetic City That Was"* Accessed at: http://www.corpse.org/archives/issue_9/critiques/ferling.htm?Src=longreads. April 3, 2025.

iv   Gizzi, Peter. *The House That Jack Built: The Collected Lectures of Jack Spicer* (Hanover, NH: University Press of New England, 1998) p.243

v   Ibid

vi   Rexroth, Kenneth, *"San Francisco Letter". Evergreen Review* No.2. (New York: Grove Press Inc., 1957) p.5-6

vii   Rexroth, Kenneth, *American Poetry in the Twentieth Century* (New York: Herder and Herder, 1971) p.136 -137.

viii   Ibid. p.139
ix   Allen, Donald. *The New American Poetry, 1945-1960* (Berkeley: University of California Press, 1999) p.xii
x   Ibid. p.xiii
xi   Admiral, Virginia. "Love Generation: Virginia Admiral Remembers Robert Duncan". *First of the Month*. March 1, 2020. Accessed at: https://www.firstofthemonth.org/love-generation-virginia-admiral-remembers-robert-duncan-2/ on September 24, 2024.
xii   Ellingham, Lewis and Killian, Kevin, *Poet Be Like God: Jack Spicer and the San Francisco Renaissance* (Hanover, NH: University Press of New England, 1998) p.11
xiii   Ibid. p.10
xiv   Holmes, John Clellon. *"This is the Beat Generation"*. *The New York Times Magazine*. November 16, 1952. Accessed at: https://litkicks.com/thisisthebeatgeneration/ on May 3, 2025.
xv   Davidson, *The San Francisco Renaissance: Poetics and Community at Mid-Century*, p.3
xvi   Rexroth, *American Poetry in the Twentieth Century*, p.178
xvii   Hirschman, Jack. American Legends interview. Accessed at: https://americanlegends.com/Interviews/jack_hirschman.html#:~:text=When%20I%20got%20to%20the,so%2Dcalled%20San%20Francisco%20Renaissance. November 13, 2024.
xviii   Bartlett, Lee. *William Everson:* The *Talking Poetry Interview*. From *Talking Poetry: Conversations in the Workshop with Contemporary Poets*. Albuquerque: U of New Mexico P, 1987. Accessed at: http://maps-legacy.org/poets/a_f/everson/talkingpoetry.htm on May 4, 2025.
xix   Meltzer, David, *Golden Gate: Interviews with 5 San Francisco Writers*, (Berkeley: Wingbow Press, 1976) p.23.
xx   Spicer, Jack, *my vocabulary did this to me: The Collected Poetry of Jack Spicer*. Gizzi, Peter and Killian, Kevin, editors. (Middletown, CT: Wesleyan University Press, 2008) p.45
xxi   Mazer, Ben, "The Berkeley Renaissance" in *Fulcrum: An Annual of Poetry and Aesthetics*. Number Three, 2004. Nikolayev, Philip and Kapovich, Katia (Editors). Saline, MI. 2004, p.391
xxii   Ibid.
xxiii   Ibid.
xxiv   Davidson, *The San Francisco Renaissance: Poetics and Community at Mid-Century*, p.40
xxv   Duncan, Robert. Maynard, John (Editor). *Collected Essays and Other Prose* (Berkeley: University of California Press, 2019) p.230
xxvi   Katz, Daniel. *The Poetry of Jack Spicer*. Edinburgh. Edinburgh University Press. Page 6.
xxvii   Peters, Robert Peters and Trachtenber, Paul, "A Conversation with Robert Duncan (1976)". *Chicago Review*. 45: 02. February 3, 2020. Accessed at: https://www.chicagoreview.org/a-conversation-with-robert-duncan-1976/ on March 24, 2025.
xxviii   Mazer, Bem, "The Berkeley Renaissance," *Fulcrum Number Three*. 2004. (McNaughton & Gunn: Saline, MI, 2004) p.392
xxix   Tallman, Walter and Spicer, Jack, "Jack Spicer. Excerpt from

Vancouver Lecture 3 (June 17, 1965). Poetry in Process and Book of Magazine Verse." Accessed at: http://jacketmagazine.com/07/spicer-lect3main.html. May 7, 2025.

xxx   Allen, *The New American Poetry, 1945- 1960*, p.146

xxxi   Spicer, *my vocabulary did this to me: The Collected Poetry of Jack Spicer*, p.361.

xxxii   "JACK SPICER." Verdant Press. https://verdantpress.com/checklist/jack-spicer/. Accessed at: https://verdantpress.com/checklist/jack-spicer/ on May 22, 2025.

xxxiii   Heilig, Steve, *"Poetry review: 'My Vocabulary Did This to Me'"*. San Francisco Chronicle. Dec 5, 2008. Accessed at: https://www.sfgate.com/books/article/poetry-review-my-vocabulary-did-this-to-me-3182610.php on June 6, 2025.

xxxiv   Elder, Sean, "National Treasure: Gary Snyder." *Lion's Roar*. May 8, 2020. Accessed at: https://www.lionsroar.com/national-treasure-gary-snyder/. February 17, 2025.

xxxv   Rexroth, *American Poetry in the Twentieth Century*, p.177

xxxvi   Silberman, Steve, "The Beat of Philip Whalen." *Lion's Roar*. Accessed at: https://www.lionsroar.com/the-beat-of-philip-whalen/. April 7, 2025.

xxxvii   Perry, Tony, "Philip Whalen, 78; Zen Priest, Mentor Among Beat Poets," *Lost Angeles Times*. June 28, 2002. Accessed at: https://www.latimes.com/archives/la-xpm-2002-jun-28-me-whalen28-story.html on February 2, 2025.

xxxviii   Hibblen, Michael, "Beat Generation poet Michael McClure Dies at 87." Hibblen Radio. May 7,2020. Accessed at: https://hibblenradio.com/beat-generation-poet-michael-mcclure-dies-at-87/#:~:text=21%2C%201999%20while%20he%20was,classes%20and%20things%20like%20that on October 5, 2024.

xxxix   Private correspondence with the author. August 29, 2025

xl   Correspondence with the author August 20 – 24, 2025.

xli   Ferlinghetti, Lawrence, *Wild Dreams of New Beginnings* (New York: New Directions, 1988) p.61

xlii   Rexroth, *American Poetry in the Twentieth Century*, p.162.

xliii   Offen, Ron, "An Open Letter to Kenneth Rexroth," *Mainstream: A Quarterly Journal of Poetry The Arts and Contemporary Comment. Vol II. No II, Summer-Autumn 1957. San Francisco Issue*. (Palatine, IL) p.19 -20

xliv   Rourke, Mary, "Poet, part of Berkeley Renaissance, made a comeback decades later," *Los Angeles Times*. November 29. 2007. Accessed on August 27, 2024 at: https://www.latimes.com/archives/la-xpm-2007-nov-29-me-everson29-story.html.

POEM FOR JACK MICHELINE
BY A.D. WINANS

Hey Jack,
The Poetry Flash
Finally gave you space
Even if you had to die for it.

Funny when you were alive
You never heard this
The Poetry Flash
      The Iowa Review
The Paris Review
      The American Poetry Review
This is not Poetry.

The holy grail has gone the way of grand slams
These people dance with the dead
they have never drank a cup of black coffee
At an all night truck stop diner
Or walked with holes in their shoes
Or sang the blues.

They shop at Macy's browse the web
They don't make love they fuck
They do not eat their food
They nibble
They do not drink they sip
Drunk on a 2 4/7 ego trip.

They drink bottled water eat sushi
trade favors like baseball cards
they are living proof of mediocrity
in the arts.

They are the gravediggers of the Beats
Play trick-and-treats
They never miss being quoted in an obituary
They are the paparazzi of the poetry world
Always seeking a photo opportunity.

They don't know the meaning of shame
To them poetry is a game
Hungry for money hungry for power
Hungry for fame.
Would be mountain men
Who set their traps with the skill
Of a paid grave digger.

This is the new breed poetry politician
Seasoned alley cats hiding in sandboxes
Looking for the right back to scratch.

They stake out their territory
At the NEA and State grant agencies
Like a vampire in need of flesh blood.

Their faces are puffy
Their handshake weak
They hover in the shadows
Like an undertaker
Waits to dress the dead.
Beware my friends
Do not die
They will be sniffing
at your grave.

TO FIND DAWN'S MOON
A REVIEW

BY DAVID S. WILLS

As Gregory Stephenson notes in his latest book, *To Find Dawn's Moon: Details and Dimensions of The Dharma Bums by Jack Kerouac*, this 1958 novel has been pretty thoroughly analysed in the nearly seventy years since its publication. It was widely trashed by "serious" critics in the beginning but is now generally lauded as a modern classic. Many have written about it in books, essays, articles, and blog posts, so what more is there to say? Stephenson writes:

> I wish to revisit and reappraise the novel, attempting to avoid repetitions and overlappings with information and ideas already treated of by other commentators. My aim here is merely to supplement what has already been written, to extend by a little what has to date been known and thought concerning *The Dharma Bums*.

It is a modest but admirable aim and in this very short book (a little over 100 pages), Stephenson guides us in almost a stream-of-consciousness fashion through his thoughts on Kerouac's second most famous book.

He covers religion, of course, telling us that this "is a religious work, implicitly urging readers to consider seriously the teachings of Gautama Buddha." He looks at "certain words in the text

[that] recur and connect, accumulate and cohere, implicit with meaning" in order to look at "the images they evoke [and survey] the dimensions of their suggestive power." He asks the reader to "defocus on the immediate particulars of the story [so that] some simple but salient features become visible" and notes that the novel begins with a man looking up at the clouds and ends with him above them. Such are the areas of discussion in this book.

Stephenson analyses domiciles and their symbolism. Think of Japhy's shack for example or Alvah's cottage, compared with Ray's brother-in-law, who "exemplifies the Faustian bargain [...] or trading life and precious time for ownership of property." There is much in this short book about this sort of symbolic representation—of characters, of buildings, of actions, of geographic features, and so on. Stephenson even discusses the suggestions inherent in cardinal directions: east means conservativism, west is freedom, and so on.

I enjoyed his dissection of names. I had of course read many interpretations of Kerouac's pseudonym for Kenneth Rexroth and I have formulated my own ideas, too, but here Stephenson presents his views on the origins and purposes of "Japhy Ryder" and "Ray Smith." He makes an interesting and persuasive case.

Towards the end of *To Find Dawn's Moon*, there is a section called "Afterlives" that explores the way that *The Dharma Bums* has impacted our world. As well as noting the famed "rucksack revolution" it inspired, Stephenson lists the (rather ironic) products that are sold alongside businesses named for the novel and various artistic endeavours. Of course, he notes that visiting Desolation Peak has become something of a pilgrimage, with dharma bums tracing Kerouac's footsteps for more than a half century.

Altogether, this is a useful book that will be of interest to Kerouac fans. Stephenson has achieved his goal of discussing the book without repeating much of what others have said and thereby provides further illumination of this critical Beat text.

To Find Dawn's Moon is published by Felix Culpa Press and can be found at the usual online retailers.

DUNCAN AMONG THE "STARS"

AN ESSAY ON ROBERT DUNCAN'S POETICS OF "OPEN FORM" PART II

BY YORIO HIRANO

TRANSLATED BY MATTHEW MCLAUGHLIN

This is a continuation of an essay begun in *Beatdom #24*.

III. SOARING TO THE "STARS" (CONT.)

Stars are related to his poetic craft. In the poems we have seen so far, we assume that the stars send back these "rimes of light" to the eye of the poem's narrator,[1] and to H.D. who does not have any stars, who has lost both language and song, the narrator asks, "we

---

1 See "Crosses of Harmony and Disharmony" on page 26 of my paper "Duncan Among the 'Stars': An Essay on Robert Duncan's Poetics of 'Open Form'" (Part 1). *Sugiyama Jogakuen University Journal*. Vol. 24. (1993). An English translation of this essay (Part 1) was published in *Beatdom #24: The West Coast Issue* (95-139).

once were too under what star?"[i] No, this is far from having to do with the craft of poetry. These "stars" are one's very "soul" and a "field of ensouling" as Duncan says:

> If the soul is the life-shape of the body, great stars, that are born and have their histories we read in the skies and will die, are souls. And this poetry, the ever forming of bodies in language in which breath moves, is a field of ensouling. Each line, intensely, a soul thing, a contribution; a locality of the living.[ii]

Let us soar off with Duncan to the extremely romantic "starry skies" in which the breath of the "soul" is linked to the lines of the poem.

1. "LONGING"

The star is symbolic of the laws and order that reside within all things. The orderly movement of the stars performs *"the music of the spheres."*

> *The actual stars moving are music in the real world. This is the meaning of the music of the spheres.*[iii]

And there is one "law" under the stars. That law must be the Earth's laws of motion, which correspond to the motions of the galaxies that drift into a new space:

> Best of ways. That there be a law under the stars. For the galaxies drift outward to enter a new universe.[iv]

Therefore, like "The Law"[v] teaches us, there is no final order. This is because there are smaller "laws" which are pulverized by an even larger "Law,"[vi] and it is the poet who unconsciously sings these frightening "laws" that reside intrinsically in all things.[vii] And this is because it is nothing more than the actual "Law" which commands. In order to capture real existence, which sheds its skin like a snake, the "deceitful ... institutions" which coil themselves up, must be violated.[viii]

This kind of poet's covenant is guarded by the starry skies.

O poet! If you would share my way,
come in under the Law, the great Longing.

                *   *   *

        come
   under the Moon, keep
         secret allegiance to the out-pouring stars
                   in Night's courts,

move into the Dance   Whose bonds men hold
   holy: the Light

life lights in like eyes.[ix]

    This Law is longing. This secret covenant to the stars that pour out their light obeys longing. However, it is a longing for what? Is it for holiness? Is it for the dance? Or is it a longing for the harmony that should exist between poets, formed by this covenant to the stars? And while it appears to be all of these things, it is not clear what this actual longing is here. However, "Apprehensions"[x] teaches us that the poet's law-bound longing appears to have something to do with the Watts Tower of Simon Rodia.

    THE DIRECTIVE

    is a building. The architecture of the sentence
        allows
  personal details, portals
  reverent and enchanting,
  constructions from what lies at hand
        to stand
  for what rings true.[xi]

    It is building a noble and attractive "construction" which is composed of "what lies at hand," including "personal details." It is about building "Watts Tower" using words that ring out the truth. Who can say that this is not the longing of the poet? This "construction" is an "island" made from language, a "tower"[xii] which has "the dome of many-colored glass."[xiii] A "hush" which is peculiar to these "high halls" is also absolutely necessary. The holy spirit which descended from up high clearly defines those who are humble.[xiv] It goes without saying that this "construction" is a building of the soul. And the poet, who is the "Sage Architect of the soul and its images,"[xv] is the person to awaken "the proportions and scales of the soul's wonder" about the stars of the sky and the waters of the Earth. While this water flows deep, it must be the water that captures the stars of the spheres. This flow, seen by the narrator of the poem, is the reason for mankind's existence written in the stream when man was still a fish, before letters were born.[xvi] Therefore, this stream that turns into the simultaneous existence of all of Mankind must capture the light of these stars. And the depth of the stream where this "Architect of the soul," that is the poet, should descend to go is even deeper than the depths which store the "jewels" formed by the pressures of the Earth and its inner fires.

> There must be a pool, dark and steady mood,
> stone and water, where this magic crossing,
> this ray of a star, catches in flow
> another time of what we always are,
>
> from which we start up into the live jewel,
> see joy hid where death most is,
> ready like a seed encased in its shell.
> O let the shadows and the light rays mix![xvii]

From deep down in the earth we depart upwards, entering "the live jewel," searching for a hidden joy "where death most is." This is the poet's mission. The hallucinatory visions of the poet pierce through to the lives and deaths of many from long ago, and when he sees that there is "a continent of feeling" that goes beyond our feelings, living in the present,[xviii] we must enter the "big house of the spirit,"[xix] which is a composite body of all the spirits of Mankind that permeate history. "I have seen the jewel"[xx] means the "construction" of an unsurpassably beautiful spirit of what Mankind has given birth to, and what Mankind may potentially generate in future. This place where the jewel will be born is where the stars of the sky and the waters of the Earth meet. Therefore, this longing must surely be a love for this spot or location. "The Apprehensions" brings out a key image that we have seen before and tells of the way that this longing can be fulfilled through the metaphor of music.

the orders of the dead and the unborn that swarm in the floods of a

man embracing his companion;

* * *

the orders magnetic of the jewel that is secreted by the toads and coils

of the brain;

the orders of the Architect building in the Likeness a
    temple;

the orders of the day that include the actual appearance of the pit in

the garden;

the orders of stars and of words;

in these most marvelous.

> There is no life that does not rise
> melodic from scales of the marvelous.
> To which our grief refers.[xxi]

    1) "[T]he orders of the dead and the unborn"; 2) "the orders magnetic of the jewel that is secreted by the toads and coils of the brain"; 3) "the orders of the Architect building in the Likeness a Temple"; 4) "the orders of the day that include the actual appearance of the pit in the garden"; and 5) "the orders of stars and of words" are the (musical) scales, and any kind of living creature obeys the scales of this order, and the poem tells us that they rise as music. In other words, in this place, "the orders of the dead and the unborn" refer to all of Mankind, from the past and the future, and "the orders magnetic of the jewel that is secreted by the toads and coils of the brain" refer to the accord between the highest and the lowest, and the "jewel" where they secretly reside. The "orders of the Architect building in the Likeness a Temple" refers to the release of the soul through building a likeness of the temple that keeps Mankind away from "base servitude."[xxii] The "orders of the day that include the actual appearance of the pit in the garden" suggest the dark depths stored within the "jewel," cut off from sunlight, but something nearby.[xxiii] The "orders of stars and of words" is a vision sung at the top of one's lungs to unify these orders. However, why must this mention of "life" that rises up from the music of the "scales of the marvelous" be

"our grief"? The answer is most likely because these orders that demonstrate the overall harmony of variances or opposites are unfulfilled dreams which are difficult to realize. Therefore, it is by no means easy to fulfill this longing. In fact, it appears that it is not supposed to be easy. Why is this? We must ascertain what is occurring.

"The Structure of Rime" XIX is the longing of the poet-narrator, which takes the form of a "cup" that is raised by a trembling hand. However, the field of vision for this cup of longing has its limits.

> my old longing rises, a raised cup from a
> hand that trembles, where sight itself is a brim of water surrounded
> by waters of what it does not see.[xxiv]

If this field of vision is nothing more than a "brim of water" (in a cup) surrounded by waters that one does not see, this field of vision of longing must surely gaze beyond one's own boundaries. This is where longing must transcend actual longing itself.

In the STRUCTURE OF RIME XX,[xxv] the "Master of Rime"[xxvi] is ordering the poet-narrator to break through the limits of one's own field of vision. He says, "Are you so blind / you cant see what you cant see?"[xxvii] However, for our field of vision to gaze into the unseen world, we must throw away all those things that make the visible world visible. For the narrator-poet, the order from the "Master of Rime" is something harsh. What he is ordering him to do is to throw away the poetic world that he currently possesses:

> You keep the unknown bird hidden in your hands as if to carry sight into the house. But the sightless ones have opend the windows and listen to the songs outside. *Absence*, the Mother of this Blindness tells them, *rimes among the feathers of birds that exist only in ight. The songs you hear fall from their flight light like shadows tars cast among you.*[xxviii]

Here, what is giving the poet-narrator sight is the "unknown bird" that he holds in both of his hands. However, the "Mother of this Blindness" says this to the "sightless ones" who open the window to listen to the songs outside, to those people who cannot hold the bird that the poet-narrator is holding. It is "Absence" that performs the "rimes among the feathers of birds that exist only in sight." The "songs you hear fall from their flight light like shadows stars cast among you" are those things that have scattered down onto the ground from the birds' soaring. What do these mysterious words from the Mother of this Blindness mean? These "birds that exist only in sight" are most likely birds that are visible to the eye but are only emblematic birds with no real physical body. If so, to the "sightless ones," these birds do not exist. What they can hear is nothing more than the songs of birds that do not exist. In that case, they are rimes that echo back and forth from "Absence" to "Absence." However, to the poet-narrator, they "exist only in sight." Therefore, as long as the poet-narrator has sight, he will be unable to hear these rimes that are echoed back and forth from absence to absence. In other words, in order to hear the songs outside, the poet-narrator must release the unknown bird, which is his sight, and become blind. The "Master of Rime" has been saying this from the beginning: "You must learn to lose heart."[xxix] And this is what he has ordered the poet-narrator to do.

> And from the care of your folded hands unfold a feeling in the room of an empty space. For the pit of despair wants you to come there.[xxx]

He is saying to release "a feeling" into the empty space, which is the "bird" of the poet-narrator's vision. The world of the poet-narrator, which was stable due to the bird of his vision, an emotion, must fall into this "pit of despair." This is because the Master of Rime says that the "thrush waits trembling in the confinement of his master's doubt"[xxxi] and that "every bird among the water eaves sings as his brother."[xxxii] If the birds of reality are the poet-narrator's bird, which is a thrush, along with his brothers, then he must release them back to where they came from. However, the Master of Rime who is the "twin lord of the net rime" has been tied "in the tongues of fire."[xxxiii] As a result, even though the bird of vision, which was "a feeling" for the poet-narrator, and the birds of reality are two different things, he had no choice but to lose them. Both hands of the poet-narrator are now empty. In order to see what he cannot, he must throw away altogether the visions of the world that he sees. However, how is this different from the poet-narrator becoming one of the "sightless ones"? This is not merely a matter of losing his vision. The poet-narrator must approach death. When the Master of Rime orders him to "learn to lose [his] heart"[xxxiv] he also means the biological heart. In the sentence that follows, the second order is "let the beat of your heart go. Missing the beat." In other words, to catch the rime that is being performed from absence to absence, the poet-narrator must go so far as to lose his own existence.

This is probably the place where he penetrates the boundary of vision. The poet-narrator possesses an eye that can see the unseen, and the underground waters can reflect the stars in the sky. We should see that hand of the smiling Master of Rime again, who has appeared to him. Just like the hands of the poet-narrator who released the birds into the void, his hands are cupt.

> And the Master of Rime appeared again, smiling. His hands cupt as he went. His head bowd, looking down, seeking his way away from me.[xxxv]

Having learned "despair" with his "head bowd," he sets off dejectedly "seeking his way." He might be the future form of the poet-narrator. This is because both the poet-narrator and the Master of Rime let the birds soar off into the void, and the person who tries to seize the atmosphere with his two empty hands is the "twin" of the poet-narrator.

We should not doubt the fundamental connection between these "stars," "water," "birds," and "what it does not see" and his poetic craft. In order for him to penetrate the boundary of vision by releasing the "birds" that comprise the visible poetic world, he is not only becoming blind, but also putting his life in jeopardy, and the *poet* in Duncan's poetics is someone who waits for the light of the stars to turn into music and descend into his two empty hands. He turns into the underground "water" as he approaches death. It is this person who can understand "the breath of the stars" as the "breath of great Nature," which can become his own "Logos."

> The breath of the stars, moving before the stars,
>   breath of great Nature,   our own,   Logos,
>   that is all   milk and light[xxxvi]

Now we know. The reasons why it is not easy to fulfill this longing are because the poet-narrator must transcend his longing and, more importantly, he is required to penetrate his own

boundaries without fail, in order to fulfill this longing.
2. PENETRATING THE BOUNDARIES
Penetrating the boundaries or "transcending the limits" is intense. "In the Place of a Passage 22"[xxxvii] tells us this. After the poet-narrator who is the "seed" that can only know "the green law of the tree" has extended his "roots" and "life" and "branches" into the "green law" without any obstructions, the poem tells us that this fact which is bound to the law of a "seed" becoming a "tree" demarcates the "boundary" of the poet-narrator.

> the vast universe
> showing only its boundaries we imagine.[xxxviii]

According to this poem, these "boundaries" are the limits of our imaginative capabilities. Therefore, seeking sleep within the tree does not result in decay, but becomes the "light that reaches us from the first days of the cosmos" and from the "Grand Mother of Images" that flares up, the poet-narrator should "draw[...] such milk" to have the necessary nutrients in order to transcend the boundaries. Sure enough, he who has become the "tree" causes the "shadow" of the poet-narrator to "waver." Through a condensation of the animal and mammalian elements within the poet-narrator, the days of the poet-narrator who stays deep within the shadows become uncertain. However, it is this uncertainty that is the key to transcending his own "boundaries" as the "tree." The poet-narrator must "draw" this "milk" from "the mother of stars."

> the shadow of a tree wavering and yet staying
> deep in it,
> the certain number of his days renderd uncertain,
> gathering,
> animal and mammal,   drawing such milk
> from the mother of stars.[xxxix]

What this means is there is no way the boundaries can be transgressed when one is at peace with the "green law" in which the seed becomes the tree.

In the poem we just looked at, it is "the mother of stars" who helps transgress the boundaries, which is what the stars command. In "Transgressing the Real, Passages 27,"[xl] a "canopy of night" which wields a "diamond radiance" within the "cluster of stars" overhead is made, and the poet-narrator who sees there the "light or joy of intellectual brilliance" declares the following: "my thoughts are servants of the stars."

> for my thoughts are servants of the stars, and my words
>   (all parentheses opening into
>   come from a mouth that is the Universe   *la bouche d'ombre*[xli]

And he says "my words" come out of the "mouth" of the "Universe." What kind of splendid unity with the universe is this? In this complete unity, the "mouth of darkness" (*la bouche d'ombre*) means the darkness of space in the cosmos and at the same time means the darkness within the mouth of the poet-narrator. However, this "mouth of darkness" might also be "the mouths of ghosts." In order for the "mouth" of the poet-narrator to be united with the universe, he must be made giant beyond the size of the cosmos, and as a result, the poet-narrator loses his existence as an individual because he has no choice but to become the "mouths of ghosts" hiding within the shadows of the mouth. This is when the poet-narrator hides his form within the poem that is emitted from the "mouth of the universe," making the poet-narrator someone who cannot be seen. As was expected, he becomes invisible and speaks as if the world were speaking.

> (under the cloak of his poem   *he* retires
>   invisible
>   so that it seems no man   but a world speaks[xlii]

However, even though transgressing the boundaries through becoming one with the universe appears to be something of extreme happiness, what we must acknowledge is that this comes with the danger of losing one's self. It is also true that he can envision these supreme matters by taking this very risk.

    The poet-narrator knows that integrating the visible and invisible worlds is the same as governing the stars.[xliii] The sea that the poet-narrator overlooks from the heights of the "endless tower" that he has reached through "faith" looks like the "clear blue" of the Virgin Mary that looks over us. These heights that "transcend language" that the poet-narrator sees are the "President of the Grand Symphony."

> From the height of the tower that has no roof:
> I have seen the ship of shadows cross the sea of light
>
> / and, beyond words,
>
> I have contemplated the Regulator of the Stars,
>   Commissar of Invisible and Visible Worlds.
>
>   The President of the Grand Symphony[xliv]

  The heights that the poet-narrator has reached transcend the visionary bounds of Dante's *Paradiso*, contemplating God, the threshold of confession, in which one cannot express God through words.[xlv] Therefore, the "President of the Grand Symphony" who regulates the "Invisible and Visible Worlds," controlling the "stars" that constitute the order of the universe, is undoubtedly just another name for God. For Duncan, though, this God is always the God of Poesy. This means that the "President of the Grand Symphony," who manifests Himself to relinquish the contraries of the visible / invisible, is the God of Poesy who above all else supports Duncan's poetic practice of developing the void between the "right and left hands" and between the "right and left eye." Therefore, the "President of the Grand Symphony" that the poet-narrator sees at the Empyrean that he has reached through "faith" must not be far removed from the "the Whole" that he saw in the "Watts Tower."[2]

  However, the road to the "the Whole" is long. "Epilogos," which closes *Bending the Bow* with "like entering the words that the old man had long awaited" as its epigraph,[xlvi] is a poem that laments the inability to contain the "feeling" that the "tree," which metaphorically stands for the possibilities of the poet-narrator, and the "cup" which is a metaphor for his soul, become and return as "rivers," "stars," and "birds."

>   The speech comes back to where it left off

---

2 For more information on "Watts Tower," see pages 25-26 of my paper "Duncan Among the 'Stars': An Essay on Robert Duncan's Poetics of 'Open Form'" (Part 1). *Sugiyama Jogakuen University Journal*. Vol. 24. (1993). An English translation of this essay (Part 1) was published in *Beatdom #24: The West Coast Issue* (95-139).

>   in me.   A tree, a cup,
> cannot contain themselves for a feeling that
> returns in whatever it can—a river,
>   a single star,
> a bird I cannot see sings—
> and I would rehearse the sounds of the names of
>   everything
> to release this old necessity and shake
>   with its need.[xlvii]

"[T]his old necessity" is his "feeling" that takes root within the poem but for the poet-narrator who is aware that he is approaching death while this remains unfinished, as suspected, there is no other path for escaping these "moans" than through language. The poet-narrator is a man of language who is propelled forward by the "Word."

>   The Word moves me.   I give in to it.
> I give into it my will, into it
> the intent of the poem.[xlviii]

In order for the "feeling" that does not take root to do so, the poet-narrator must walk into the language, just like the old man in the Epigraph. In fact, he must continue to fly towards the "the Whole" that the "President of the Grand Symphony" knows.

However, when will the poet-narrator arrive at "the Whole"? The one thing he knows is that he should obey the commands of the stars. He has already decided that he is ready for them. This is because he has declared that he has accepted having his heart broken, if it means obeying the commands of the stars.

>   I saw
> willingly the strain of my heart break
>   and pour its blood thundering at the life-locks
>
> to release   full   my man's share of the stars'
>
>   majesty   thwarted.[xlix]

This is where the poet-narrator chooses to die as a martyr

at the stars' command, being unable to stand the "majesty of the stars" being warped by man. We should take a look at "O! Passages 37."[l] For this poet-narrator, under the starry sky, uttering poems after transforming into "the world cow" is unbounded happiness. There is a splendid overlap between how the songs are born from the "tip of the tongue" of the poet-narrator and the "calf," which is the poem, born from "the world cow."

>   The tip
> of the tongue
>   before the mouth sings,
>   in labor
> the world cow's lips
>   from which
>   *   *   *
>
>   her dewy calf
> from his confinement
>   the poem from the heart in labor
>
>   springs.[li]

After the "labor" pains, we must know the joy of the "song" which is represented by the "calf," which is the "poem" that "springs." What the poet-narrator is hoping for is to catch the "scent" of "these stars."

>   These stars
> are fragrant and I follow their scent.
> I am their hunting hound,
>
>   predator of the marvelous.[lii]

The poet-narrator, who is the "predator of the marvelous," feels with his soul the "hues" and "scents" of the stars, like a "music" given off by the flowers. This is the "pivot" within the "torrent" that overflows within him. This is precisely what the poetic craft is to the poet-narrator.

However, no matter how determined he is to martyr himself to "the command of the stars," is it not fundamentally impossible for the poet-narrator to realize "the Whole"? What this means is that a single poem in one verse will be judged on whether it is sufficient as one "individual" or whether it conforms with the supreme goal indicated by the Whole. And because the Whole is only part of the imaginative capabilities of the individual, whether a collection of individuals will be able to form a whole, a *Whole* will be unclear until the point when the poet stops composing individual poems. In other words, as long as the writer continues to be a writer, the realization of the Whole is postponed. Furthermore, this Whole is not only all of Duncan's collective works as a writer, but when it also refers to "the Whole of civilization" it is impossible to judge the form of this Whole without first waiting for the end of civilization. What appears here is the assumed need for a "reader" at this end of the world. In other words, when no single person is left able to judge the form of the Whole, we encounter an extremely paradoxical situation in which we can ask whether the Whole has been formed or not.

Therefore, we only have recourse to an approval of the direct experience by imagining the Whole. "We" who cannot hold the Whole of civilization inside of us have no other choice than to assume that our imagination of the Whole is a "pivot" towards it.

> and only in the imagination of the Whole
> the immediate percept is
> to be justified—Imagining
> this
> pivot of a totality
> having
> no total thing in us, we so
> live beyond ourselves
> --and in this unitive.[liii]

This is because the "sum is beyond us."[liv] This "sum" is about poetic craft entering "into the Process of Man" in order to form "the Whole."[lv] And this is not inside of us, but the "pivot of what we are doing" that "sing(s)."[lvi] If the poem captures the harmony, he must have fulfilled the "command of the stars" which was to break through the boundaries.

3. INVADER OF THE SKIES

The best way to fulfill the "command of the stars" is for the poet-narrator to turn into a bird and break through the boundaries, reaching the starry skies. It is the very order of the starry skies that embodies "the Whole" because the starry skies are its emblem. We must feel this in the pulsating rhythm of "Letting the Beat Go" which closes Book One of Dante Études.

LETTING THE BEAT GO

Letting the beat go,
the eagle, we know, does not
soar to the stars, he rides
the boundaries of the air –

but let the "eagle"
soar to the stars! there
where he's "sent"![lvii]

The eagle that dances in the sky transgresses several boundaries of the air but is not yet ascending vertically. It is not enough to take in the scent of the stars and realize the order of the starry skies through making the poem. This is the place where the poet-narrator orders the eagle to soar upward to the starry skies. As the starry skies are assumed to be "blazons … of a high glamor,"[lviii] soaring to these skies is impossible without elevating an "increasing exaltation."[lix] To the poet-narrator, the way the eagle circles around as he soars looks like he is building a tower. The starry skies towards which the eagle is soaring is infinite space. The top of the "tower" being built by the eagle pierces through these starry skies, which means infinite space, as the eagle bursts into the middle of the Whole. However, the poet-narrator is drifting in the space between the starry skies and the ground, and so he does not reach the starry skies like the eagle. He looks down upon "the 'facts' of the world," such as "the glutted cities" and the "choked streams," dancing mid-air.[lx] The poet-narrator can only wish to attain the heights reached by the eagle, and his soaring, which can penetrate through to the starry skies, has to be put off. This is how the poem concludes:

"high",
beyond this matter of our speech here,
into this furthest reach, this

incidence of a rapacious

silence,

gnostic invader of the "Sky"!^{lxi}

We should look at the complexity of the heights reached by the poet-narrator. He is supposed to be drifting mid-air, looking down over "the 'facts' of this world."^{lxii} Judging from the context, even though the quoted "here" ought to refer to the poet-narrator drifting mid-air, beyond "our conversation," we cannot read it as this, but we must take this "this" to mean instead the "ground" which modifies our "speech." Therefore, even though the first of these three "this" words is trying to go beyond the ground, it refers to the contradictory limitation of being earthbound. As the second "this" refers to the cap, or "furthest place" from the Earth, it refers to the place mid-air to which the poet-narrator has soared, and must refer to somewhere near to the poet-narrator in the air. However, this "furthest place" is "the furthest place" that his field of vision can reach, in other words a point that is not invisible in the "starry skies" to which the eagle has soared. And if we assume that the "incidence of a [rapacious] silence" that the third "this" refers to is the "invader of the 'Sky,'" not only does this incidence refer to the poet-narrator flying mid-air, but also means the adventurous visions of the poet-narrator looking over the eagle's soaring to the starry skies. And we can also see that it speaks of an invasion into the territory of the silence of the starry skies by the poet-narrator and the eagle. The "this" which is supposed to refer to somewhere close gradually shifts from the ground to mid-air, and from mid-air to the starry skies. The poem is written so that progressively the heights to which the subject soars, through a fusion of the eagle with the poet-narrator, go further upward. It is the poet-narrator who wishes to reach the starry skies more than anybody.

However, how should we perceive the vision of the Whole which in principle cannot be reached? And what is the extremity indicated by the starry skies?

The "Eidolon of the Aion"^{lxiii} provides an answer to these questions. The poet-narrator who calls out "who are you?" to the "[i]mpersonator of a universe / root-voice of first dream," after calling to the "Dark Star" which ties together an unknown "you" to the incidences in a configuration, says the following in what appears to be something he has finally recalled:

> I remember,　O　I return
> IT
> constantly recurring
> transcends its inner organization
> The fundamental unit of (this) music
> not the note but the series as a whole:
> TOTAL
> involving every note in a piece
> overrides
> independent of tempo
> and does not conform to a regular unit —[lxiv]

The poet-narrator "remembers" and this "IT" that he is trying to return to is the laws of that universe, the roots of his poetic craft. While it is a "TOTAL" that includes various elements, this "IT" is also the laws of the universe and the poem that goes beyond the structures of the whole. We cannot help imagining this to mean the end of the "transcended boundaries." We might say that this "IT" is the same supreme being as "the President of the Grand Symphony" that we saw in "Eye of God, Passages 29." However, the poet-narrator in "Eye of God, Passages 29" reached Dantesque heights through "faith" and the god of Dante's poesy was praised as "the President of the Grand Symphony." However, in this poem, the poet-narrator must not miss this point of "here / now," or a point in the process of making the poem, which remains unchanged as the laws of space and the laws of poetry, which constitute exactly the same principle—a principle that transcends its own organization. This principle of "IT" is neither theological nor divine. The poem tells us that in order for "thought" which had been split into two to return once again as one "thought," it is persistently this principle of making two into one, through the blind sexual union of lovers.

        as Eidolon of the AION
            you would return
      the two halves of the one thought
           close in their   knot, nut, noeud,

     as if only in this moment   lovers
         but "making" love   blindly

    form the shell to enclose
        --so I *do* know what *IT* is—
        the round of all meetings,   all
                coming together
    in the sweetness of a note growing[lxv]

    The principle of "IT" is meeting amidst the beauty ("sweetness") of a "note" in which everything is growing. What could this be other than a vision of the Whole, or "the Ensemble," in the form of the process? If this is true, there can be nothing beyond this vision. This is because one poet has reached the ultimate point that he can reach within the poem. This is not only the end of his career as a poet, but also because this is a process generated by components or "individuals" that comprise the TOTAL, the inescapable abstraction of when he tries to capture within the verse of one poem the Whole, something which he must continually postpone until the end of civilization, changes into longing which gives off the scent of abstraction, and this is the ultimate POEM.

    Therefore, in the indescribably beautiful serial poem "VEIL, TURBINE, CORD & BIRD,"[lxvi] which was written after this ultimate poem, we are unable to distinguish between the music performed at this place where we used to be and "Miraflor," which is assumed to be a "star" despite its ghostly beauty. In other words, the star is no longer in a sky towards which we should soar.

THE RECALL OF THE STAR MIRAFLOR

            1
      The turban and the veil
      lead us to the turbine in the vale

> 2
> where we have been before
> flowers forever bloom—it is the dale of profusions,
> of the mind's lingering, of the heart's stop,
> here, where perfumes and colors pour,
> here, where the magic top spins,
>
> 3
> Miraflor
>
> 4
> is the name of the place we were
> --you and I are—in this music
> for *Ever*?[lxvii]

Led by the customs of the "turban" and "veil" of exotic countries, we visit "the turbine in the vale," words which share almost the same pronunciation, a place where we were once happy—a "dale of profusions" where "flowers forever bloom," a place the mind does not try to leave, where the heart stops, "where perfumes and colors pour", and "where the magic top spins"—and because we call it "Miraflor," the so-called "Miraflor" star is a "longing" for this place of bliss. This cyclical "longing" is subtly suggested through the cyclical syntax of the first verse which weaves together the same original sounds of "turban" and "turbine," and "veil" and "vale." The "morning bird" who sings the songs of "our lives"[lxviii] invites us to our vale of bliss. The poem tells us that the song of this "morning bird" which is "awakening each day / beyond in us,"[lxix] is "Miraflor."

> Miraflor is thy song
> to us ever venturing
> tones we hear[lxx]

It is a place of happiness, and also a "longing" for a place of happiness, and Miraflor which is the singing voice of the "morning bird" which awakens the "beyond" in us is also assumed to be a star-nest of various birds.[lxxi] Words dance on top of other words and disappear, and "Miraflor" is where the ghostly poem is born as the "radiant message." Within this mirage, the bird has seen the poet-narrator and his spirit return cyclically to the "large cup in which various voids are present."

> I pour forth my life
> ever light star magic bird
> being cord veil and turbine,
> transmitter of retractions and emissions
> in the course of things
> recoursing, sounding changes, things resounding,
>
> so that the source has changed in me
> and what was bound to be is free
> --so said the bird upon the tree[lxxii]

What the bird says is that it is just one "star [...] bird" in its own "Miraflor" nest and this is the very title of this serial poem, which is an apparatus for producing poems. However, the existence of this bird is too faint to be called real. It is nothing more than "the shape drawn within the grass pattern of the veil," and even the branch that the bird alights upon is nothing more than "embroidery" in the veil to "put over or take away" for the "soul-drenched song." In spite of this, at the end of the "VEIL, TURBINE, CORD & BIRD" serial poem, the poet-narrator along with the faintly present bird loudly declare that they are servants of "Miraflor," the "bright star," the power of song.

> For I your boy of brass bright star the force[lxxiii]

Here, "Miraflor" which we assume is the "bright star," has come to be called a variety of things: "the dale of profusions," a "longing" for a place of bliss, "the morning-bird's song" to "awaken [...] each day / beyond in us," a "starnest of every bird" and "my guiding hand." However, its true character can be nothing other than the "longing" as a mother that gives birth to the poem that goes beyond oneself.

In other words, after "Eidolon of the Aion" which indicates the ultimate point, the star is not in the sky beyond but resides within the poet-narrator as "a force of longing that gives birth to the poem" and also something that orients towards the beyond. If this is so, then what we should ask is not *what* is this starry sky beyond, but *where* is this starry sky beyond.

IV. THE STARRY SKIES OF THE "BEYOND" / "BEYOND" THE STARRY SKIES
1. THE STARRY SKIES OF THE "BEYOND"

The starry skies beyond are the poetics of the ultimate made up of the laws of space and the laws of poetry. They are the poetics of the Whole. However, they materialize within the text. The poetics of the Whole has shed light on the metaphor of the starry skies from a variety of angles. The above is the generation of "eternity" mentioned in Chapter I of this paper's discussion, and to talk about its relationship to reading Whitman in Chapter I Section 2, what we saw in the starry skies above we could say is where the philosophy of the "Ensemble," which supports Whitman's theory of democracy, and the Neo-Platonism that pervades Dante's *De Monarchia*, fuse together.[3] What the poet-narrator saw in the starry skies when he transformed into a bird and soared off was everything in multitudes. Be it "Nature" in Whitman, or be it "God" in Dante, the ultimate point where they fuse together as one is the "IT" in "Eidolon of the Aion."

However, perhaps he is not supposed to reach this point. This is because reaching this ultimate point means the end of a process in which a poem turns into Poetry, a man becomes Man, and an individual becomes Whole, with the likely result of the poet-narrator's death. This is because if we assume the Whole to refer to all of civilization, the only result can be the end of the world. The poet-narrator, Duncan, civilization, and space must not meet the end. The ultimate point should reside within the imagination only.

Duncan himself knew this better than anyone else. It limits itself to an extremely abstract expression of mastering the ultimate IT, which integrates the right and left hand, and the visible and invisible; not something that could be expressed in specific terms in the first place. His being unable to capture the image of the right eye and left eye as one, and the right and left hands together constituting a void, were all in order to put off the ultimate IT. That is why Duncan's bird had to continue to soar mid-air forever between the ground and the starry skies.

Now is the time for the gaze to be shifted from the starry skies beyond to beyond the starry skies.

---

3   See pages 3-4 of my paper "Duncan Among the 'Stars'"" in *Sugiyama Jogakuen University Journal*. Vol. 24. (1993) or *Beatdom #24* (95-139).

2. BEYOND THE STARRY SKIES

This ultimate IT that we saw along with Duncan is something which surprisingly extends out further. What orients the "beyond" is the "Intention of a Universe."

>   but Now   is wedded thruout to   the Intention of a Universe.
>   Verse,   linkt to the Idea of that Governance,
>   moves "beyond";[lxxiv]

Having said that, even if "Now" is linked to this Intention of a Universe, the beyond that the poem should be aiming for under its governance is not identified in "Jamais." This poem tries to point out matters that cannot be named, through a privileged series of abstract concepts—silence, the eternal, inertia—but in the end it fails to accomplish this, and the poem closes very abruptly.

>   Love
>
>   flings itself forward
>   at sea   in its work   harmony   dark-wingd
>   creature of the air
>
>   "the"[lxxv]

The God of Love flings itself into the sea, manifesting its "harmony" in its "work," changing into a "dark-wingd / creature of the air," and the way this poem ends, it is hard for us to say whether the beyond has been actually defined or not, leaving the reader at a loss. However, when it comes before "The Dignities [Passages],"[lxxvi] the reader must be at even more of a loss. This means that we can develop the theory that as long as the poet-narrator is not Whole, he cannot fully capture the object of his vision. Following this line of reasoning, there is no way around this: every recognition becomes dubious. Therefore, the supremacy of this ultimate IT that we see in "Eidolon of the Aion" becomes doubtful, and this "What Is" of reality becomes nothing more than a hypothesis on top of reality for the poet-narrator who is incomplete.

> I ... liberal, radical, pluralistic, multiphasic   my mind   most
> a part   not whole   nowhere total, no "where" to be fulfilld—
> the *Virtu* of What Is is prepositional   realms within realms secreted
>   "seem."[lxxvii]

However, this is a hypothesis and the issue of the poem for the poet-narrator is continuing to sing "Gloria." This is how "The Dignities [Passages]" wraps up:

> there is this last voice, first voice this   "Gloria"   this one beginning
>   flower of song
>   this lingering of a scent in every thing.[lxxviii]

This "What is complete," to begin with, was nothing more than an illusion. In addition, the truth that we know is nothing more than "truth's rumors," so what we can do is listen to "the wind heard" and float into Eternity while calling the Muse.

> 　　　　　　　　　　　　　　　our having
> 　　　no more than truth's rumors and our learning no knowing is
> 　　　　broken themes in passages of the wind heard
> Erato   here   Muse of the Kithara, sing for me   sing me blowing
>   upon that reed
> yet the charge of a note coming into our histories   that allure touching
>   songs rise and fall   enchanting   what government regulates
>   this state of Mind   the beat steady   where we wonder.[lxxix]

However, we must not think of this as a withdrawal of the poem from the ultimate point. It suffices to look at the threshold of this ghostly poem, where the section from "yet" onwards dissolves into the void. The "wind" of the poetic craft blown "upon that reed" becomes a "song" that vibrates on the harp and enters "our history," and is this not our resolute existence above the ground as we go drifting along? If this is so, this "beyond" of the starry skies ought to refer to this "above the ground." To put it more precisely, it ought to mean "above the ground" in the form of the "starry skies."

However, Duncan's poem asserts that there is a further beyond. The poem "AT the Door" says that this "ground," which means "the ground of poetry," opens to the "beyond" within the poet-narrator. And it is through his "fall" to the beyond that he wishes for the actual text that he is writing be fused with something holy.

> Pass on.   In the passage beyond   faire mon habitation
> I pass out in reading   divine the text   intoxicate
>   mine to divine.[lxxx]

In other words, this "beyond" of the starry skies is the point where the poet-narrator's text and the "divine" fuse together in the ultimate. The "above the ground" which has become the "starry skies" is undoubtedly at some remove from this point. But what kind of locus is it actually, at the point where his text fuses with the "divine"? Also, is this beyond a point that can connect with an image inside the poem?

In order to answer this question, we should once again consider the topic of "transgressing boundaries" in Duncan's poetics.

Duncan's poetics assume the transgression of boundaries to be a supreme command:

> *tree that you are, toward a foliage that breaks at the boundaries of known things.*
> ("THE STRUCTURE OF RIME VII," *The Opening of the Field*, 20)

> the vast universe / showing only its boundaries we imagine.
> ("IN THE PLACE OF A PASSAGE 22," *Bending the Bow*, 74)

> They [the workers] must go beyond the bounds of their art.
> ("STRUCTURE OF RIME XXVII," *Ground Work: Before the War*, 55)

With the purpose of transgressing the boundaries, in "Structure of Rime" XV, XVI, XVII, the bestiality that resides within oneself is confirmed in the shape of the lion,[4] which then transforms into a bird, and this soaring away from bestiality is portrayed in "Structure of Rime" XVIII and XIX (*Roots and Branches*, 67, 169-

---

4   The poet-narrator of "The Structure of Rime" XV dances around wearing the mask of a mandrill, and communicates with a lioness. The poet-narrator of XVI enters the body of the animal, and with an erect penis returns back to the "source" while dancing in time to the music. In XVII, the poet-narrator turns into Kundry, drinks Helen's aphrodisiac, and knows the anger in the eyes of the lioness.

70)⁵. In "Structure of Rime" XXV (*Bending the Bow*, 37) the poem is born at the very point where the inner bestiality blends with the human voice; this is the Robert Duncan who descended to his resolute inner self and soared to the skies. However, in the end, the Master of Rime makes Duncan descend from "the ladder of vision."

> the fierce sparrow nests down meek in the cold of the blast
>   the tiger seeks shelter from his element of fire
>   Who then sings this
> sweet song? Who then roars?
>
>   Who then is this passion
> that returns for me?   who then
>   that remembers and goes back for me?
>
> "I" – "me" no longer mine --your
>   sudden call I did not mean
>   to climb the ladder of
>
>   Feb. 19, 1982[lxxxi]

  This means that the sparrow no longer soars and the tiger that metaphorically represents the fire of the soul evades its own essence and cannot spur on the poet-narrator. Even if there is passion that cyclically returns to the poet-narrator, the feeling that can respond to the call of this passion is no longer inside him. He no longer tries to climb "the ladder of vision."

  Not answering the call from within his own poem, the poet-narrator seems to have given up writing the poem with his own force and within the poem "Close," written on the same day—February 19, 1982—now that he has reached the final stage of his poetic work, he awaits the words that will issue from his own lips.

---

5 The poet-narrator of "The Structure of Rime" XVIII depicts the figure of a person wearing a dog and mandrill mask dancing along to the music of Wagner, and a sparrow flying between the branches of a firethorn. The poet-narrator of XIX depicts a "phantom cup" for a "surviving artist" who tries to see "the invisible."

CLOSE

> At the brim,   at the lip
> the water   the word   trembles   fills
> to flooding   every thing[lxxxii]

Here, the secret of "the water" is assumed to be the torrent that floods "every thing," and "the word" that trembles and fills "every thing" is not within time but fills time to its last reaches.[lxxxiii] This "mystery" is referred to as the "force before the gods came," the "wish," and "the daimon of this field"[lxxxiv] but what it actually is remains unclear. This "mysterious force" must unmistakably be a force that gives an orientation towards the beyond. That is why the poet-narrator is left waiting for the arrival of something that transcends what is given. And the poet-narrator who approaches the conclusion of this poem thinks of his whole poetic oeuvre as a "cultivation of unreality" and tells us that his own existence will probably not be recognized within history and sheds a tear.

> History
> will disprove my existence.
>
> The Book will not hold his poetry   yet
>   all the vain song I've sung comes into it
>
>   spirit-bird cuckoo's   Song of Songs
> one tear of vexation as if it were beautiful
>
>   falls into the elixir
>
> one tear of infatuation follows
>   as if it were love
>
> Let something we must all wonder about   ensue
>
>   one tear I cannot account for   fall
>
> this: flooding into the flooding
>
> this: the gleam of the bowl in its not holding—
>
>   Feb. 19, 1982[lxxxv]

History will not just disprove his existence. If we assume that "what is ultimately written" will not accept his poem, the "Song of Songs" sung by his "spirit-bird" has no recourse other than to disappear into the void. One "tear of vexation" falls into the elixir "as if it were beautiful," wishing it to turn into gold, that this "tear of infatuation follows" as if it were love, as Duncan (the poet-narrator) reminisces back upon his whole poetic oeuvre. However, the tear that he "cannot account for" is one that surprisingly brings something "we must all wonder about." And this final tear is probably a tear because he tried to capture unsuccessfully the flooding forces of nature. And what had intended to be "the gleam of the bowl in its not holding" is also a "tear" because it was not able to hold it all. Therefore, this final tear is unmistakably a lament in which he confesses that he was heading straight for the ultimate poem but was unable to attain it. That's why through the forces of nature that were overflowing within him, both body and mind, it is to this very point where the poem "gleams" in "the bowl" of the void, made between his right and left hands, that all of Duncan's poem aspires. And that's where he wished his oeuvre to converge. It goes without saying that this point is the beyond past the IT from "Eidolon of the Aion."

This point is where the text changes to something divine. The beyond in the starry skies is the beyond of the text, and is the place where the divine power, which renders the text holy, resides. But we must not call this divine power "God" because while Duncan is a poet who continues to soar towards the residence of this divine force, he is not a religious poet. However, how can he arrive at this beyond which is nothing more than "God's …hint at the Sublime"?

--"God"'s but Mind's hint at the Sublime
I'd not think to surpass[lxxxvi]

In spite of this, Duncan's poetic craft eternally tries to listen to himself and the poem, heading towards the beyond of the starry skies, which in principle he cannot reach. In his poetic text, Duncan is attempting the following: 1) trying to catch the stars of the beyond in their descent from above ground to underground; 2) waiting to hold in both of his empty hands on the ground the descent of the starry skies of the beyond into the air; 3) soaring to the starry skies beyond the ground of the earth; 4) returning to the starry ground from the starry skies of the beyond; and 5) trying to reach beyond the starry skies. In other words, it is a continual effort to boldly recapture or usurp Poetry from within the poem.

Therefore, there is no end to Duncan's poetic craft. If the end were to finally come, that would only be at the time of the writer's (i.e. Duncan's) death but death is not the ultimate of anything. The writer can only expand his life by heading towards the world of death, where the only thing that will arise is "eternal arrest." It suffices to look at the final line of the poem that closes Duncan's total poetic output.

> In the real I have always known myself
> in this realm where no Wind   stirs
>   no Night
> turns in turn to Day,   the Pool of the motionless water,
>   the absolute Stillness.   In the World, death after death.
> In this realm,   no last thrall of Life stirs.
>   The imagination alone knows this condition.
> As if this were before the War,   before
>   What Is,in the dark this state
> that knows nor sleep nor waking, nor dream
>   --an eternal arrest.[lxxxvii]

In "this realm" where the poet-narrator is in reality, no wind blows and night does not turn into day; there is just "the Pool of the motionless water." In other words, "the absolute Stillness." It is like this "eternal arrest" before the "war" of making poetry and before soaring to "What Is" is right in front of us here now. In that case, what was Duncan's entire poetic oeuvre? In these ten or so lines that begin with, "In the real I have always known myself / in this realm," and conclude with "this state [of eternal arrest] that knows nor sleep nor waking, nor dream," does it not appear as if Duncan is confessing that his whole poetic oeuvre comes to nothing?

Even when we reach the very end, Duncan does not try to head towards a final destination; his poem is still opening outwards. The philosophy of "field composition," also known as "open form," makes Duncan bear the burden of it being "open" from beginning to end. However, the result of the poetic act of trying to be endlessly "open," removing any ultimate point, may be nothing more than a prayer assuming that the writer's life and whole poetic works have formed a part of civilization at the end of all human history. In other words, it is a prayer with the connotations of "ultimate writings." This is because open form is when the surface level of the poetic text does not close its parentheses and it is a philosophical way of seeing poetry as a process. Aesthetically, it is about each individual verse actively "shining" at the atomic level without it converging anywhere.

Duncan's poem, which tries to be "open" from start to finish, opens out in the direction of the beyond that transcends the ultimate IT reached in "Eidolon of the Aion." At this point, Duncan takes the step towards the beyond of his planned harmonic world view, at the center of which lies his vision which is a convergence within his poem of the point where Whitman's nature and Dante's God are fused together. This beyond is one of time and space that he does not know and above all else is a beyond of his own poem. What Duncan reaches in his final poem, "After a Long Illness," must be none other than this locus. And at the edge of this beyond, it is impossible for there to be anything other than a vacuum.

If that is so, we who have seen a vacuum at the ultimate point beyond the starry skies must now go back to the starry skies once again. However, this time it is not to the starry skies of the beyond, but towards the Duncan of the starry skies.

V. DUNCAN OF THE "STARRY SKIES"

Duncan of the starry skies envisions a "city" that is given a shape in the starry skies by poets and it is Duncan who is trying to enter it. That's why what we should consider here at the end is this main topic of the *city* for Duncan. We ought to be able to find answers to the questions: "Where does the text shift to something divine?" and "What is the ultimate point of the beyond?"

Duncan's city is a city within the soul of Mankind. The model for Duncan's city is Wagadu, which continues to live on to this day in our hearts, as it fell four times to vanity, falsehood, avarice, and strife and each time it was rebuilt.

> Gassire's lute, the song
> of Wagadu, household of the folk,
> commune of communes
> hidden seed in the hearts of men
> and in each woman's womb hidden.[lxxxviii]

The poem says that the "song / of Wagadu" performed by "Gassire's lute" is the song of the folk, which means the "commune of communes" which lies "in the hearts of men" and "in each woman's womb." It goes on to say that man's goodness lies in the community of every thing and that the "character" that lies within the great household in the hearts of living beings is the character of Mankind. In other words, the city is first linked to the principle that it lies within the hearts of men. Therefore, for people who are working hard on their life's work in the noisy metropolis, this city can exist even within their room.

> And we have made a station of the way to the hidden city in the rooms where we are.[lxxxix]

If we assume that the "we" in the quotation are the people who are trying to make "the grand opus of their humanity,"[xc] then the city means something that has ties to a positive creative spirit.

However, "Dante Études" clearly teaches us more about what this city means. It means that through a reading of Dante's texts—*De Vulgari Eloquentia*, *De Monarchia*, *Convivio*, and *Epistles*—the central topic of Duncan's serial poem, which is a confirmation and verification of the grounds for his own poem and the direction in which it is heading, is the building of this city within the heart. After "The Work," which is assumed to be the realization of his innate capabilities as an individual, the city appears when everyone strives fully to realize his own capabilities towards "the good of the whole." He has a feeling of a sense of unity with the cosmos before the word, that is the old layers of history, and using this, he captures "the old oracular voice."[xci] By writing the voice he can soar to the starry skies. "Dante Études" says that the city is grounds for the manifestation of the sum of all the harmonious force.

> ... for the sweetness
> of the whole harmony
> the city designd.[xcii]

The starry skies to which the eagle has soared were this city.

> for this (polity)
> can never be attaind without
> strenuous effort of genius,
> constant practice in the art
> (of government)   (of lines, stanzas)

> and the habit of the sciences."
>
> --the eagle
>
> soaring to the stars.[xciii]

At the end of his movement, which opens up outwards endlessly, becoming a citizen of this city is his final goal and wish as the poet-narrator.

Residents of the starry skies are great poets—here we can assume that this is Dante and Shakespeare. Joining their spirits and their "sublime community" means becoming a citizen of this city.

>   his mind
> ours   a sublime community[xciv]

The poem goes on to tell us that this community of sublime creative spirits comprises the core of this city and has the driving force which can give birth to "civilization."

> the "city" is
> *civitas*
> civil in this
> a civilization depending upon each
>   one   in time
> having his right
>   one poetry
> the poem belongs to—[xcv]

As the quotation says, civilization rests on the shoulders of each individual. However, when the innate capabilities of each individual bloom and come together as civilization manifests, civilization should transcend individual capabilities. In Duncan's texts, the process of the individual becoming the whole, the poem becoming Poetry, and man becoming Man is eternally opening outwards. At the same time, Duncan's texts are an endless fight to recapture or usurp the individual from the whole, the poem from Poetry, man from Man, with no end in sight. By entering the process of becoming "Man,"[xcvi] while he envisions his own poem becoming Poetry, he continues to soar towards the city of the starry skies which is comprised of each individual "star" of the great poets. The above is what his serial poem "Dante Études" tells us.

On the other hand, there is an incredibly dangerous aspect to this soaring. When Duncan opens himself outwards as a poet, when he opens himself towards the poets, but because of this obsession with the city of the starry skies, his counterpart towards which he opens himself, the union he envisions is excessively erotic. For example, there is his kiss with William Blake. The poet-narrator of "Variations on Two Dicta of William Blake" calls Blake, who moves his own hand as a "bright star,"[xcvii] and he sees himself inside of Blake.

> I recognized in you my own presence
> beyond touch, within being.[xcviii]

The poet-narrator has not only entered the body of William Blake, for Blake has also entered inside of him, to the point where distinguishing between oneself and another has become meaningless.

> I do not dare
> rescue myself in you
> or you in me.[xcix]

If we were to say what caused this mutual invasion between Blake and the poet-narrator, he himself is "only a factor" of what he is and nothing more, and through the authors that came both before and after the author, this person who pushes forward towards "the eternal / sparks of desire" is the poet-narrator. And this is because the quotation below from Duncan's "Traditions" draws its inspiration from two lines from Blake used as an epigraph for the poem: "Mental things alone are real" and "The Authors are in Eternity."

> What I am is only a factor of what I am.
> The authors of the author
> before and after
> wait for me to restore
> (I had only to touch you then)
> the way to the eternal
> sparks of desire.[c]

After this, the poem proceeds towards a feeling of connection that transcends space and time between these authors. The eye sees beyond what it can see, as he must know the joy of "the inner world" and "outer world" becoming one.[ci] Responding to the call of "the lineaments of eternity" which are carved into the human brain,[cii] the poem tells us that it manages to "transgress boundaries" and must awaken the "sensory chains between being and being."[ciii] The poet-narrator who affirms this thought in all respects, outside of the "whole of time,"[civ] becomes an "eternal being" alongside Blake,[cv] and while waiting for Time to be complete, the poet-narrator begs for a kiss from the forbidden "lover."

> The authors are in eternity
>
> That is
>
> in thought intensely between us,
> restraint that acknowledges
>
> the lover's kiss.[cvi]

Or there is the "blazing star"[cvii] in "Circulations of the Song," which is a sexual union with Jalal Al-Din Rumi.

> For the embrace of our two bodies,
>   for the entwining of bodies,
> for the kiss,   even as the first kiss,
>
> for the memorial seal into silence the
>   lips bound,
> the joyous imprint and signature of our
>   being together[cviii]

Here it is easy to take this "embrace" and "entwining" of the craving two physical bodies as a metaphor for "our sweet marriage / of minds"[cix] as something vivid and excessive. The poet-narrator in Duncan's poem tries to have a sexual union with the poet that opens something up inside of him. It is true that for the poet-narrator, Jalal Al-Din Rumi was a poet who could be a new output for his emotions but the poet-narrator is undoubtedly trying to form a physical union with this kind of poet.

Or another way of seeing it is his performing fellatio on the penis of Rime.

> Phallus, erect, silent, compels   I, wet,
> bent down and took into my throat the sign,
> here alone my horizon spells its palace, head,
>   live station and arrest.   How   long,
>
> sweet festival, I mouth the opening of the song
> the only presentation of the hidden solar   one   in you
>   the pulse   the rod   the a-waiting time
>
> all requires   signal load-stone of apprehensions   spires
> the heart grows tall and reaches   comes to head in me
>   and, candling, quick enthralls and leaping
>   fires.[cx]

"'Dante's Inferno' the knowing calld this place"[cxi] and then the mention of Sodom after this is an extremely raw metaphor for his performing fellatio on Rime. After this act was over in "this / dim arena,"[cxii] a "magic tower" within the body of the poet-narrator, "full with seed," is built and his whole body is anointed in "dreaming will."

> wet in me the magic tower fills full with seed
> and all is anointed in dreaming will.[cxiii]

The seed was sown but what kind of erotic poetic imagination is this sowing of the seed? Due to its explicitness, it would not be unusual for us to be driven to the temptation to find out who this master sower is. Of course, it is perfectly reasonable for us to think of this master sower, first of all, as representing a composite of all of the poets Duncan respects. However, as a representative of all poets, we want to assume that this is the pioneer of American poetry, Walt Whitman, who sang loudly about male love. But what we should think about is not the master sower but whether he is actually opening himself towards other poets or not.

If Duncan's way of entering the process of becoming "Man" by eternally opening himself up is an impossible physical unification with predecessor poets, who are "stars," in order for

Duncan to reach the city of the starry skies, presumably he cannot avoid a unification with various poets of the past. Both Duncan and his texts must have the vision of a unification not only with poets of the past but also with the poets to come in future. If this is Duncan's way of implementing his "open form," then so be it. However, "to open" ought to mean opening oneself to something outside of oneself. And yet, in order for the counterpart, to whom Duncan opens his entire body, to be a poet that he envisions unifying with, who inevitably shares a sameness with Duncan and becomes an object of Duncan's wish for unification, the direction of his "opening" up must be to another person on the "outside." However, we must also entertain doubts over whether Duncan is not in fact opening towards the "inside." While Duncan accepts an eternal "opening" up, in order to avoid the peril of disembodying himself, in actual fact Duncan does not open himself up to any other poet, but rather internalizes the others. And is this not because he is opening up a future that should be created together with those others that he has internalized within him? If this is true, the city of starry skies that he envisions is a *starry skies of the Canon* comprised of poets who shine with the colors with which Duncan has painted them. But in the end, they can be nothing more than immaterial beings who exist only within Duncan's vision. Therefore, these immaterial beings are indeed what the starry skies of the beyond actually are.

Duncan's texts are consecrated as stars, but there is no answer to when Duncan will obtain his citizenship of this city of starry skies. If this city of the starry skies in Duncan's poem, to which he soars after turning into a bird, exists only as a canon of starry skies within Duncan's vision, then the poet-narrator of the poem must continue to fly endlessly towards the core that is constantly being formed within his own vision. Duncan's texts become stars, while envisioning at the same time the moment of canonization with which the city of starry skies shines.

But who can canonize Duncan's texts? There is the connotation that the poem becomes Poetry, that a man becomes Man, and that the individual becomes one with the Whole. When this process is completed, no poem can be written any longer and because it is supposedly the end of civilization, when Mankind has died out, as long as we see this as a process of a poem becoming Poetry, a man becoming Man, and the individual becoming the Whole, the moment when time becomes complete can be perceived as nothing other than the end of time. If that is so, the person who can canonize Duncan's texts must be someone (who is nowhere) who appears at the end of time. Putting this extraordinary situation at the forefront, what answers can we give to the questions left to us: Where is the point at which the texts turn into something "divine"? What is the ultimate point "beyond" the starry skies?

Now we must recall Duncan's reading of Whitman. Whitman's lines of verse are in the middle of a process which is constantly opening outwards and the individual person reading and comprehending his verse is also in the middle of an unending process. Then, the final destination of a comprehension of Whitman's lines is not in the infinite far-off future, but in the "present," which is the non-existent "here and now." In other words, we can assume that it is merely the place where lecture (reading) and écriture (writing) meet.

This *nowhere* person who will pass judgment on the canonization of Duncan's texts will appear at the end of history and while being a judge who knows the sum total of all realized human potential, he must also be a great "reader = writer" of not only Duncan's entire oeuvre, but also in reading / writing a variety of unplaceable texts in the non-existent "here/now." In our context, this unnamable entity, which can be nothing other than "Man," gives birth to "Poetry" under the name of "the Whole," and is the grand constituent who produces the "tradition" of the development of the "city of the starry skies." Only this unnamable entity, towards which Duncan's body (now in the form of his texts) continues to fly, can know whether his canonization will be permitted or not, and it goes without saying that this far exceeds our own judgment. What we can say is that Duncan's actual poems, which envisage this kind of philosophical constituent, remain forever "open" and for "open form," which does not try to converge towards any kind of ultimate end-point, there is a second point, a vision which the writer is actually constantly in the process of forming.

As a result, Duncan's right and left hands wait suspended in the void for Poetry to emerge shining, and the space in between when the images of his crossed left and right eyes are bound together are left as the void and the bird will continue to soar for eternity. Duncan himself becomes this nowhere man, drawing this "when time becomes complete" which is nowhere into the present, until the time when he becomes this grand constituent. We do not imagine that Duncan has what we are in fact seeking, but even if we are aware of this and still choose to seek it out, this is not a Duncan who writes "Poetry" whose poetics transcend the poem, but this is the time when Duncan as writer of poetry is born. That is why Duncan must stop longing for the "city of starry skies" and stop assuming himself as part of the process towards Man. What Duncan should do is not receive the commands of the stars through internalizing and becoming the poets of the past in order to soar to the starry skies, but rather portray the frightful vacuum beyond the starry skies. And it is through performing this very act that the present will appear before Duncan in its naked form, and through a bloody fight with the naked present, Duncan's texts ought to have come in touch with the power of "the divine." And this is when Duncan will be released from the binds of the texts of the poets who preceded him, which are far stronger than the binds of mother and father, and at the ultimate point beyond the starry skies he ought to be able to obtain his real constituency.

However, this is not the direction that Duncan took. He wished for something that would be perpetually "open." Continuing to soar to the void of a process with no beginning and no end, going beyond the boundaries of something that never ends. However, even now, there is no way of us knowing how this poet, who gave shape to a rare model for American poetry by continuing to soar throughout his whole life, intended his own death to "open" outwardly.

Therefore, whether Duncan's body which has become his texts will be granted canonization or not in the city of starry skies, which in the end will make up the Canon, and whether they will shine as stars or not, will be left to the judgment of this nowhere constituent who will manifest beyond history, this constituent who will read / write these various works in the "here and now" which is nowhere.

FINIS

(This research was conducted using a 1991 research subsidy obtained from Sugiyama Jogakuen University).

*As in the previous issue, I have revised and added to, "Duncan of the 'Starry Skies'—An Interpretation of Robert Duncan," a paper delivered at the Chubu Regional Chapter's 43rd Conference of the English Literary Society of Japan (ELSJ), held at Mie University on October 5th, 1991. The main outline of this paper and its preceding one comprise Chapter Two, "Duncan of the 'Starry Skies'" in the "Anti-Eliot 'Tradition'" (*T. S. Eliot Review*, No. 4, 1993, pp. 5-24), which is a somewhat poor argument of Olson's and Duncan's relation to Eliot.

ENDNOTES

i	See 27-28 of "Doves." Ibid.
ii	Bending the Bow, Preface ii.
iii	THE STRUCTURE OF RIME II, The Opening of the Field, 13
iv	THE STRUCTURE OF RIME XIII, The Opening of the Field, 83
v	Roots and Branches, 26-30
vi	Ibid., 26
vii	Ibid., 28
viii	Ibid., 30
ix	"The Propositions" conclusion. The Opening of the Field, 37
x	Root and Branches, 32-43
xi	"Apprehensions" Roots and Branches, 32-33
xii	Ibid., 33
xiii	Ibid., 33
xiv	Ibid., p. 33
xv	Ibid., p. 34
xvi	Ibid., 34
xvii	Ibid., 34
xviii	Ibid., p. 37
xix	Ibid., 37
xx	Ibid., 38
xxi	"Apprehension" conclusion. Roots and Branches, 43.
xxii	Ibid., p. 33
xxiii	Ibid., 32
xxiv	STRUCTURE OF RIME XIX, Roots and Branches, 170.
xxv	Roots and Branches, 170-1
xxvi	Ibid., 170-1
xxvii	Ibid., 170
xxviii	Ibid., 170
xxix	Ibid., 170
xxx	Ibid., 170
xxxi	Ibid., 170
xxxii	Ibid., 170
xxxiii	Ibid., 170
xxxiv	Ibid., 170
xxxv	Ibid., 171.
xxxvi	"Chords" Passages 14, Bending the Bow, 47
xxxvii	Bending the Bow, 74-5
xxxviii	Ibid., 74
xxxix	"In the Place Of A Passage 22." conclusion. Bending the Bow, 75.
xl	Bending the Bow, 120-1
xli	Ibid., 120
xlii	Ibid., 120
xliii	"Eye of God, Passages 29" Bending the Bow, 124-7
xliv	Bending the Bow, 126
xlv	See Canto 33 of Paradiso, from Dante's La Divina Commedia.
xlvi	Bending the Bow, 134
xlvii	Ibid., 135-6

xlviii   Ibid., 137
xlix   "The Concert, Passages 31" conclusion. Tribunals, serial poem. Ground Work: Before the War, 13
l   Ground Work: Before the War, 51-2
li   "O!, Passages 37" conclusion. Ground Work: Before the War, 51-2.
lii   "To Speak My Mind" Dante Études. Book One, Ground Work: Before the War, 100
liii   "The Meaning of Each Particular" Dante Études. Book One, Ground Work: Before the War, 106-7
liv   Ibid., 107
lv   "The Whole Potentiality" Dante Études. Book One, Ground Work: Before the War, 108
lvi   Ibid., 108
lvii   Ground Work: Before the War, 112-3
lviii   Ibid., 113
lix   Ibid., 113
lx   Ibid. 113
lxi   Ibid., 113.
lxii   Ibid., 113
lxiii   Ibid., 155-8
lxiv   Ibid., 155.
lxv   Ibid., 156
lxvi   Ground Work II: In the Dark, 26-30
lxvii   Ibid., 27
lxviii   "The Naming of the Time Ever" Ground Work II: In the Dark, 27
lxix   Ibid, 28
lxx   "The Naming of the Time Ever" Ground Work II: In the Dark, 28
lxxi   Ground Work II: In the Dark, 28
lxxii   "I Pour Forth My Life from This Bough," Ground Work II: In the Dark, 29.
lxxiii   "The Turbine," Ground Work II: In the Dark, 29
lxxiv   "Jamais, Passages" Ground Work: Before the War, 147
lxxv   Ibid., 148
lxxvi   Ground Work II: In the Dark, 57-60
lxxvii   "The Dignities [Passages]" Ground Work II: In the Dark, 59.
lxxviii   Ibid., 60
lxxix   "YOU, Muses, [Passages]." Conclusion. Ground Work II: In the Dark, 73.
lxxx   "At the Door." Conclusion. Ground Work II: In the Dark, 85
lxxxi   "Whose [Passages]" Conclusion. Ground Work II: In the Dark, 82
lxxxii   Ground Work II: In the Dark, 83
lxxxiii   Ibid., 83
lxxxiv   Ibid., 83
lxxxv   "Close" Conclusion. Ground Work II: In the Dark, 84
lxxxvi   "The Dignities [Passages]," Ground Work II: In the Dark, 59
lxxxvii   "After a Long Illness," Ground Work II: In the Dark, 90.
lxxxviii   "Orders, Passages 24," Bending the Bow, 77
lxxxix   "Structure of Rime XXIV," Conclusion. Bending the Bow, 36
xc   Ibid., p. 36

xci "Secondary is the Grammar," 97
xcii "The Household" Dante Études. Book One, Ground Work: Before the War, 111
xciii "Let Him First Drink of the Fountain," Dante Études. Book One, Ground Work: Before the War, 112
xciv "In Nothing Superior," Dante Études. Book Two, Ground Work: Before the War, 117
xcv "Enacted" Dante Études. Book Two, Ground Work: Before the War, 117-8
xcvi Dante Études. Book One, Ground Work: Before the War, 108
xcvii Ibid., p. 49
xcviii Roots and Branches, 49
xcix Ibid., 49-50
c Ibid., 50.
ci Ibid., 50
cii Ibid., 50
ciii Ibid, 51
civ Ibid., 52
cv Ibid. 52
cvi "Variations on Two Dicta of William Blake," Conclusion. Roots and Branches, 53.
cvii Ground Work: Before the War, 167
cviii Ibid., 169
cix Ibid., 169
cx "An Eros / Amor / Love Cycle," 5. Ground Work II: In the Dark, 42.
cxi Ibid., 42
cxii Ibid., 42
cxiii "An Eros / Amor / Love Cycle" 5 Conclusion. Ground Work II: In the Dark, 42

GHOST MANTRAS

MICHAEL MCCLURE REMEMBERED

BY D.S. BLACK

I was fortunate to have Michael McClure as one of my first poetry teachers. David Meltzer's zestful book of interviews, *The San Francisco Poets* (1971) was a helpful guide when I signed up for poetry workshops at Naropa, as I quickly checked Michael's name on the list of offerings.

My first impression of this "prince of the San Francisco scene" was his jousting verbally with Lawrence Ferlinghetti at the opening ceremony of the 25th anniversary *On the Road* conference at Naropa's Jack Kerouac School of Disembodied Poetics. It was affectionately dubbed by its participants "Camp Kerouac."

Allen Ginsberg was at the podium, making introductions and setting the tone for the week ahead. "If you brought drugs or psychedelics, take them," he urged us.

The message was that even in 1982, with Reagan President, we weren't going to let it tie our spirits down or keep us from dreaming.

From the audience, Ferlinghetti touted the need for the artist to be *engagé* with the issues of their day, prompting McClure to counter that without a foregrounding of the environment, human life and politics were doomed.

"Hundreds of known species became extinct in the last year," I remember him saying, "and thousands more will follow if we don't act to protect the environment. Biology will have the last word. If we fail today, we may be gone tomorrow."

Many are the times I subsequently encountered Michael. In the winter following Camp Kerouac, he gave a reading at the University of Chicago. Spotting my Naropa t-shirt, he recalled the joys of that conference, and at a student after-party invited me to join his workshop the next day at the Art Institute of Chicago.

When I told him of my plan to move that summer to San Francisco, he encouraged me to contact him via City Lights. His reply to my arrival missive was an invitation to his reading at the Palace of Fine Arts in support of Nicaragua (with Ferlinghetti, Alice Walker, Ernesto Cardenal, and others) in opposition to Reagan's U.S.-backed Contra insurgency.

"None of my poems is about Nicaragua," he admitted, but on this day he stood against neo-colonial interventions in Central America.

My first San Francisco apartment was in the lower Haight. Michael lived on Downey St., not far from Haight-Ashbury, up the hill from me. I visited him there once, and he came to my apartment tempted by the lure of books, which I have always surrounded myself with in abundance.

On an early weekend in January 1984, we tooled around the city in his car, careening over the Twin Peaks with the manuscript of his new play *Vktms*, which he was ready to post to his agent. He did not trust the post office in the Haight as it was rumored to be staffed by '60s burnouts.

Besides seeing him at readings, we had a number of pleasant chance encounters over the years. At the Clarion Café on Mission St., I happened upon and joined a small group at his table as he shared his critiques of two then-popular theater personalities: Spalding Gray (the monologist, whose minimal staging centered on the performer seated at a desk) and George Coates (whose multimedia shows were visually arresting, flashing light-enhanced spectacles). Both were drawing appreciative audiences. After seeing a couple of Coates' shows, I shared Michael's view that they were a triumph of strobing form over substance.

Soon after I began work in the UC Berkeley Library, Michael sought my help obtaining early books on Custer. When he returned them, I saw and gently chided him for leaving his light pencil marks annotating passages of interest. I wondered if he was going to give the Boy General a memorable stage treatment akin to his notorious play *The Beard*, which had featured Billy the Kid and Jean

Harlow in Hell, but if that seed germinated, I have not yet read it.

Michael's second book of poems was *For Artaud* (1959). In this regard, he connected me with an avantgarde performance documentarian named Kush, who I recalled seeing on the streets of Boulder during Camp Kerouac. With much spit flying, Kush acted out the death of Edgar Allan Poe.

According to Michael, Kush possessed a recording of Antonin Artaud's suppressed radio performance *To Have Done with the Judgment of God*, which I was eager to listen to. I found Kush at a large anarchist commune called the Farm, and he agreeably shared this recording.

One of my library colleagues, Richard Ogar, had the blessed good fortune to meet the love of his life, Leah, at one of Michael's poetry readings in Berkeley, and their courtship was attended at various gatherings in Michael's performative company.

In October 2014, I hosted a Litquake/Bancroft Library event marking 30 years from the approximate death of Richard Brautigan by his own hand in Bolinas. McClure was a close friend of Brautigan, and was joined in this discussion by daughter Ianthe, Joanne Kyger, David Meltzer, Robert Hass, Ishmael Reed, Herbert Gold, V. Vale, and others.

When someone leaves before their time—and for poets, musicians, and storytellers, it's almost always too soon—those who remain have to fill in the gaps.

My first meeting with Michael's wife Amy was an evening when he took her and some of his students to a show at one of Berkeley's fine theatres, either Berkeley Rep or the Aurora Theatre, in the early 2000s.

After Bancroft Library acquired Michael's literary archive, they commissioned Amy to make a homuncular sculpture of Menches the village scribe or *komogrammateus*. This figure greets visitors to the suite of offices for the Center for Tebtunis Papyri, where Egyptian text fragments are studied by scholars from around the world.

The source of these papyri was in large measure mummified crocodiles, domestic pets, and people—all revered enough by the living to be wrapped in these lineaments of desire for eternity, which are now enjoying a text-centric afterlife elucidated by scholars.

In describing the vast and varied holdings of the Bancroft Library, its late curator of Rare Books and Literary Manuscripts, Anthony Bliss, liked to remark that it ranges from Pharaohs to

Menches Komogrammateus [village scribe] *of Tebtunis, circa 119 BC, conceived and sculpted by Amy Evans McClure, 2008*

Beat poets. He might have been talking about Amy's and Michael's works in plotting that continuum.

> *People who wear black are in mourning for themselves.*
> —Michael McClure (October 20, 1932 – May 4, 2020)

Michael provided many quotable sayings (above his paraphrasing Chekhov) that were repeated at the in-person memorial in September 2021. Even after three bicoastal memorials over Zoom marking the anniversary of his passing in May 2020, Amy McClure recognized that Michael's many friends would not be satisfied until there was an in-person gathering.

A strict proof of vaccination requirement, masking, social distancing at the outdoor CalShakes Theatre in Orinda provided a relatively safe space for that to happen. Around 250 people attended, and many stories, tears, songs, poems, and laughter were shared.

One story I'll propagate came from Juvenal Acosta, who was Michael's department chair at the California College of Arts and Crafts. Michael had told him of an early visit to Big Sur, in which he had visited Henry Miller around the time described in Miller's *Big Sur and the Oranges of Hieronymus Bosch* (1957).

On meeting Miller's wife, Eve McClure, Michael chatted to her about their shared surname. She was 4 years older than Michael and 37 years younger than Henry. It wasn't long before Henry Miller was ready to boot out the dashing and beautiful upstart he believed was making moves on his wife.

"You are a supercilious young man," he said, pointing an angry finger in the young poet's face.

Michael was perplexed, having never before heard that word applied to him and not knowing exactly what it meant.

Ferlinghetti, also present, and hosting McClure at his cabin just up the road, was quick to reassure the elder bohemian that it was all a misunderstanding, and thus Michael was saved from being thrown out into the night.

As my literary perambulations recently took me south of Monterey/Carmel, my research fixed upon a sound recording Allen Ginsberg made with Michael on one of their later trips to Big Sur. This recording is in Lawrence Ferlinghetti's papers, also at the Bancroft Library.

The year was 1966. The three poets had taken acid. Michael was playing autoharp as Allen chanted *ommmm* in Ferlinghetti's Bixby Canyon cabin.

The sound quality is poor but I manage to make out Michael's quip: "sounds like anger, wisdom, joy, nature. *And nature was a one-line poem.*" After an artful pause, he adds: "It sure doesn't lack stature."

They all laugh. A child then approaches—it might have been Ferlinghetti's or McClure's—the recording includes many sounds of family, the rituals of domestic life, going on in the background.

In this moment, captured for eternity: *a child offering enchiladas.*

www.ingramcontent.com/pod-product-compliance
Lightning Source LLC
Chambersburg PA
CBHW020340010526
44119CB00048B/542